Sourcework
Academic Writing From Sources

Nancy E. Dollahite
Portland State University

Julie Haun
Portland State University

Houghton Mifflin Company   Boston

Publisher: Patricia A. Coryell
Director of ESL Publishing: Susan Maguire
Senior Development Editor: Kathleen Sands Boehmer
Development Editor: Kathleen M. Smith
Editorial Assistant: Evangeline Bermas
Senior Project Editor: Margaret Park Bridges
Manufacturing Coordinator: Chuck Dutton
Senior Marketing Manager: Annamarie Rice
Marketing Assistant: Andrew Whitacre

Cover image: Paul Taylor/Getty Images

Photo Credit: © Lester Lefkowitz/CORBIS

Printed in the U.S.A.

Library of Congress Control Number: 2004116654

ISBN: 0-618-41287-5

456789-VHO-09-08 07 06 05

Contents

CHAPTER 4 Building a Paper: **Create** 72

CHAPTER 5 Building a Paper: **Refine** 98

CHAPTER 6 Building a Paper: **Independent Research   135**

PART TWO: **Sources for Research 155**

For chapter notes, answer key, and other related instructor material, got to http://college.hmco.com/esl/instructors.

To obtain access to the Houghton Miffllin ESL instructor sites call 1-800-733-1717.

For additional student activities related to this book, go to http://college.hmco.com/esl/students.

A Guide for Students
Where to Find Answers About Writing a Research Paper:

How do I:

- get ideas for a research topic? (Chapter 6, pages 136–139)
- figure out what an assignment means? (Chapter 6, pages 146–153)
- find good sources? (Chapter 6, pages 141–145)
- understand what a source is about? (Chapter 1, pages 3–6)
- paraphrase information from sources? (Chapter 1, pages 6–14; Chapter 4, pages 79–88)
- respond to another writer's ideas? (Chapter 1, pages 15–20)
- write a summary of a source? (Chapter 1, pages 21–32)
- create a research question? (Chapter 2, pages 35–40; Chapter 6, pages 140–141)
- take notes to keep track of all the information? (Chapter 2, pages 40–43)
- make a rough outline? (Chapter 2, pages 44–47)
- make a detailed outline? (Chapter 3, pages 67–71)
- write a thesis statement? (Chapter 3, pages 49–60)
- find good evidence from sources? (Chapter 3, pages 61–67)
- organize a good paragraph with a good topic sentence? (Chapter 4, pages 73–78, 88–94)
- write good topic sentences for body paragraphs? (Chapter 4, pages 74–76)
- put evidence from sources into my paper? (Chapter 4, pages 77–94)
- know when to use a direct quote? (Chapter 4, pages 77–78)
- know what plagiarism is and why it's a problem? (Chapter 4, pages 77–78, 96; Chapter 5, page 116)
- keep writing when I can't think of anything to say? (Chapter 4, pages 95–96)
- write an interesting introduction? (Chapter 5, pages 99–101, 104–107)
- write a conclusion? (Chapter 5, pages 101–107)
- make my paper sound good? (Chapter 5, pages 108–115)
- document evidence in my paper? (Chapter 5, pages 116–131)
- make a references page? (Chapter 5, pages 122–129)
- improve my first draft? (Chapter 5, pages 131–134)

Sourcework: Academic Writing From Sources applies process-approach writing to the academic setting to take students beyond writing based on personal experience. This text is a guide for students writing academic papers for mainstream university courses, in which students must use sources to develop and support their ideas. *Sourcework* is designed for advanced students who have had some exposure to basic rhetorical styles and who have had experience in writing essays with a thesis statement and supporting points.

 ## An Overview of *Sourcework*

Sourcework guides you and your students through the process of writing an academic research paper. Part One presents a five-step process for writing research papers. Each chapter in Part One corresponds to a step in the writing process: Exploring, Focusing, Organizing, Creating, and Refining. An additional chapter on independent research and finding and evaluating sources is also included.

Part Two provides four thematically organized sets of university level articles that function as sources for students as they practice the art of writing, using evidence to support their ideas. The themes presented in *Sourcework* include:

- Heroes—the people who inspire us
- Globalization—changes that draw us together
- Non-violent Social Change—working for a better world
- Bioethics—when science and values collide

Suggestions for additional themes and sources appear on the *Sourcebook* website at http://esl.college.hmco.com/students.

Instructors may access an instructor site that includes chapter notes, an answer key, assessment tools and example essays at www.college.hmco.com/esl/instructors.

How to Use *Sourcework*

A central goal of *Sourcework* is to build a "community of learners." That is, when students work together to explore and write about a common topic over the course of several weeks, they develop a shared sense of curiosity about the topic, a desire to help one another overcome difficulties encountered as they write, and a greater willingness to take risks in their writing.

To achieve this goal, *Sourcework* is designed for students to work together on a theme chosen from Part Two. You may choose the theme or ask your class to vote on a theme. Once the theme is selected, the students read, discuss, and write their papers using the articles you have selected from Part Two and following the steps in the writing process in Part One, Chapters 1–5.

We recommend the following sequence:

1. Select a theme from Part Two and complete the "Getting Started" activity presented in the introduction.
2. Work with students to develop a basic understanding of the ideas and issues related to the theme by doing an open reading of each article and then using the 3 strategies presented in Chapter 1: Exploring. You probably will not have time to use all four strategies for each article.
3. Once students have a general understanding of the theme, they will be ready to focus on a specific aspect of it. You can assign a research question from the list of Writing Questions that appears at the end of each reading unit in Part Two, or you can have students develop their own research question using the methods described in Chapter 2: Focusing.
4. With this foundation of knowledge on their theme and their research question, students can work through the rest of the chapters in Part One to complete a three to five page guided research paper.
5. Once students complete the writing process in Part One and produce a guided research paper, they can repeat it to produce additional essays. Following this process more than once in a term helps students become familiar with writing an academic essay based on sources. When students repeat the process you may ask them to:

   - continue with the same theme but focus on a different topic within it.
   - select a new theme from Part Two (or from the *Sourcework* website at http://esl.college.hmco.com/students).
   - select their own themes and find their own sources using the guidelines in Chapter 6: Independent Research.

6. How much time you spend on each step of the writing process will depend on your time constraints and your students' needs. *Sourcework* includes an "optional" icon for sections that students may skip the first time they work though the Part One chapters to write a paper.

Organization of Chapters and Units

Contents of Chapters in Part One

The organization of chapters in Part One varies from chapter to chapter. However, each chapter includes the following components.

Chapter Introduction

This summarizes the chapter including what the student will practice and accomplish by the end of the chapter.

Writing Concepts

Each chapter presents two to four overarching concepts that underlie the steps in the writing process. Explanations of these concepts include methods, techniques, characteristics, or strategies that students can use as guidelines. Examples derived from authentic student writing are included to illustrate each of the concepts.

Now You Try

This is a 5- to 10-minute activity that is done immediately after the presentation of a writing concept and is intended to serve as a quick comprehension check for teachers and students.

Activities

Several more complex activities are included after each writing concept. These are designed to help students practice several related skills before applying these concepts to their own writing. Teachers may choose from among the activities to suit their students' needs.

Building Your Paper

As students work through the Writing Process in Chapters 1–5, they create their own research papers. Building Your Paper assignments occur after most writing concepts. This is where students apply the concepts to the research papers they are writing. The Building Your Paper steps in Chapters 1–5 work cumulatively to help a student produce a research paper.

Contents of Units in Part Two

Table of Contents

Each theme has a table of contents on the unit's first page of the unit that lists the articles for that theme.

Getting Started

This is a short discussion activity that students can do in class to help them begin thinking about their themes.

Introduction to the Theme

The introduction provides an overview of the unit and a one-sentence summary of each source.

Articles

Four to seven articles are included for each theme. These articles are designed to work together as sources of information for students as they write their research papers. A bibliography of additional sources for each theme is also included on the *Sourcework* website at http://esl.college.hmco.com/students.

Questions for Writing

A list of possible research questions is included for each theme. Teachers can assign one of the research questions or ask students to choose one on their own. Teachers who decide to have students write more than one paper on a theme, may want to use more than one question from the list.

More Questions for Writing

This list of additional questions and ideas is included for teachers who want to expand the theme beyond the topics covered in the articles in Part Two. Some of the questions are based on sources included in the bibliographies on the *Sourcework* website. Other questions would require students to find their own sources.

Acknowledgments

This book developed out of our work with writing classes in the Intensive English Language Program at Portland State University (PSU) and, thus, depends in large part on those friends, colleagues, and students who worked with us.

We thank our colleagues at PSU and elsewhere who generously shared their time and expertise in various ways and field-tested much of this material in partial form: John Armbrust, Leslie Batchelder, Andrea Binder, Liz Brunkow, Ruth Chapin, Dan Clausson, Debra Coultard, Greg Davis, Kirsten Freeman-Benson, Suzanne Fontaine, Michael Harvey, Trina Hing, Deanna Hochstein, Lena Koessler, Tom Kuehn, Sandra Lee, Susan Lindsay, Judy Reed, Talisman Saunders, Laura Shier, Leslie Siebert, Stephen Storla, Linda Walton, Regina Weaver, Susan Westby, Judith Wild, Hilary Williams, Norman Yoshida, Margaret Young, Belinda Young-Davy.

Thanks also to our students who enthusiastically gave us feedback and allowed us to use their writing: Dhowaihi Al-Dhowaihi, Turki M. Al-Sudiary, Yousif Al-Qatami, Jaturapat Bhiromkaew, Pimala Bhiromkaew, Pimyukol Bunnag, Hai Cao, Alex Chan, Jariya Chatcheydang, Hui-chuan Chen, Ying-Jen Chen, Sungwook Choi, Jung-min Po, Yuafeng Dong, Javier Espinoza, Ayako Fujisaki, Fransiska Gunawan, Keiko Hirano, I-Jung Chiu, Vanessa Hasenmeyer, Cindy Huang, In Ah Hwang, Yoshimi Hyodo, Yachiyo Iisako, Vutthisak Kanchanaporn, Junichi Koga, Keumjoo Jwa, Lim Myung Joon, Toshiaki Kameyama, Yuki Kanai, Aya Kawano, Yumie Kajino, Seok Ju Kim, Onyou Kim, Richard Ko, Naoshi Kobayashi, Masako Kondo, Minsun Koo, Seda Kose, Kanako Kunihisa, Haruna Kunisawama, Jui-Lin Lee, Mi Jung Lee, Sung Hoon Lee, Peiju Lin, Chia-ying Lu, Jan Makovsky, Maiko Muto, Kimiko Nakagawa, Gyongnam Nam, Sayuri Naruse, Mayumi Oura, Kana Obayashi, I-Ping Pai, Kyeonywon Park, Nghia Pham, Claudia Prado, Pornpun Ratanapitakkul, Masami Sagara, Chie Sakai, Ban Shakir, Bomi Shin, Sok Sreypich, Heidi Stadler, Lee Suntlwa, Shoko Taniguchi, Kotone Tomobe, Anh-Thu, Truong, Han-Fang Tsai, Naoko Tsujimoto, Kuo Cheng Tung, Adisorn Tuntikul, Jadwiga Witkowska, Elmer Wong, Xiaojin Xu, Jie Yang, Harn-Sung Yoo, Pilwon Yoon, Ryoko Yoshimitsu.

At Houghton Mifflin, we have been fortunate to have the support of Susan Maguire, Kathy Sands Boehmer, Kent Watson, and many others. We would also like to thank our Development Editor, Kathleen Smith and Helen Gagnon of Laurel Tech, whose patience and insight helped make *Sourcework* a better book.

We would also like to thank the instructors who provided us with valuable feedback: Carolyn Baughan, Illinois State University; Donald Beck, University of Findlay; Ellen Butki, University of Texas, Austin; Joy Campbell, Michigan State University; Karen Chaparian, Quinsigamond Community College; Reka Clausen, University of Southern California; Nick Hilmers, DePaul University; Barbara Jordan, Mesa Community College; Patricia Juza, LaGuardia Community College; Robert Maguire, Boston University; Carole Miele, Bergen Community College; Sydney Rice, University of Missouri; and James Zorn, Norwalk Community College.

Most of all, to our family and friends who cheerfully relinquished time and offered moral support that we might get the writing done, we express our deepest appreciation.

While we received help from many, we ourselves are, of course, responsible for any inaccuracies in *Sourcework*.

PART ONE
The Writing Process

 ## Introduction to Part One

The chapters in Part One of *Sourcework* present a five-step process for writing research papers. Your teacher will choose one of the themes in Part Two and guide you through the process of writing a research paper using articles in that unit. As you and your classmates read the assigned articles, you will use the strategies in Chapter 1 Explore to deepen your understanding of the theme.

In Chapter 2 Focus, you will begin to develop a specific topic for your paper. Your teacher will assign one of the Writing Questions from Part Two or you will work with your classmates to develop a research question based on the theme you have been reading about. The information, activities, and Build Your Paper assignments in Chapters 3 through 5 will help you continue this step-by-step approach to writing a research paper. By the end of Chapter 5 Refine, you will have written a complete research paper.

Once you have completed a guided research paper, you can repeat the writing process (Chapters 1–5) with another research paper. When you repeat the process you may choose to

- continue with the same theme but focus on a different topic within it.
- select a new theme from Part Two (or from the *Sourcework* website).
- select your own theme and find your own sources. Chapter 6 Independent Research will help you get started on an independent research paper.

Repeating the writing process more than once will help you become familiar with the process of writing an academic essay based on sources. A description of the five main steps in the writing process follows.

The Writing Process

These steps correspond to Chapters 1–5 of *Sourcework.* "A Preliminary Step" corresponds to Chapter 6 Doing Your Own Research.

Step 1	**Explore** The writing process begins by exploring your theme. Contrary to what many people think, the first step in writing involves more reading, thinking, and discussion than actual writing. When exploring, you are building an understanding of the ideas and issues related to the topic you will eventually write about.
Step 2	**Focus** In this part of the process, you develop a focus for the topic of your research paper. You decide on a specific issue to discuss in your writing and then reread each source article to find ideas that will help you develop and explain your main point(s).
Step 3	**Organize** Once you have a clear focus for your essay and have collected relevant information, you can begin organizing your ideas. It is at this stage that you write your thesis and develop a detailed outline that maps how you will organize the information in the body of your essay.
Step 4	**Create** When you have reached this point, you are ready to write your first full draft, following the organizational plan you developed in Step 3. Step 4 includes combining your own ideas with information from sources you have been working with to create an essay that is rich in both.
Step 5	**Refine** In this final step, you consider the reader of the essay. Your goal is to fix, edit, and shape your writing so it is smooth, clear, and easy for your reader to understand.
A Preliminary Step	**Independent Research** If you choose a topic *not* included in Part Two of *Sourcework,* you will need to find and evaluate your own sources. If you're working with a complicated assignment from your teacher, you'll have to read it carefully in order to know what is required. After you have done these steps, you'll be ready to focus on your research, beginning with an open reading of your sources in Chapter 1.

CHAPTER

1

Building a Paper:
Explore

Writing often begins, not with a pen on paper or fingers on a computer keyboard, but with thinking, talking, and reading about a topic. Although we, as writers, are impatient to get on with the actual writing, the preparatory work we do exploring and evaluating themes, topics, and sources actually saves time and effort later.

In this book, you will become familiar with the process of writing an academic essay by writing a guided research paper using information from the articles in Part Two. To begin your paper, your teacher will choose a theme from Part Two of *Sourcework*. After completing the Getting Started activity about your theme, you will read several articles that your teacher assigns from that section. After you and your classmates read each article, you will use the strategies in this chapter to deepen your understanding of the theme.

You will be learning about the issues involved and the opinions of experts in the field, getting acquainted with the vocabulary used in your subject, and considering your reactions to, and opinions about, the subject. You will use some of these ideas from the sources to write your research paper.

> This chapter describes an approach to use when reading a source for the first time
>
> * Open reading
>
> and three strategies to further explore ideas in that source:
>
> * Paraphrasing
> * Responding
> * Summarizing
>
> You may choose to use one or more of these strategies with each article you read for your research paper. By the end of this chapter you will have gained a clearer understanding of the theme you will write about in your paper.

 Open Reading

Before reading the articles from Part Two, spend a few minutes thinking about what you already know about the theme. Doing the Getting Started activity will help you. Then, either individually, in a small group, or as a class, write a list of questions about it.

Next, begin exploring your theme by doing an **open reading** of one of the articles in Part Two. This reading is done quickly. Your goal is to develop an understanding of the ideas, issues, and terminology related to the topic you have chosen. You do not need to memorize the information or even understand every sentence in the article. Remember, your goal is to explore ideas. Choose from the following three techniques to help you think about ideas in the article as you read.

Three Open-Reading Techniques

1. **Focus on ideas that interest you.**

   - Highlight sections that capture your interest and make you pause and think.
   - Highlight sections that relate to your experiences or to ideas you have seen elsewhere.

2. **Write questions and comments in the margins.**

   - Note words or sentences that you don't understand.
   - Note examples or explanations that are unclear.
   - Write your reactions such as "I don't believe this!" or "This is exactly what happened to me" or "This idea is the same as what I already know or have read."

3. **Skim the article.**

   - Read first and last paragraphs.
   - Look for subtitles.
   - Look for key words and repeated words.
   - Develop a general sense of the topic.
   - Then read through the entire article.

Activities to Do After Open Reading

To practice open reading, do one or more of the following activities with an article you read from Part Two.

ACTIVITY 1

Discussing an Interesting Idea

A. Do the following on your own.

   1. Select one idea from the article that you think is interesting. Write the sentences about that idea below.

_____

_____

2. What do you think the sentences mean?

_____

_____

3. Why does this idea interest you? What does it make you think about?

_____

_____

B. Now you are ready to share your ideas with a partner, a group, or the class.

1. In the article, mark the sentences you wrote in Part A. Read them aloud to the others in your group. Explain what you think the passage means. Discuss why the idea is interesting to you.

2. As you listen to each other share ideas, ask questions when you don't understand something and comment on group members' ideas that also interest you.

ACTIVITY 2   *Writing Questions*

With a small group, return to the questions you generated about your topic before you began your open reading, or as you read your article (item 2 under Open-Reading Techniques on page 4).

1. Do you have other questions to add?
2. Can you begin answering some of the questions?
3. Share your questions and answers with a group.

ACTIVITY 3   *Freewriting*

After reading an article, freewrite for five to ten minutes and answer these questions.

1. What ideas in the article get your attention?.
2. What have you learned so far about your topic?
3. What other questions come to mind?

ACTIVITY 4   *Skimming*

Do this activity after you have skimmed a source you are reading in Part Two. Remember, to skim means to read first and last sentences in paragraphs and to look for subtitles, key words, and repeated words.

1. Freewrite for one to two minutes on any ideas you remember from skimming the article.

_____

_____

_____

2. With a partner, a small group, or the whole class, share what you have written.
3. Write a list of questions that you and your partner or group develop about the topic.

> ## BUILDING YOUR PAPER
>
> ### Do an Open Reading
>
> The Building Your Paper assignments in Chapters 1 to 5 guide you through the steps of writing your research paper. When you have completed these assignments, you will have finished your paper.
>
> - The first step in creating your paper is to do an open reading of each article from Part Two that you are working with.
> - Later, to continue exploring the ideas in each article, you can choose one of several strategies described later in this chapter—paraphrasing, responding or summarizing.

Paraphrasing

After you have done an open reading of a source, one strategy for further exploring the ideas you have read about is to paraphrase them to show you understand what they mean. A **paraphrase** is a restatement of another person's ideas using our own words.

When we describe something we have heard, we often repeat the same idea but use different words. For example, if you hear the TV announcer say, "There is an 80% chance of rain tomorrow," you may tell a friend, "It will probably rain tomorrow." This last statement is a paraphrase.

You can use this same way of repeating ideas using other words when you paraphrase in writing. Repeating the author's ideas in your own words shows that you truly comprehend the original idea.

The paraphrasing skills that you learn now as you explore your theme will also be useful later when you integrate ideas from the articles into your paper. Chapter 4 discusses how to use information from articles appropriately in academic writing.

Three Criteria for a Good Paraphrase

1. A good paraphrase has the same meaning as the original.

- All main ideas included.
- No new ideas added.

2. A good paraphrase is different enough from the original to be considered your own writing.

- Uses no more than four or five words in a row from the original source.
- Changes grammar and vocabulary as much as possible.

3. A good paraphrase refers directly to (or cites) the original source.

- Include the name of the author and/or the name of the source. (You will study citing and documenting sources in Chapter 5.)

Example:

Original: As the chain [McDonald's] expanded nationwide in the mid-1960s, it sought to cut labor costs, reduce the number of suppliers, and ensure that its fries tasted the same at every restaurant. —*Schlosser, Eric, "Why McDonald's Fries Taste So Good" 2002*

Paraphrase: Schlosser (2002) writes that while McDonald's spread all over the country during the 1960s, the company tried to spend less on its workers, get its supplies from fewer sources, and guarantee that its French fries always tasted the same.

Now You Try

The following is an original sentence and two paraphrases of the sentence. One of the paraphrases is well done. The other does not meet all the criteria for a good paraphrase. Decide which of the two paraphrases is weak. Identify which of the criteria is missing.

Original: Many of the doctors taking part in the survey on assisted suicide doubted whether they could decide if a patient had less than six months to live. —*"The Anguish of Doctors" 1996*

Paraphrase 1:   According to a survey on assisted suicide in *The Anguish of Doctors* (1996), many doctors disagree with assisted suicide because they can't know when a patient will die.

Does the paraphrase meet all three criteria?   Yes   No   (circle one)

If no, what is the problem? _____

_____

Paraphrase 2:   In a survey on assisted suicide in "The Anguish of Doctors" (1996), many doctors were not sure they could always know whether a patient would die within six months.

Does the paraphrase meet all three criteria?   Yes   No   (circle one)

If no, what is the problem? _____

Paraphrasing Techniques

Below are two ways to approach paraphrasing:

- "tell the idea to a friend" method
- chunking method

Tell a Friend Method

One effective way to paraphrase is to focus on the meaning of the passage and find a completely new way to explain it. The Tell a Friend method works well in this situation.

1. Read the original and concentrate on what it means.
2. Cover the original so that you cannot see it.
3. Imagine you are talking to a good friend. How would you explain this idea to your friend? Write down your explanation.
4. Go back and reread the original to see if it means the same as your paraphrase.

Example:

Original: Leadership by birth order apparently holds for both genders. Studies have found that female executives are much more likely to be firstborns than later-borns. —*Koselka, Rita and Shook, Carrie, "Born to Rebel? Or Born to Conserve?" 1997*

Paraphrase: Not only firstborn men, but also firstborn women are more likely to be executives than people who are later born (Koselka & Shook, 1997).

- Notice that while the key ideas from the original are included in the paraphrase, the structure of the paraphrase is very different.

Now You Try

Using the proverbs below, practice the Tell a Friend method of paraphrasing.

Example:

Proverb: Don't cry over spilled milk.

Paraphrase: When something bad happens that you can't control, it doesn't help to get upset.

1. With a partner, choose one of the proverbs below and use the Tell a Friend method to write a paraphrase of it.

   - All work and no play make Jack a dull boy.
   - All that glitters is not gold.
   - The squeaky wheel gets the oil.

   Write your paraphrase here. _____

   _____

2. Find a new partner and tell that person your paraphrase. Have your partner guess which proverb you're paraphrasing.

Chunking Method

Another way to paraphrase is to divide the original into groups of words, or "chunks," and concentrate on explaining the meaning of each chunk. This can be especially helpful when you are working with longer passages. Here's how *chunking* works.

1. Read the original passage several times to develop a basic understanding of the ideas.
2. Divide the passage into chunks by underlining main ideas.

   - As you divide the passage, focus on phrases rather than on individual words.

3. Explain each chunk using your own words.
4. Combine these explanations into one or more sentences to create a paraphrase.

   - As you combine these chunks, you will need to think about how the ideas are related to each other.
   - It is okay to rearrange these chunks into a new order for your paraphrase.

In the two examples below, the original sentences are divided into chunks. Each chunk is then explained in a new way. Finally, the chunks are combined to form a paraphrase.

Example 1:

Original: As the chain, [McDonald's] expanded nationwide, in the

Chunk #1

mid-1960s, it sought to cut labor costs, reduce the number of

Chunk #2   **Chunk #3**

suppliers, and ensure that its fries tasted the same at every

Chunk #4

restaurant. McDonald's began switching to frozen French

Chunk #5

fries in 1966—and few customers noticed the difference.

Chunk #6

Nevertheless, the change had a profound effect on the nation's

Chunk #7

agriculture and diet. —*Schlosser, Eric, "Why McDonald's Fries Taste*

Chunk #8

So Good" 2002

Rewordings of chunks:

1. McDonald's spread all over the country during the 1960s.
2. The company tried to spend less on its workers.
3. It got its supplies from fewer sources.
4. It wanted to guarantee that its French fries always tasted the same.
5. The company started using frozen French fries.
6. Not many people realized the change had been made.
7. But using frozen fries ultimately had a big influence.
8. It influenced U.S. farming and eating habits.

Paraphrase: Schlosser (2002) writes that while McDonald's spread all over

Chunk #1

the country during the 1960s, the company tried to spend less

Chunk #2

on its workers, get its supplies from fewer sources, and

Chunk #3

guarantee that its French fries always tasted the same. When

Chunk #4

the company started using frozen French fries, not many

Chunk #5

people realized the change had been made, but using frozen

Chunk #6

fries ultimately had a big influence on U.S. farming and

Chunk #7   **Chunk #8**

eating habits.

Example 2:

This example shows a paraphrase in which the chunks have been arranged in an order that is different from the original.

Original: There is an element of sacrifice and obligation: women are

Chunk #1

expected to make many things secondary once the husband

Chunk #2

comes along, to devote their energies to him and his house

Chunk #3

and the building of another family Unit. —*Wark, Penny, "What*

Does Life Tell Us About Love?" 2003

Explanation of chunks:

1. Women must give up time and energy for themselves.
2. After women get married
3. Women are expected to focus on taking care of their husband, home, and children.

Paraphrase: After they get married, women must give up time and energy

                          Chunk #2   **Chunk #1**

                   for themselves because they are expected to focus on taking

                                                          Chunk #3

                   care of their husband, home, and children (Wark, 2003).

Now You Try

A. Use the Chunking method to paraphrase this sentence.

Original: Often procrastination stems from a real or imagined fear
              or worry that is focused not so much on the thing you are
              avoiding, but its potential consequences. —*Moore, Rebecca;*
              Baker, Barbara; Packer, Arnold, "Coping With Procrastination" 1997

1. How would you divide this sentence into smaller chunks? Underline each chunk.

   * As you divide the sentence into chunks, remember to focus on phrases rather than on single words.

2. Explain the meaning of each chunk using your own words.

   a. _____

   b. _____

   c. _____

3. Using your explanations, write a paraphrase of the original sentence.

   * It is okay to arrange the chunks in a different order than they appear in the original sentence. As you put the chunks together, remember to consider how they are related to each other.

_____

_____

A third paraphrasing method involving changes in grammar, word order, and vocabulary is available on the *Sourcework* website at **http://esl.college.hmco.com/students**. Look for **Grammar Toolbox Method.**

Activities to Practice Paraphrasing

To practice paraphrasing, do one or more of the following activities.

Activity 1 · *Identifying Problems in Paraphrases*

Below are several paraphrases that have been created using the Chunking method. By yourself or with a partner, read the original sentences and then evaluate the paraphrases using the criteria for a good paraphrase on page 7. Circle OK or Not OK and give an explanation.

1.   *Original:*   The United States leads the world in its belief in

Chunk #1   Chunk #2   Chunk #3

romantic love—86 percent of American college

Chunk #4   Chunk #5   Chunk #6

students say they would not marry without love.

Chunk #7   Chunk #8

—Levine, Robert, "Is Love a Luxury?" 1993

Paraphrase: America is ahead in the world in its faith in dreamy love—three quarters of U.S. students in college declared they don't want to marry without being in love (Levine, 1993).

OK   Not OK

Explanation _____

_____

2.   *Original:*   Countries are likely to indulge in romance if they are

Chunk #1

wealthy and value individualism over the community.

Chunk #2   Chunk #3

—Levine, Robert, "Is Love a Luxury?" 1993

Paraphrase 1:   Rich, individual countries are more likely to think love is important (Levine, 1993).

OK   Not OK

Explanation _____

_____

Paraphrase 2:   Countries that are rich and value individualism are more likely to believe in romantic love (Levine, 1993).

OK   Not OK

Explanation _____

_____

3.   *Original:*   There are not nearly as many divorces in this society
                          Chunk #1

[Indian] and I think it's because one doesn't expect to
                          Chunk #2

be nurtured and communicated with and understood

every second of the day. —*Wark, Penny, "What Does Life*
                          Chunk #3

Tell Us About Love?" 2003

Paraphrase 1:   Indian couples are less likely to get divorced because they do not expect caring and open communication from each other at all times (Wark, 2003).

OK   Not OK

Explanation _____

_____

Paraphrase 2:   Indian husbands and wives don't require caring and open communication because divorce is not acceptable (Wark, 2003).

OK   Not OK

Explanation _____

_____

 ACTIVITY 2   ## *Chunking Practice*

Use the Chunking method to paraphrase the following three sentences from the article "Ray Anderson," by Jennifer Beck in Part Two, Heroes, page 159. Use separate paper. You may work alone, with a partner, or in a group.

1. By combining environmentalism with dedication to his company's success, Anderson has proven that being green can also bring in the green for big business.
2. The book *The Ecology of Commerce* suggested that industry was systematically destroying the planet, and the only people in a position to stop the destruction were the industrialists themselves.
3. Almost immediately he [Anderson] began to turn Interface, Inc. [his company] into an environmentally friendly enterprise. He began by taking steps to reduce the company's waste and conserve energy by recycling.

ACTIVITY 3   ## *Paraphrasing Proverbs*

1. Working in a small group, think of a proverb familiar to you.
2. Take a few minutes for each group member to write a paraphrase of the proverb.
3. Read each person's paraphrase aloud and discuss each of the paraphrases using the criteria below:

- It is close in meaning to the proverb.
- No new ideas are added.
- Important ideas are not deleted.

ACTIVITY **4**

Finding the Paraphrase

Use this activity when your whole class is reading the same article from Part Two.

1. With a small group, select two or three sentences from an article in Part Two to paraphrase.
2. Using the Tell a Friend method, the Chunking method, or a combination of the two, rewrite the passages you have selected.
3. Evaluate your paraphrase, according to the criteria for a good paraphrase on page 7.
4. Trade your paraphrases with another group.
5. Read the other group's paraphrases and see if you can identify the original passages in the article.

ACTIVITY **5**

Guessing the Paraphrase

Use a sentence from an article you are reading in Part Two to practice the Tell a Friend method.

1. Divide into groups of three and ask one member of each group to leave the room.
2. With the other person in the group, read a sentence or short excerpt from an article in Part Two.
3. Cover the passage and discuss the meaning of what you have read.
4. Write a paraphrase of the passage.
5. Ask the group member who left the classroom to return. That person reads your paraphrase and identifies the original passage in the article.
6. Write your group's paraphrase on the board. Then discuss each group's paraphrase as a class, using the criteria for a good paraphrase on page 7.

BUILDING YOUR PAPER

Explore Ideas by Paraphrasing

Select 3 to 5 passages from one or more articles in Part Two that you have been exploring for your research paper. Use the Tell a Friend method, the Chunking method, or both to write paraphrases of these passages. Your paraphrases should:

- Have the same meaning as the original.
- Use your own, unique way of explaining the ideas.
- Include the name of the author.
- Have accurate grammar and vocabulary.

Responding to Writing

As you read the articles in Part Two for your guided research paper, consider this second way of exploring the concepts in a source—responding to some of the author's ideas.

When we read actively, we may find that we agree or disagree with different ideas that remind us of our experiences or that we find interesting because they help us see the world in a new way. Teachers are often interested not only in your understanding of an article, but also in your reactions to it. Thus, as a university student, you may be asked to write responses to the material you are reading for a class.

Responding is a good way to figure out if you relate well enough to the ideas in an article to use it in your research paper. When you write a response, you are having a short conversation with the author, explaining what his ideas mean to you. Also, writing a response gives you a chance to practice paraphrasing, a skill you will need often as you integrate evidence into your research paper.

Three Characteristics of a Response

1. **Responses are subjective.** This means you explain *your* opinion, perception, or insight about an idea or ideas in the article.
2. **Responses vary in content.** A response may include one or more of the following approaches:

   * Personal Experience

     Write about an idea in the article that matches your own experience or reminds you of something you or someone you know has experienced.

   * Application

     Write about something that illustrates an idea in the article. This might be something you have read or heard that applies to or supports what the author has written.

   * Agree/Disagree

     Write about a point the author makes that you strongly agree or disagree with. Include in your response an explanation of why you think this way.

3. **Responses vary in length.** The length depends on such factors as the requirements of your assignment and the length of the original source.

Response Examples

Below are student examples of the three approaches to responding just described. Study each example and do the Now You Try exercise that follows.

A Response Using Personal Experience Approach

In her article "Closing the Gap," Mary Piper writes "My life is richer, too, because of the time that I've spent with my elders. Over the past three years I've interviewed my five aunts, listened to family stories, looked at pictures and eaten home-cooked meals. As a result, I better understand my own parents and our country's history." The author's point is that our life becomes more meaningful when we take time to listen to older people's stories of their experiences because we can begin to understand the history of our family and country.

In my experience, I heard from my grandfather about how my great grandmother began a business making and selling clothing after my great grandfather died. My great grandmother was a good seamstress and many people in the town wanted to buy her clothes. She hired other people to help her sew and built her shop into a successful business. Learning about my great grandmother's strength and business ability has inspired me to study business in college. I'd like to someday run my own business just as my great grandmother did and also to encourage other women in my country. As Piper wrote, listening to my grandfather has been a way to give more meaning to my own life.

Now You Try

1. Underline the author and article title in the introduction to the response above.
2. Put a vertical slash at the beginning and end of the quote from the article.
3. Circle the student's explanation of the idea that she is interested in from the article.

A Response Using Application Approach

One idea from the article that I'd like to discuss is Sudo's statement in "Larger Than Life" about a hero's focus on helping other people even when personal risk is involved. Sudo writes, "In fact, the one trait of heroes that transcends all cultural boundaries," Lesy says, "is the willingness to risk one's life for the good of others." Humans are naturally selfish. Most people live their entire lives thinking only about how to improve their own situations. However, for our society to function, we need people who are willing to consider the world beyond their own lives. Cooperation among people is the only solution to many problems such as war, environmental destruction, and poverty. Unfortunately, few people are willing to solve these problems because there is no material reward and sometimes they involve personal risk.

Martin Luther King is a hero because he was willing to lead a fight against racial discrimination. He did not lead this movement to improve his own wealth or reputation. The only reason he devoted his life to civil rights was because he knew that the discrimination blacks experienced was wrong.

We would not have improved racial equality today without him. His willingness to risk his own life for the good of others has encouraged many ordinary people to jump into other social, environmental, and political causes. His sacrifice was enhanced by the sacrifices and social movements that followed his own.

Now You Try

1. Underline the author's name and title of the article in the response introduction.
2. Put a vertical slash at the beginning and end of the quote from the article
3. Circle the student's explanation of the idea from the article that he is interested in.
4. This student gives an example of his point about heroes. Where does his example begin? Mark this place with an X.

A Response Using Agree/Disagree Approach

One important idea from "Going Over the Top" is that a need for personal challenge is a significant reason for the popularity of extreme sports. Bower writes, "Challenging yourself to go to the edge, say extreme sports enthusiasts, triggers an almost addictive sense of accomplishment and power." He also writes, "Meeting challenges and realizing goals can also yield a greater appreciation for living." In other words, putting yourself in a high risk situation and overcoming your fear and your limitations can make you appreciate yourself and your life.

While I agree with his general point, I need to ask why extreme sports? You can challenge yourself through many other things. Playing basketball can be challenging too, if you are really serious about it. You can find challenge by saying something to your boss that you couldn't say before. You can also start a new business instead of complaining about your old job. Why should people endanger their life to feel their power and appreciate their lives? I like peaceful days, but I could also get bored if I have nothing to challenge me. Challenging myself broadens my possibilities. It is exciting to me, so I can relate to extreme sports to some extent. But I will take another path which could be as wild as extreme sports, but less dangerous physically.

Now You Try

1. Circle the name of the author and the article title.
2. Put a vertical slash at the beginning and end of the quotes from the article.
3. Circle the student's explanation of this quote. What words does the student use to introduce her explanation?

_____

4. Where does the student begin to discuss how she disagrees with the author? Mark this place with an X.

Response Format

A response has two parts:

1. An introduction, which includes the author, title, and idea you plan to discuss.
2. Your response or reaction to a part of the article.

Introducing Your Response

In your introduction include:

- The name of the author and the title of the article
- A paraphrase of the specific point from the article that you plan to discuss. You may also want to include a quote of the idea you are discussing.

You may choose to use one of the following two formats:

Format 1: Including the Quote, Then Paraphrasing It

In (name of article), (name of author) writes (quote of sentence or sentences you plan to discuss). In other words . . . (paraphrase of this idea).

Example:

In "The Case for Torture," Michael Levin writes, "There are situations in which torture is not merely permissible but morally mandatory." In other words, he says that torturing people is sometimes acceptable and even necessary.

Format 2: Paraphrasing Only

One interesting idea from (name of article) by (name of author) is (paraphrase of the ideas you plan to discuss).

Example:

One interesting idea from "The Case for Torture" by Michael Levin is that torturing people is sometimes acceptable and even necessary.

Explaining Your Response to the Idea

Once you have identified the specific idea you plan to discuss and provided an explanation of what this means in your own words (a paraphrase), you can begin to discuss your reaction to this idea using one of the approaches suggested in Characteristics of a Response, page 15.

Now You Try

A. Choose one of the two response formats and write an introduction using the information below.

Name of article: "The Friendship of Boys"

Name of author: Mike Barns

Quote: "When boys compete with each other it can be a form of bonding."

Paraphrase: Some boys develop friendship through competitive activities.

Introduction:

_____

_____

_____

Activities to Practice Writing Responses

To practice responding, do one or more of the following activities.

ACTIVITY 1   *Discussing Your Reaction*

Read the short article "Coping with Procrastination" on page 21. In a small group or with the class, discuss your response to the article based on these characteristics.

Personal Experience

Discuss an idea in the article that reminds you of something you have experienced. Have you put off something for one of the reasons the authors mention?

Application

Discuss how you could apply an idea in the article. Can you think of an example of how someone has applied one of the solutions to procrastination mentioned in the article?

Agree/Disagree

Choose an idea from the article that you agree or disagree with. You might choose one of the reasons for putting things off and explain why you agree that it is a powerful reason for people to procrastinate.

ACTIVITY **2**   ***Paraphrasing One Interesting Idea***

1. Choose an article you have read from Part Two. Select one or two sentences that you find interesting. Look for an idea that corresponds to one of the response types:

   - Personal experience
   - Application
   - Agree/disagree

2. Write a paraphrase of the sentences.
3. With a partner,

   - read the original sentences.
   - use your paraphrase to explain what you think the sentences mean.
   - discuss your reaction to this idea. If you have had an experience that is related to the idea, tell your partner the story. If you can think of a good example to illustrate an idea, describe your example. If you agree or disagree, explain why.

4. For more practice, you may repeat step 3 with several partners. Each time you explain the author's idea and your response to it, the process will become easier and your response will become clearer.

ACTIVITY **3**   ***Comparing Articles***

When you have read more than one article on the same topic, you can compare what they say about the topic. Do the following with a partner or a small group.

1. Choose two or three articles from the same unit that you are exploring in Part Two.
2. Look for an idea that is repeated in more than one article. Highlight or write on a separate piece of paper all the sentences from each article that discuss this idea.
3. Discuss how this idea is treated in each article. Is it defined? Is an example given? Does the author express an opinion?
4. Orally summarize how the different articles discuss this idea. Present your ideas to the class.

BUILDING YOUR PAPER

Explore Ideas With a Response

Write a response to one of the articles you have been exploring in Part Two for your guided research paper. You may respond to one or two ideas or to the entire article. As you write your response, remember the following:

- Responses are subjective. They explain *your* opinion or perception about an idea in the article.
- Response introductions include the name of the author and the title of the article.
- The introduction to your response should also identify the specific idea—either quoted or paraphrased—that you plan to discuss in your response.

# Summarizing

A final method for exploring ideas in sources for a research paper is to summarize an article. Summarizing, like responding, demonstrates to yourself and others that you understand the material you have read. We often use summaries in both speaking and writing to tell listeners or readers our ideas quickly and clearly. In academic writing, a summary of someone else's text has four important elements.

Four Criteria for a Good Summary

1. **A good summary acknowledges the original author.**

   - It refers to the writer and the title of the work in a formal way.
   - It presents the writer's ideas objectively, without your interpretation or opinion.

2. **A good summary contains only the most important information.**

   - The topic (the general subject of the article)
   - The main point that the author makes about that topic (the *thesis*)
   - The supporting points that support or explain the thesis

3. **A good summary is much shorter than the original writing.**

   - A one-sentence summary describes only the author's thesis, or main idea.
   - A fuller summary explains both the thesis and main supporting points.

4. **A good summary paraphrases any information taken from the original writing.**

   - Paraphrasing shows that you understand what the author is saying.

Summary Examples

Below is an article about why people procrastinate. After the article are two summaries. The first is a one-sentence summary that explains the author's thesis. The second is a longer, complete summary that includes both the thesis and main supporting points of the article.

"Coping with Procrastination"

Rebecca Moore, Barbara Baker, and Arnold Packer
College Success, 1997

Any discussion of time management would not be complete without an examination of the most well-intentioned person's worst enemy—procrastination. The dictionary (*Webster's new Collegiate*) defines *procrastination* as "the act of putting off intentionally and habitually the doing of something that should be done." Interestingly, most procrastinators do not feel that they are acting intentionally. On the contrary, they feel that they fully *intend* to do whatever it is, but they simply cannot, will not, or—bottom line—they *do not* do it. Procrastinators usually have good reasons for their procrastination (some would call them excuses): "didn't have time," "didn't feel well," "couldn't figure out what to do," "couldn't find what I needed," "the weather was too bad"—the list is never-ending.

2   Even procrastinators themselves know that the surface reasons for their procrastination are, for the most part, not valid. When procrastination becomes extreme, it is a self-destructive course, and, yet, people feel that they are powerless to stop it. This perception can become reality if the underlying cause is not uncovered. Experts have identified some of the serious underlying causes of procrastination. Think about them the next time you find yourself struck by this problem.

3   Often procrastination stems from a real or imagined fear or worry that is focused not so much on the thing you are avoiding but its potential consequences. For instance, your procrastination over preparing for an oral presentation could be based on your fear that no matter how well prepared you are, you will be overcome by nerves and forget whatever you are prepared to say. Every time you think about working on the speech, you become so worried about doing "a bad job" that you have to put the whole thing out of your mind to calm down. You decide that you will feel calmer about it tomorrow and will be in a much better frame to tackle it. Tomorrow the scenario gets repeated. The best way to relieve your anxiety would be to dig in and prepare well so that you can't possibly do poorly.

4   Being a perfectionist is one of the main traits that spawns fear and anxiety. Whose expectations are we afraid of not meeting? Often it is our own harsh judgment of ourselves that creates the problem. We set standards that are too high and then judge ourselves too critically. When you picture yourself speaking before a group, are you thinking about how nervous the other students will be as well, or are you comparing your speaking abilities to the anchorperson on the six o'clock news? A more calming thought is to recall how athletes measure improvements in their performances by tracking and trying to improve on the own "personal best." Champions have to work on beating themselves in order to become capable of competing against their opponents. Concentrating on improving your own past performance, and thinking of specific ways to do so, relieves performance anxiety.

5   On the surface this would seem to be the reason for all procrastination, and the obvious answer is for the procrastinator to find a way to "get motivated." There are situations where lack of motivation is an indicator that you have taken a wrong turn. When you seriously do not want to do the things you need to do, you may need to reevaluate your situation. Did you decide to get a degree in Information Systems because everyone says that's where the high paying jobs are going to be, when you really want to be a social worker or a travel agent? If so, when you find yourself shooting hoops or watching television when you should be putting in time at the computer lab, it may be time to reexamine your decision. Setting out to accomplish something difficult when your heart isn't in it is often the root cause of self-destructive behavior.

6   Often procrastination is due to an inability to concentrate or a feeling of being overwhelmed and indecisive. While everyone experiences these feelings during a particularly stressful day or week, a continuation of these feelings could indicate that you are in a state of burnout. Burnout is a serious problem that occurs when you have overextended yourself for too long a period of time. It is especially likely to occur if you are pushing yourself both physically and mentally. By failing to pace yourself, you will "hit the wall," like a long distance runner who runs too fast at the

beginning of the race. Overworking yourself for too long without mental and physical relaxation is a sure way to run out of steam. Learning to balance your time and set realistic expectations for yourself will prevent burnout.

Sometimes you put off doing something because you literally don't know how to do it. This may be hard to admit to yourself, so you may make other excuses. When you can't get started on something, consider the possibility that you need help. For example, if you get approval from your favorite instructor for a term paper topic that requires collecting data and creating graphics, you can be stymied if you don't have the necessary skills and tools to do the work and do it well. Does the collection and analysis of the data require the use of a software program that you don't have and cannot afford to buy? Sometimes it is difficult to ask for help and sometimes it is even hard to recognize that you need help. When you feel stymied, ask yourself, "Do I need help?" Do you need information but haven't a clue as to where to go to get it? Have you committed to doing something that is really beyond your level of skills? Being able to own up to personal limitations and seek out support and resources where needed is a skill used everyday by highly successful people. ●

One-Sentence Summary

A one-sentence summary includes only the author's thesis, plus the name of the author and the title of the article.

Example:

In "Coping with Procrastination," Moore, Baker, and Packer discuss the fundamental reasons why people put off doing things and how to overcome these issues.

Full Summary

A full summary includes the name of the author, the title of the article, the author's thesis and the main ideas that support it.

Example:

In their article "Coping with Procrastination," Moore, Baker, and Packer suggest that, in order to change the habit of procrastination, it is essential to look below the surface for the real reasons why one puts off doing things. Worry about bad results can cause procrastination, but a better way to approach the task you dread is to be very sure you are so ready that nothing bad can happen. If a person expects nothing less than perfection from himself, he will fear failure and simply not begin the task. A suggestion for dealing with this is to copy athletes who strive to achieve their own best effort rather than comparing themselves with the champion in their field. Sometimes motivation is the problem; a person may feel trapped by a bad decision that no longer matches his or her desires. Re-examining one's goals may help. Burnout, or exhaustion from pushing oneself too hard for too long, can lead to procrastination. In this situation, it is essential to set doable goals. Finally, a person may avoid doing a task because of a real lack of knowledge or experience about the job at hand. Seeking assistance from others can make the task less forbidding.

Techniques for Identifying Main Ideas for a Summary

One of the challenges of summarizing is that we must choose which information to include, keeping in mind the principles of being complete and objective. You can choose one of the three techniques that follow to help you identify main ideas in an article.

Technique 1: Underlining Key Ideas

1. Read the article completely several times to develop a basic understanding of the ideas presented.
2. With a highlighting pen, mark each idea in the article that you believe is important.

   - Often, although not always, you will find that each paragraph has a key sentence. It is often the first or last sentence in a paragraph.
   - If you find that you have highlighted most or all of the sentences in a paragraph, you may be highlighting supporting details rather than main ideas.
   - If so, go back and underline only the main ideas in the sentences that you highlighted.

3. When you finish highlighting, reread each sentence to make sure you understand it.
4. Use either the Tell a Friend or Chunking method to paraphrase each sentence you highlighted.
5. You can use these paraphrased ideas in your summary.

Now You Try

Re-read the article "Coping with Procrastination." As you read, underline the one or two sentences from each paragraph that you believe are the most important points. Check the sentences you have chosen against the full summary of the article on page 23.

Technique 2: Dividing and Describing

1. With a pen in hand, read the entire article, "Coping with Procrastination." Each time you sense that the topic is shifting, draw a vertical line where you think the shift begins.

   - Don't analyze how the topic is changing. Let your intuition do the work.
   - Throughout the article, draw a line each time you feel the topic shifts.

2. By drawing these lines you have created sections. In a longer article, you will discover that paragraphs are grouped together according to common topics.

   - Analyze the topic of each section you have created.
   - Write a phrase or short sentence that explains the topic of each section.

3. The topics of these groups of paragraphs are usually the author's main supporting points. Examining how many paragraphs an author uses to discuss a single idea can help you decide which information is most important and should be included in your summary.

4. Use your list of phrases describing the sections to write your summary.

Now You Try

> In the article "Coping with Procrastination" on the website at **http://esl.college.hmco.com/students**, a line has been drawn each time the topic shifts. In the first two sections, a short phrase describing the topic has been given. Write a short phrase or sentence describing the topic of the other three sections of the article.

Technique 3: Summary Grid

Sometimes it is helpful to lay out your notes in a visual way. Using a grid is one way to help organize the information in an article.

1. Using a grid like the one below, take notes on each paragraph or section of several paragraphs.

   - Writing main ideas and supporting details in separate columns is a good way to help distinguish between the two.

2. Use your notes to create a summary of your article.

   - Remember, a summary focuses on main ideas. Details are usually not included in summaries. In some cases, a specific example from the article might be included.

Example Summary Grid

Here is an example of a summary grid created by a student after reading an article on negative aspects of drinking bottled water.

Paragraph(s)	Main Idea	Some Supporting Details
1	• Bottled water may not be any safer than tap water.	
2–3	• Bottled water manufacturers don't have to disclose the source of their water.	• Yosemite brand comes from a Los Angeles suburb. • Everest brand comes from Texas.
4	• The EPA requires fewer contamination tests for bottled water than city water.	• The FDA only tests once a year, or if there is a complaint.
5	• Plastic bottles are a source of water contamination also.	• Bacteria develop in bottles. • Chemicals leach from plastic material.

Now You Try

Use the grid below to take notes on each paragraph of the article "Coping with Procrastination."

Summary Grid

Paragraph(s)	Main Idea	Some Supporting Details

To print out a copy of this grid, go to the *Sourcework* website at **http://esl.college.hmco.com/students**

Summary Formats

A summary of an article includes two parts:

1. An introductory sentence or two that includes three pieces of information:

- The title of the article, or source
- The name of the author(s)
- The author's thesis, or main idea

2. The body, which may be one or more paragraphs depending on the length of the original writing, describes the main ideas in the original source.

Introducing Your Summary

You can choose how you want to arrange the information in your introduction. Below are two possible formats.

Format 1: One Sentence

In (title of article), (author's name) writes/discusses (article thesis).

Example:

In "Why McDonald's Fries Taste So Good," Schlosser (2002) writes that while McDonald's spread all over the country during the 1960s, the company tried to spend less on its workers, get its supplies from fewer sources, and guarantee that its French fries always tasted the same.

NOTE: This format appears in the example summary on page 23.

Format 2: Two Sentences

(Name of author) writes about (article topic) in (his/her/their) article, (name of article). The second sentence of the summary introduction describes the thesis.

Example:

Schlosser (2002) writes about the spread of McDonald's restaurants in his article "Why McDonald's Fries Taste So Good." He says that while McDonald's spread all over the country during the 1960s, the company tried to spend less on its workers, get its supplies from fewer sources, and guarantee that its French fries always tasted the same.

Now You Try

Using Format 2, write an introduction for a summary of "Coping with Procrastination."

_____

_____

_____

Describing the Main Ideas

After you introduce the author, title, and main idea or thesis of the original, use the notes you made with one of the Techniques for Identifying Main Ideas on page 24 to write the body of your summary.

Combining a Summary and a Response

Sometimes you might want to combine a summary with a response as a means of exploring sources for your research paper. In this case, your summary appears first and your response is second. Your summary may be a single sentence summary or a fuller summary, depending on your assignment. Your response may focus on just one or two ideas or it may discuss the entire article.

Summary and Response Format

A summary and response has two parts:

1. An introduction that summarizes the article and tells the reader which ideas you plan to discuss.

   - The name of the author and title of the source
   - A summary of the article
   - A statement of the idea or ideas you will respond to

2. Your response, or reaction, to ideas in the article. This includes paraphrases of specific ideas you will discuss.

   - Your response to one or more ideas from the article
   - Paraphrases of each idea as you discuss it

Summary and Response Example

Here is an example of a combination summary and response.

author ——————— Susan Scarf Merrell (1995) writes about birth order in her book *The Accidental Bond.* She explains whether it is true or a myth that birth order can predict a person's future. Even though many people think that birth order defines a person's life, other important factors such as culture, gender, social and economic status affect a person's achievement. Two important issues from the book that I would like to discuss are Merrell's statements about gender and culture. For me, they are connected to each other.

The first issue is about gender. Merrell (1995) indicates that if the firstborn in the family is a girl, she has different experiences than her brothers. I agree with her because her statement applies in my own culture. Even though Mexican culture about "machismo" is changing, it still exists in our society. By the term "machismo," I mean that men are considered more important than women. In some Mexican families the gender of the firstborn is very important. If the firstborn is a boy, he will receive more benefits or advantages than a girl. Also, he will receive more privileges and he will have access to more things. For example, in my father's family he was the firstborn, so he had the opportunity to study in Mexico City from the time he was 12 years old (the family used to live in a little town far from Mexico City). However, his sisters had to wait to study outside the town until they were more than 18 years old. They went to live in a city close to their parents' house so their parents could visit them every weekend.

The next important idea is about culture. Merrell (1995) indicates that if a firstborn in a wealthy family is a boy, he receives the economic and powerful benefits of his family. In the "machismo" culture the primogeniture is supposed to inherit the control of the family's business and money. Therefore, for the family, it is very important that the firstborn is a man because they think that a man has more intelligence or capacity than a woman. For instance, a very famous Mexican family from the North of the country, which owns a big company, had as firstborn a girl, but they did not give her all the control of the business. They gave her a comfortable and nice life as a member of the family. However, the second born was a boy, and he has in his hands the control of the business because he is a man. Nowadays, he is the president of his family's business.

In conclusion, in these cases, gender and culture affect a person's development more than birth order, therefore it is only a myth. Merrell's thesis is interesting and I agree with her. It is important to remember that factors such as culture, gender, social and economical status influence the development of a person.

Now You Try

Work with a partner to label the following parts in the summary and response example on birth order.

1. Author of book discussed in summary (this one has been done for you)
2. Title of the source (a book)
3. Summary of the source
4. Two ideas in the book that the writer will respond to
5. Paraphrase of first idea writer will respond to
6. Writer's explanation of her response
7. Paraphrase of second idea writer will respond to
8. Explanation of her response to second idea
9. Conclusion

Activities to Practice Summarizing

To practice writing summaries, do one or more of the following activities.

ACTIVITY 1 *Finding Main Ideas and Writing a Summary*

With a partner or a small group, apply the numbered directions to one of the paragraphs that follow. Your teacher may put the paragraph on an overhead transparency for you.

1. Identify key words and phrases that express the main ideas.
2. On the board or an overhead transparency, present your paragraph with key phrases underlined. Explain why you chose those phrases as key and why you didn't choose others.
3. Write your summary on the board or on another transparency and show it to the class. Explain how your summary satisfies the four criteria for a good summary on page 21.

Paragraph 1

Sometimes the original writing includes lots of specific facts, such as proper names or statistics, so you have to choose which to include. If the facts all have equal emphasis in the original, it does not matter which you choose to use in the summary.

The New Jersey Turnpike runs through the heart of the flavor industry, an industrial corridor dotted with refineries and chemical plants. International Flavors and Fragrances (IFF), the world's largest flavor company, has a manufacturing facility off Exit 8A in Dayton, New Jersey; Givaudan, the world's second largest flavor company, has a plant in East Hanover. Haarmann & Reimer, the largest German flavor company, has a plant in Teterboro, as does Takasago, the largest Japanese flavor company. Flavor Dynamics has a plant in South Plainfield; Frutarom is in North Bergen; Elan Chemical is in Newark. Dozens of companies manufacture flavors in the corridor between Teaneck and South Brunswick. Altogether the area produces about two thirds of the flavor additives sold in the United States.
—*Schlosser, Eric, "Why McDonald's Fries Taste So Good" 2002*

Paragraph 2

Another type of source paragraph tells a chronological history but, in summarizing, you can include only a few details that you consider most important or interesting. Also, when special terms are used, such as "methyl anthranilate" in the paragraph below, you do not need to explain the technical words in a summary, but can simply use a general term, such as "a chemical."

The flavor industry emerged in the mid-nineteenth century, as processed foods began to be manufactured on a large scale. . . . In the early part of the twentieth century, Germany took the technological lead in flavor production, owing to its powerful chemical industry. Legend has it that a German scientist discovered methyl anthranilate, one of the first artificial flavors, by accident while mixing chemicals in his laboratory. Suddenly the lab was filled with the sweet smell of grapes. Methyl anthranilate later became the chief flavor in grape Kool-Aid. After World War II much of the perfume industry shifted from Europe to the United States, settling in New York City near the garment district and the fashion houses. The flavor industry came with it, later moving to New Jersey for greater plant capacity. Manmade flavor additives were used mostly in baked goods, candies, and sodas until the 1950s, when sales of processed food began to soar. The invention of gas chromatographs and mass spectrometers—machines capable of detecting volatile gases at low levels—vastly increased the number of flavors that could be synthesized. By the mid-1960s, flavor companies were churning out compounds to supply the taste of Pop Tarts, Bac-Os, Tab, Tang, Filet-O-Fish sandwiches, and literally thousands of other new foods. —*Schlosser, Eric, "Why McDonald's Fries Taste So Good" 2002*

Paragraph 3

In summarizing original writing that uses a casual attitude or makes a joke, you should mention the humorous tone of the original, but write a serious summary. Also when the original contains many questions, choose only one or two questions that seem to represent the most important ideas to rephrase as statements and use as part of the summary.

Obviously, sports connect with something deeply rooted in the male psyche, dating back to prehistoric times, when guys survived by hunting and fighting, and they needed many of the skills exhibited by modern athletes—running, throwing, spitting, renegotiating their contracts, adjusting their private parts on nationwide television, etc. So that would explain how come guys like to *participate* in sports. But how come they care so much about games played by *other* guys? Does this also date back to prehistoric times? When the hunters were out hurling spears into mastodons, were there also prehistoric guys watching from the hills, drinking prehistoric beer, eating really bad prehistoric hot dogs, and shouting "We're No. 1!" but not understanding what it meant because this was before the development of mathematics? —*Barry, Dave, "Sports Nuts" 1991*

Paragraph 4

When you summarize a serious opinion piece, the opinion of the author must be maintained throughout the summary.

I am not advocating torture as punishment. Punishment is addressed to deeds irrevocably past. Rather, I am advocating torture as an acceptable measure for preventing future evils. So understood, it is far less objectionable than many extant punishments. Opponents of the death penalty, for example, are forever insisting that executing a murderer will not bring back. his victim . . . But torture, in the cases described, is intended not to bring anyone back but to keep innocents from being dispatched. The most powerful argument against using torture as a punishment or to secure confessions is that such practices disregard the rights of the individual. Well, if the individual is all that important—and he is—it is correspondingly important to protect the rights of individuals threatened by terrorists. If life is so valuable that it must never be taken, the lives of the innocents must be saved even at the price of hurting the one who endangers them.
—*Levin, Michael, "The Case for Torture" 1982*

ACTIVITY **2**   *Finding Main Ideas in a Complete Article*

Do this activity when everyone in the class is reading the same article in Part Two for possible use in your guided research paper.

1. For homework, read through an article from Part Two. As you read, underline what you believe are the key ideas, or complete a summary grid (review the sample grid on page 26). Bring your underlined article or summary grid to class for discussion.
2. In a small group, work through the article paragraph by paragraph discussing which ideas you have selected and why.
3. Share your list with the class.
4. If there is time, work with your group to write a summary using the ideas from your list.

ACTIVITY **3**   *Dividing and Describing*

1. Working by yourself, read through an article from Part Two and draw a vertical line at each point where you feel the topic shifts.
2. In a small group with others who have read the same article, share where you have drawn lines and discuss why you think your divisions make sense.
3. Try to come to agreement with your group about where the topic shifts and how the article should be divided.
4. With your group, describe the main idea of each section of the article in one or two sentences.
5. Share your divisions and descriptions with the rest of the class.
6. As a class or in your small group, use your descriptions to write a summary of the article.

BUILDING YOUR PAPER

Explore Ideas With a Summary

Write a summary, or a summary and response, of an article that you have been reading and exploring in Part Two.

- The summary introduction should include the title of the source, the name of the author, and the author's thesis.
- Remember that a summary contains only the most important information and is shorter than the original source.
- Use one of the strategies described in class (underlining key ideas, divide and describe, or a summary grid) to help you identify main ideas.

CHAPTER

2

Building a Paper:

Focus

After exploring the theme in a broad sense, we are ready to write a research paper about one specific aspect of the theme. Here you will begin to develop a specific topic for your paper. Your teacher will assign a Question for Writing from the end of the theme you have been reading about in Part Two, or you will work with your classmates to develop a research question.

Using your writing question—or research question—as a guide, read your sources in Part Two again, but in a different way than you did in Chapter 1. This time, make notes only about the parts of the source that help to answer your research question. As you read each source and take notes, you'll start to accumulate useful ideas that will contribute to the content of your paper.

When you review these notes, look for patterns of similar or related ideas. Then organize these concepts into a rough outline of the potential supporting points for your paper.

In this chapter you will practice

- Creating a research question
- Identifying the focus of your research question
- Doing a focused reading and taking notes
- Organizing notes into a rough outline of your research paper

By the end of this chapter you will have written a research question and used it as a guide in taking notes on the articles that you will use from Part Two. You will also have organized your notes into a rough outline for the paper you'll write.

A Research Question

To explore your topic in Chapter 1, you did an open reading of several articles from one of the themes in Part Two. In this next step of the writing process, you will do a second reading of the same articles. As you reread your sources, you will look for specific information about your topic, using a research question to guide you.

Using a Research Question

A research question is a tool that enables you to read your sources more efficiently by providing you with a specific focus. The research question helps you decide which information might be useful for your research paper, that is, which information can help to answer your research question, and which information will not be relevant.

Often, you can use a research question that your teacher provides. For example, your teacher may assign you a question from the "Questions for Writing" listed at the end of each unit in Part Two, or you may be asked to choose one of these questions. If you already have a research question, you will not need to read the next section on creating a research question.

Creating a Research Question

If your teacher does not give you a research question, it is worthwhile to create your own because using it will save you time and help you read sources more effectively. You can create a research question from the notes you took during your open reading of sources in Chapter 1.

Two Ways to Create a Research Question

1. Consider the ideas you shared with classmates or wrote about after you did your open reading in Chapter 1. For example, in a discussion on heroism, one student shared her thoughts with her classmates on the following quote from "Eve's Daughters," Part Two, page 163.

    > "The hero has an original perspective that distinguishes her from others who settle for agreement and conformity or are too beaten down to ask necessary questions. The relationship between the hero and the established order of things is fluid; she insists on her freedom to perceive, within the context of things-as-they-are, the way things *could* be."—*Polster, Miriam, 2001*

    Talking about this quote led to a more general discussion of the definition of a hero. This student eventually developed the following research question:

    What is a hero?

2. Look at some of the sections you highlighted in your sources during your open reading. These ideas can turn into more general questions. For example, in an article on mind-body medicine, a student highlighted the following sentence:

> "Equally intriguing are studies that tackle the mind-body equation by finding links between severe stress and illness."—*Goode, Erica, "Your Mind May Ease What's Ailing You" 1999*

After thinking about this quote, the student developed her research question:

> How is stress related to illness?

Now You Try

Write one or two possible research questions based on this excerpt from "If Poor Get Richer, Do We See Progress?" in Part Two, Globalization, page 171.

> "Rising consumption has helped meet basic needs and create jobs," says Christopher Flavin, president of the Worldwatch Institute, a Washington, D.C., think tank. "But as we enter a new century, this unprecedented consumer appetite is undermining the natural systems we all depend on and making it even harder for the world's poor to meet their basic needs."
> —*Knickerbocker, Brad, 2004*

Research questions:

_____

_____

_____

BUILDING YOUR PAPER

Create a Research Question

If your teacher has not given you a research question, create one now. In developing your research question, you may want to use an idea from the discussion and writing you did after your open reading of the articles on your theme in Part Two.

Focused Reading and Taking Notes

With your research question as a guide, you can begin to decide which information from the articles will be useful for the research paper you are building. To use your research question effectively, you need to be clear about its focus: What is it asking you to look for in your reading?

Focus of a Research Question

A research question includes two parts:

1. The topic for your paper, usually in the form of a noun or noun phrase.
2. The focus, which suggests what you will say about the topic and tells you what kind of information to look for as you read.

Sample Research Question

Why do people become addicted to alcohol?

- The general topic of this question is the noun phrase "addicted to alcohol," and the focus is about why people become addicted—**causes** of addiction.

Using this sample research question, you would look in your sources for information about the causes of addiction. You would disregard any information about the effects of drinking alcohol or about types of alcohol addiction, since the focus of the question does not mention these ideas.

Types of Focus

The focus of a research question may be one of several types.

Cause

This kind of question asks you to explain the causes or reasons for something. See the example about why people become addicted to alcohol.

Effect

Writing about the consequences or effects of an event or action is another common focus of academic writing, as in this research question:

What are the negative consequences of alcohol addiction?

- The writer using this research question will read sources looking for effects of alcohol addiction.

Comparison

Your research question might ask you to compare two or more concepts:

How are attitudes toward drinking alcohol similar or different in the United States and Japan?

- The focus for this question is comparing attitudes in the two countries. As the writer reads through sources, he will search for information that describes the attitudes towards drinking in the two countries.

Definition

Some research questions ask for an in-depth definition of a topic:

What are the signs of alcohol addiction?

- Here the focus is on explaining what alcoholism is, so the writer will read sources and note any information that helps define alcoholism.

Classification

Other research questions are about ways of classifying a topic:

What are the different patterns of alcohol use?

- The focus in this paper will be how people use alcohol. The evidence the writer looks for in reading sources will be about various ways people incorporate alcohol into their lives.

Process

A research question may ask how to do something:

How can a person who is alcoholic stop drinking?

- With this focus about how to stop using alcohol, the writer will read for information about methods for quitting drinking.

Argument

Some research questions may be in a yes/no format and ask you to explain an opinion:

Should the legal age for drinking be lowered from 21 to 18?

- In this case, the focus is an opinion and why that opinion is right. The writer using this research question will decide his opinion about the question and look for information about why that opinion is correct.

Again, notice that a research question helps you look for certain information and discard other information. In the argument question, for example, you would look for information to support your opinion, and you would ignore information that discusses causes or effects of alcoholism or any other focus. In this way, as you read through sources, the research question helps you select only the information that will be useful in writing your paper.

Now You Try

For each research question that follows, identify the topic and the type of focus: cause, effect, comparison, definition, classification, process, or argument. Then describe the kind of information to look for in sources to answer the question.

1. How does early home schooling affect students' later academic performance?

   Topic _____

   Type of focus _____

   Kind of information to look for _____

2. Should assisted suicide be legal?

   Topic _____

   Type of focus _____

   Kind of information to look for _____

3. How do the public school systems in the United States and Canada compare with each other?

   Topic _____

   Type of focus _____

   Kind of information to look for _____

Research Questions With More Than One Focus

Sometimes a research question combines more than one focus idea. In this case you need to identify each focus and consider how they relate to each other.

Example 1:

Research Question: In what ways can understanding the causes of alcohol addiction help a person stop drinking?

- This research question includes two focuses:

    1. the causes of alcohol addiction (cause)
    2. the methods for stopping addiction (process)

- The writer must also discuss how methods for stopping relate to causes of drinking.

Example 2:

Research Question: How does the value of individualism influence people's expectations of marriage?

- This research question has two focuses:

    1. the definition of the concept of individualism (definition)
    2. the effects of individualism on ideas about marriage (effect)

Now You Try

For each research question, write the topic and the type of focus: cause, effect, comparison, definition, classification, process, or argument. Then describe what kind of information to look for in order to answer the question. Remember there is more than one focus in each research question.

1. How does blues music reflect the values of U.S. culture?

Topic _____

Types of focus _____

Kind of information to look for _____

2. What are the different kinds of yoga and how do they compare in methods and health benefits?

Topic _____

Types of focus _____

Kind of information to look for _____

BUILDING YOUR PAPER

Identify the Focus of Your Research Question

Look at your research question again for the paper you are building and identify the topic and the focus.

- Recall that the topic of the research question is usually a noun or noun phrase. The focus suggests what you will say about that topic.
- Remember that your research question may have more than one focus.

Focused Reading Guidelines

With the topic and focus of your research question clearly in mind, you are ready to do a focused reading of the articles on your theme in Part Two. As you read through your sources:

1. Read quickly.
2. Highlight any information that looks like it might answer your research question. Use a different color marker than you used for open reading.
3. Don't analyze what you highlight. Just mark anything that seems useful.

4. Notice that some sources will be covered with highlights while others will have only a few marked areas. However, it is not the quantity of information that makes a source valuable, but whether the information actually relates to your research question.
5. Go back and reread only the information you just highlighted. Look up any confusing words, then reread those sections until you understand them.

Now You Try

To understand how a research question can guide and focus your reading, do two focused readings of "Coping with Procrastination" on page 21, using different research questions.

1. Use a color marker to highlight any information that you think will help answer the question, *Why do people procrastinate?*
2. Read the article a second time. This time look for information to answer the question, *How can people overcome procrastination?* Use a different color marker to highlight useful information.
3. Share the information you highlighted for each question. Is it the same or different from what your classmates highlighted?

Note-Taking Methods

With many sources to read and evaluate, you need a way to keep track of the material you may use in your research paper. You need to record where you have looked, what you have found, and how to find each piece of information again. In short, you need a system for taking notes. There are many ways to keep and organize information. Choose a system that's useful for you and that you will use every time you do research for your paper.

It's not a good idea to neglect taking notes on an article "just this one time" because you are in a hurry or because you plan to come back to it later and read it in more detail. You will save yourself time and frustration if you take notes on everything you think may be of even the slightest use. You can always throw away any notes you don't use. You can't always retrace your steps and find the same quote again if you haven't kept track of it. Below are four common methods for taking notes.

Using Your Highlighted Sources

For a short paper, or if you are reading only two or three sources, you may be able to simply use as your notes the parts that you highlighted during your focused reading.

The advantage of this system is that you've already done the work—the notes are right there in the articles you've read. The drawbacks are that you can't move the notes around to group similar ideas together, and you still have to paraphrase the ideas in order to use them in your writing.

Taking Notes on a Computer

1. Type your research question at the top of the page.
2. Type the source information under the research question: the title of the article, the author, the publication where the article appeared, the date it appeared, and the page numbers.
3. Type any sentences from the article that you think can help provide an answer to your research question.
4. Next to each piece of information, type comments about how you might use this information in your paper.

The advantage of this system is that you begin to develop material that is directly related to your paper. This method allows you to focus on useful source information without being distracted by other information in the article. The disadvantage is that you must have access to a computer when you are doing your focused reading.

Writing Margin Notes

At this stage in the writing process, some writers prefer to simply refer to the text they highlighted during their focused reading rather than creating a separate set of notes. In addition to the highlights, you can write comments in the margins of the article next to highlighted information.

The advantage of this system is that it is quick and easy. The disadvantage is that you must photocopy all your sources and have them with you whenever you work on your paper. In addition, you will not be able to move these notes around as you begin to sort and organize them in later stages of the writing process.

Using Note Cards

1. Use a separate card for each sentence or group of sentences from the source article that might help you answer your research question.
2. Write the title, author, date of publication, and page number of the source on the card.
3. In addition to the quote from the article, write notes to yourself about how you might use this information.

The advantage of this method is that you can easily reorganize the information by rearranging the cards. However, taking notes this way is time-consuming and the stack of note cards can be awkward to carry.

The key point is to take some time at this focus stage of your research process to devise a way to take notes that works for you. Your method should be easy, accurate, and comfortable enough that you will follow it for taking notes on all your sources.

Activities to Practice Taking Notes

To practice note-taking methods, do one or both of the following activities.

ACTIVITY 1

Sharing Highlighted Information

Do this in a small group with others who have the same research question.

1. For homework, do a focused reading of at least one source in Part Two that you are reading for your research paper. Bring your highlighted article to class.
2. In small groups, share three pieces of information you highlighted. Discuss how this information could be used to help answer the research question.
3. If the whole class is working on the same research question, share up to four pieces of information that your group believes would be most useful in answering the research question. There will probably be more than four pieces of useful information, but limit yourself to four.

ACTIVITY 2

Explaining Information From Sources

Do this with several classmates who are working with different research questions and/or different sources of information from Part Two.

1. Complete a focused reading on at least three sources in Part Two.
2. In a small group or with a partner, share your research question and then explain some of the information you found to help you answer the research question.
3. Use your own words when discussing the information from your sources; in this way, you will begin to develop a greater level of comfort in using and writing about the ideas in a source. The more you practice talking about this information, the easier it will be to write similar explanations when you begin your paper.

BUILDING YOUR PAPER

Read and Take Notes on Your Sources

1. Using your research question as a guide, complete a focused reading of the articles in Part Two that you plan to use. Remember to highlight any information that may help to answer your research question.
2. Write a set of notes for each source you selected. You can write your notes with a computer, in the margins of the articles, or on note cards.

Creating a Rough Outline

Now that you have a collection of notes, you have much of the substance of your research paper. However, you have to decide how this information can be combined and organized into your paper. Look again at the focus of your research question. The focus will guide the way you analyze your notes and eventually, how you organize your paper.

For example, if your research question asks for the effects of something, you would look through your notes to find related ideas that could be grouped together. Each group of similar ideas would relate to one effect.

Example:

Using the research question presented at the beginning of this chapter, one writer did a focused reading about the causes of alcohol addiction. Then she analyzed the notes from her reading, looking for causes. She identified three main categories of answers to her research question and created a rough outline of these ideas that looked like this:

Rough Outline

Research question: Why do people become addicted to alcohol?

Causes:

1. Emotional distress
2. Social pressure
3. Genetic predisposition

A rough outline begins with your research question and contains a short, simple list of the main ideas found in your reading notes.

You will develop the groups of ideas that you identify in the analysis of your notes into the main supporting points of your paper. When you refine this rough outline and draft your research paper, you may change how you describe these supporting points, what information you include with each point, or the points themselves. But a rough outline is a first step in organizing your ideas.

Following are a few techniques to choose from to help you group your notes into categories of similar ideas or supporting points for your research paper.

Three Techniques for Analyzing Notes for a Rough Outline

Technique 1: Brainstorming a List

To use this technique you need to have your notes written on a piece of paper separate from the source article, or on note cards.

1. Read all your notes quickly to refresh your memory and then put them aside.
2. On a fresh piece of paper, or on your computer, write your research question.

3. Without looking at your notes, brainstorm a list of words and phrases from your notes that come to mind as you consider the answer to your research question. Write quickly without analyzing or judging the ideas.
4. Return to your notes and check to see if you have missed any ideas during your brainstorm.
5. Read over your list to see which words or phrases seem to go together. Label each group of words that go together with a different number. Work quickly, letting your intuition do the work. Don't stop to figure out how the words in each group are related.

For an example, in a brainstorm about the characteristics of a successful city, a group of students created the list that follows and numbered the related ideas.

Research question: What makes a successful city?

Strong neighborhoods 1	Natural beauty 3
Good economy 2	Safe 2
Cultural amenities 3	Dynamism 3
Arts community 3	Diverse industry 2
Major league sports team 3	Flexibility 2
Volunteerism 1	Opportunities for variety
Interesting places to go 3	of people 2
Easy to get around 3	Good citizens 1
Affordable housing 1	Strong leadership 1
Good air and water quality 3	Attractive urban design 3
Strong sense of itself 1	Good colleges 2
Good schools 1	Low crime 1

6. Once you have created and numbered a list, look for ways to describe the different groups of ideas. Ask yourself: What do all the ideas with the same number have in common?

Using the list above, the students decided that all the items numbered "1" were about social structure; all "2s," about the economy; and all "3s," about the environment. They then created a rough outline using these categories.

Rough Outline

Research question: What makes a successful city?

Characteristics:

1. Strong social structure
2. Solid economy
3. Good physical and cultural environment

Technique 2: Sorting Your Notes

1. Read your notes and put a check mark next to each piece of information that you find particularly useful in answering your research question. Try for 15 to 30 check marks.
2. If your notes are on a single piece of paper, cut them apart so that each piece of information is on a separate strip. If your notes are on note cards, you already have your separate pieces of paper.
3. Put all the notes that seem to belong together into the same pile. Don't spend time analyzing how they are related; just work intuitively. You will probably find that some ideas don't fit easily into any category, so you may decide to omit them. You may also notice that some categories have many ideas and others have very few.
4. Now analyze what connects the ideas in each pile and give each pile a category name—a descriptive word or phrase, as the students did in the list about a successful city on page 45. These categories will become the main supporting points in your rough outline.

Technique 3: Color Coding

1. Assemble all your reading notes and several different colored highlighting pens.
2. Read all your notes quickly and decide on some categories for the different kinds of information. Between three and eight categories is usually a good number.
3. Assign a different color to each category and make a key showing which color represents which idea.
4. Highlight all the notes in a category with the same color.
5. Name each category and use these categories as the main supporting points in your rough outline.

Activities to Practice Organizing Your Notes

To practice organizing notes, do one or more of the following activities.

ACTIVITY 1   *Brainstorming a List From Your Notes*

1. With a group of classmates who are working on the same research question, brainstorm a list of ideas from your notes that will answer the question. One person should be the secretary while the others suggest ideas.
2. Write your list on the board for the whole class.
3. With your class, look at each list and begin to categorize the ideas into groups, numbering each group.
4. In your small groups, write a phrase or sentence that describes each category of ideas. Share these descriptions with the class.

ACTIVITY **2**

Sorting Your Notes

Do this activity with a partner or group using the same research question as you.

1. For homework, create a set of strips from your notes following steps 1 and 2 in Technique 2: Sorting Your Notes, page 46. Bring these strips to class. As an alternative, your teacher may complete this step and provide each group with a set of strips.
2. In your group, read each strip. Make sure you understand each separate idea. Throw out any duplicate information.
3. With your group, begin to sort the strips into piles.
4. Once the strips are sorted, analyze the common idea in each pile of notes. Develop a category name—a descriptive word or phrase—that describes each pile.
5. Share your categories with the class and ask for feedback about whether the notes in each category fit the category name.

ACTIVITY **3**

Color-Coding Your Notes

1. For homework, color-code your own focused reading notes from an article in Part Two.
2. With a partner, compare how you've labeled your notes.

   - Do some sources have ideas that are similar?
   - Which point(s) seems to have the most supporting information?
   - Do any points have only one piece of supporting information?

3. Create a category name—a descriptive word or phrase—for the ideas in each color.

   - Do you have any questions about how some of the information in your sources relates to these categories?

BUILDING YOUR PAPER

Create a Rough Outline

Create a rough outline for your research paper that includes your research question and a list of potential supporting points from your notes.

- Remember that *brainstorming a list, sorting your notes,* and *color-coding* are three useful ways to identify key ideas for your paper.

Building a Paper:

Organize

Sooner or later we have to write the first sentence of our research paper. It might seem like the most difficult sentence of all because we are facing a blank page.

However, now that you've explored and analyzed so much information—facts from and opinions about articles in Part Two and thoughts of your own about the topic—your paper may be blank, but your mind certainly isn't. Several things you have already written will help you with that first important sentence.

Look at your research question and rough outline that you created in Chapter 2 and you will find that, together, they lead to a thesis statement: that single sentence that, all by itself, gives the basic idea for your paper. Once you have a thesis statement, you can use it to help organize the rest of your paper.

In this chapter you will mostly use notes you took while reading articles from Part Two. As you read your notes, you will look for information, or evidence, that you can use to explain the ideas in your paper.

In this chapter you will practice

- writing a thesis statement
- selecting supporting evidence from sources
- creating a detailed outline

By the end of this chapter, you will have written your thesis statement, chosen the most useful evidence to support your ideas, and organized your evidence into an outline that is easy to use in writing your paper.

Writing a Thesis Statement

Your rough outline from Chapter 2 reflects the focus of your reading question and provides some general ideas about how to answer it. The next step is to plan your answer to your reading question in more detail.

The short answer to your research question is your thesis statement. This is the single sentence that tells the point you want to make in your paper. Articulating your thesis, or the main thing you want to say, right at the start will help in two ways:

1. You will find out at the beginning whether you have a clear, workable idea.
2. You will be able to use the thesis statement as a guide while writing the essay.

The thesis statement you develop in this chapter will be your **working thesis.** This means it's still tentative. Further along in the writing process, you may discover that you need to revise your thesis statement because of additional information you find or a new direction your research takes.

Your thesis is different from your topic. A topic is a short phrase that states the general subject of your paper, such as:

Expectations of marriage

* In contrast, a thesis statement sets up a framework for your essay. It tells the reader not only your topic but also the focus, or what you plan to say about that topic.

Three Characteristics of an Effective Thesis Statement

An effective thesis statement has these qualities:

* It states the focus, or what you will say about the topic.
* It includes supporting points that are logically connected to the focus and that show how the paper will be organized.
* It uses formal language that is easy to understand.

1. An effective thesis states the topic and focus of the essay.

As you create your thesis statement, you will return to your research question from Chapter 2. Recall that the research question defines the focus of your paper. This focus should be clearly mentioned in your thesis statement.

Example 1:

Research Question: How are expectations of marriage in the United States and India similar or different?

* This research question asks for a comparison of attitudes toward marriage in two countries.

Thesis statement: Belief in romantic love, the division of family responsibilities, and attitudes toward divorce are *three differences between American and Indian expectations of marriage.*

- The topic, "expectations of marriage," and the focus, "three differences between the United States and India," are directly stated in the thesis.

Example 2:

Research Question: Why do people become homeless?

- The research question asks for a discussion of the causes of homelessness.

Thesis statement: The lack of affordable housing, inadequate public assistance, and the breakdown of the family are *three causes of homelessness.*

- The topic, homelessness, and the focus, "three causes," are directly stated in the thesis.

Now You Try

For each thesis statement below, circle the topic and underline the focus.

A. Three major factors cause teenagers to commit murder: the influence of the media, the easy availability of guns, and the lack of family contact.

B. The death penalty should be abolished for two reasons: it might kill innocent people and it is unfairly applied to the poor and minorities.

C. Two results of promoting birth control are increased education for women and greater economic opportunity for everyone.

2. An effective thesis statement provides an overview of supporting points that are logically connected to the focus.

In Chapter 2, you developed a rough outline of ideas to answer your research question. This list of ideas will be developed into the main points you will discuss in the body of your research paper.

A good thesis statement includes the categories from the rough outline that you plan to use. This overview of the supporting points clarifies for the reader the key ideas you will discuss and how they will be organized in your essay.

Example 1:

Research Question: Why do people become homeless?

Rough Outline: 1. Lack of affordable housing
2. Inadequate public assistance
3. Drug and alcohol problems
4. Breakdown of the family
5. Mental health problems

Thesis statement: The lack of affordable housing, inadequate public assistance, and the breakdown of the family are three causes of homelessness.

- In this example, the writer selected three ideas from the rough outline to include in his thesis statement: "lack of affordable housing," "inadequate public assistance," and "breakdown of the family."
- As a reader, you would expect the paper to follow the order of the supporting points as they are presented in the thesis statement.

   1. First, a section that discusses the problem poor people have in finding housing they can afford.
   2. Second, a discussion of the inadequate amount of money the government provides to support poor people.
   3. Third, a discussion of how family breakups can lead to homelessness.

Example 2:

Research Question: What are the signs of alcohol addiction?

Rough Outline: 1. An urge to drink
2. Inability to stop
3. Physical dependence
4. A need to drink more

Thesis statement: Alcoholism is a disease that has four symptoms: physical dependence, a need to drink more to feel its effects, a strong urge to drink, and an inability to stop drinking.

- In this example, the writer used all four signs of alcohol addiction from his rough outline. Notice, however, that he has changed the order of the supporting points so that each idea will flow logically from one to the next in his essay.

Your overview of supporting points may change as you work. You may decide that you need to modify it after you have written the first full draft of your essay. For example, you may decide to add or delete categories or rearrange the order.

Now You Try

Look at each research question and rough outline and then decide whether each thesis statement is a good answer to the research question.

- Does it include an appropriate focus?
- Does it include an overview of supporting points?

Circle OK or Not OK and explain your reasons.

1. *Research Question:*   Should marijuana be legal?

    Rough Outline: a. Damages the brain
            b. Causes memory loss
            c. Leads to birth defects

Thesis Statement A: Marijuana should not be legal because it is too dangerous.

OK   Not OK

Why? _____

Thesis Statement B: The use of marijuana and alcohol should be legal.

OK   Not OK

Why? _____

Thesis Statement C: Using marijuana should be against the law because it damages the brain, causes memory loss, and leads to birth defects.

OK   Not OK

Why? _____

2. *Research Question:*   How does junk food affect health?

    Rough Outline: 1. Poor nutrition
            2. Weight gain
            3. Inability to concentrate

Thesis Statement A: Eating junk food results in poor nutrition, weight gain, and inability to concentrate.

OK   Not OK

Why? _____

Thesis Statement B: Junk food and health food are different in several ways.

OK   Not OK

Why? _____

Thesis Statement C: Every culture has its own junk food.

OK   Not OK

Why? _____

3. An effective thesis statement uses formal language that is easy to understand.

Below are three aspects of language in thesis statements for you to consider as you write your thesis.

Structure

The topic, focus, and overview of supporting points can appear in any order in your thesis statement. The example illustrates three correct versions of the same thesis.

Topic: Vegetarianism

Focus: Reasons for becoming a vegetarian

Supporting points: Health, ethics, and ecology

Possible thesis statements:

- Three reasons why people become vegetarians are health, ethics, and ecology.
- Health, ethics, and ecology are three reasons why people become vegetarians.
- People become vegetarians for three reasons: health, ethics, and ecology.

Style

Thesis statements are written in third person rather than first person. Phrases such as "I'm going to talk about" or "I think" are not appropriate in a thesis.

Example:

Inappropriate language: I'm going to talk about two reasons why video games have a negative impact on children: isolation from other people and overexposure to violence.

Appropriate language: Two reasons why video games have a negative impact on children are isolation from other people and overexposure to violence.

Vocabulary

Because you need to include a lot of information in a thesis statement, precise vocabulary is essential. You can sometimes repeat carefully chosen vocabulary in a thesis statement throughout the research paper, providing an effective unifying thread. In particular, choosing appropriate words for the focus can help clarify and strengthen the thesis.

The following is a list of words and phrases associated with several common types of focus.

Focus	Vocabulary	Example
Cause	reasons, influence lead to cause result in	Cultural values influence expectations of marriage in three ways.
Effect	consequences, results, outcomes, benefits, advantages/disadvantages	Inadequate transportation planning can have several negative consequences.
Comparison	differences/similarities X differs in these ways X is related to Y in these ways X has these points in common with Y	Attitudes towards marriage in the United States and Iran differ in four ways.
Definition	characteristics, components, qualities, traits	Two qualities of a successful city are strong schools and diverse economic opportunities.
Classification	types, categories	Heroes can be divided into two categories: personal and public.
Process	steps, stages, phases	The change in men's role in the family during the past 50 years has occurred in four distinct phases.
Argument	reasons positive/negative helpful, harmful	Two reasons why standardized testing is a good idea are to increase student motivation and to measure school performance.

Now You Try

Use the vocabulary in each thesis statement in the left-hand column to identify its focus. Draw a line to connect the thesis statement with the type of focus in the right-hand column.

Thesis Statement	Type of Focus
1. High school education in Japan has two points in common with high school education in Korea: a rigorous testing system and strict expectations of classroom behavior.	Process
2. To develop a successful space program, the United States has gone through three stages of planning: research, development, and testing.	Effect
3. Although globalization produces a few negative results, it is largely a positive force in the world today for three reasons: increased opportunities for employment, higher education, and greater equality for women.	Classification
4. An effective public transportation system is based on four components: regional growth plans, available resources, community needs, and sustainability principles.	Comparison
5. Two types of video games teach children valuable skills: educational and cooperative.	Definition

OPTIONAL Common Problems With Thesis Statements

A thesis statement is one of the most important sentences in your research paper. The purpose of a thesis statement is to help the writer to focus and the reader to predict the content of the paper. As mentioned earlier, an effective thesis statement should have:

- A statement of the focus, or what you will say about the topic
- Supporting points that are logically connected to the focus and show how the paper will be organized
- Formal language that is easy to understand

There are five common problems writers face when creating thesis statements.

1. Some thesis statements lack a focus.

Weak Thesis Statement:

The United States has a lot of crime.

- This statement does not tell whether the paper will discuss the causes of crime or its effects; contrast the amount of crime now compared with ten years ago; argue in support of certain ways to reduce crime; or present some other ideas. To improve this thesis, the writer must include a focus. Here are two possible ways to revise the thesis statement to include a focus.

Stronger Thesis Statement (focus on cause):

The rising crime rate in the United States has caused a loss of talented young people to crime, high government costs for law enforcement, and a drop in tourism.

Stronger Thesis Statement (focus on comparison):

Crime today is more widespread among many economic groups, more violent, and more costly to society than it was ten years ago.

2. Some thesis statements have no supporting points.

Weak Thesis Statement:

> Three types of crime have been increasing in U.S. cities.
>
> • By briefly describing as supporting points the types of crimes that have increased, the writer can have a more effective thesis statement that tells the reader what kinds of crime she will be discussing.

Stronger Thesis Statement:

> Three types of crime have been increasing in U.S. cities: personal assault, car robbery, and home burglary.
>
> • The new thesis tells us that the first part of the paper will be about increases in personal assault; the second section, increases in car robberies; and the third, increases in burglaries of homes.

3. Some thesis statements have supporting points that are not logically connected to the focus.

Weak Thesis Statement:

> Many factors influence the hunting behavior of sharks: the type of shark, its age and strength, its migration patterns, people's misunderstandings about sharks' hunting behavior, and the current overfishing of sharks.
>
> • The focus of this research paper is "factors [that] influence the hunting behavior of sharks" or causes of sharks' behavior while hunting. However, when we examine the supporting points:
>
>   **1.** the type of sharks
>   **2.** a shark's age and strength
>   **3.** migration patterns
>   **4.** people's misunderstandings about sharks
>   **5.** overfishing of sharks
>
>   We find that while points 1, 2, and 3 support the focus by explaining causes for the sharks' behavior, points 4 and 5 do not. A better thesis statement would include only the supporting points related to the focus of causes for sharks' hunting behavior:

Stronger Thesis Statement:

> Many factors influence the hunting behavior of sharks: the type of shark, the age and strength of the shark, and the shark's migration pattern.

4. Some thesis statements contain more information than is necessary.

Weak Thesis Statement:

> Although some people argue that voting should be mandatory because it is a civic duty, it would increase voter turnout among poor people and would cause politicians to consider the needs of every citizen, compulsory voting is not a good idea because it is every citizen's right to choose to vote or not, it would not be feasible to enforce mandatory voting and people who are forced to vote may not vote carefully.
>
> • This statement is too long. These details are more appropriate as supporting information in the body of the paper. This thesis statement would be more effective if some of the ideas were condensed.

Stronger Thesis Statement:

> Although some people argue that voting should be mandatory, there are three reasons why it should not.

5. Some thesis statements use inappropriate language.

Weak Thesis Statement:

- In this paper, I will write about why I support capital punishment and what people on the other side have to say about it.

This thesis statement includes the opinion of the writer directly with the words "why I support." A more appropriate thesis statement for an academic paper indicates your opinion indirectly, without using "I."

Stronger Thesis Statement:

> Although some people disagree with capital punishment, it is necessary for three main reasons.

- The use of "it is necessary" tells the reader that the writer thinks capital punishment is essential. The inclusion of the phrase "although some people disagree" shows that she will also explain some of the reasons others disagree with capital punishment.

Now You Try

For each thesis statement, identify the problem from the list and revise the statement to be more effective.

Common Thesis Statement Problems

- Inappropriate language
- Focus not clearly stated
- No overview of supporting points
- Supporting points not logically connected to thesis
- More information than is necessary

1. I believe assisted suicide causes two main problems: difficulty in regulating it and difficulty for patients in making a rational choice.

Problem _____

Revised thesis _____

2. The Internet leads to improved communication.

Problem _____

Revised thesis _____

3. Several cultural factors lead to the prevalence of child labor in Latin America: family values, the company managers back in the United States, inflation, poor transportation systems, a lack of emphasis on education, and the Catholic Church.

Problem _____

Revised thesis _____

4. This paper is about cloning.

Problem _____

Revised thesis _____

5. Home schooling results in closer family ties, flexible time schedules for parent and child, and a desire for more educational choices.

Problem _____

Revised thesis _____

Activities to Practice Writing Thesis Statements

To practice writing thesis statements, do one or more of the following activities.

ACTIVITY **1**   *Identifying Parts of a Thesis*

Work with several classmates to identify the parts of each thesis statement.
- Circle the topic.
- Underline the focus once.
- Underline the supporting points twice.

1. Although our memory of John F. Kennedy has been frozen, he is remembered for many reasons; his political achievements, the way his public behavior reflected American values, and the mystery of his assassination.

2. Three important factors that make Bruce Lee extraordinary: his dramatic life, his skill as a martial artist, and his philosophy of life.

3. It is time for everybody in society to become aware of factors, such as family problems and media portrayal of violence that motivate children to commit violence as well as to consider some of the possible ways, such as better support for parents and monitoring of media, to prevent such violence.

4. Simplicity, emptiness, directness, and naturalness are four traditional characteristics of Japanese art inspired by Buddhism.

5. There are several reasons why people smoke even though they know it is a habit that can bring death: social pressure, psychological need, and physical addiction.

ACTIVITY 2   *Improving Thesis Statements*

With your group, consider each thesis statement that follows and decide how to improve it, following the criteria for a good thesis:

- Does it state the focus, or what will be said about the topic?
- Does it include supporting points that logically connect to the focus and show how the paper will be organized?
- Does it state the topic in formal language that is easy to understand?

1. I think genetically modified food is terrible.

Problems: _____

Revision: _____

2. Public transportation has some advantages and disadvantages.

Problems: _____

Revision: _____

3. The topic of this paper is women's rights.

Problems: _____

Revision: _____

4. Confusion and trouble will probably come from the recent changes in laws about medical privacy in the United States.

Problems: _____

Revision: _____

5. Space travel for ordinary people is exciting and will probably happen soon.

Problems: _____

Revision: _____

ACTIVITY 3   *Writing Thesis Statements*

Work in pairs or groups to write a thesis statement that reflects each research question and rough outline. Compare your thesis statements with others in your class.

1.   *Topic:*   Youth crime in America

Research question: Why do young people commit crimes?

Rough outline: 1. Influence of the media
2. Availability of weapons
3. Lack of family contact

Thesis statement: _____

2.   *Topic:*   International students

Research question: What problems do international students face when they study in the United States?

Rough outline: 1. Language difficulties
2. Money problems
3. Adjusting to a new culture

Thesis statement: _____

BUILDING YOUR PAPER

Write a Thesis Statement

Using the research question and rough outline you developed in Chapter 2, write a thesis statement for the research paper you are building.

- Remember that your thesis statement should have a clearly stated topic and a focus that matches your research question.
- The overview of supporting points should logically connect to the focus and show how the paper will be organized.
- The language should be formal and easy to understand.
- Remember that your thesis statement may change as you begin to write your paper.

Getting Feedback

1. Bring your thesis statement to class. Share it with the class or with a small group by writing it on the board or on an overhead or giving a written copy to each person in your group.
2. Look at each person's thesis and evaluate it according to the criteria for a good thesis listed.
3. As your thesis is evaluated, ask questions, and take notes on changes you may make.

Expanding Your Outline With Evidence

Now that you have a thesis statement and a rough outline listing the supporting points for your research paper, it's time to return to the notes you took from your sources in Part Two. So far, your sources have served two important functions. First, in Chapter 1, you explored your theme by reading the sources for general information. Then, in Chapter 2, you took notes while doing a focused reading of your sources that helped you answer your research question. In addition, using the ideas from your sources as a guide, you created a thesis statement and rough outline that will become the framework for your paper.

In this next stage of the writing process, the information in your sources will have a new role. You will select specific information from your notes to use as evidence—to help you explain each of the main supporting points in your thesis statement.

Choosing Effective Evidence

When we use information from articles to explain the main points in our paper, we call that information "evidence." Your reading notes from Chapter 2 include all the information you found to answer your research question. However, it's likely that only some of that information will work as evidence in your paper. You need to decide which information to use as evidence. Your paper will be more convincing if you follow these guidelines when choosing evidence:

Guidelines for Choosing Effective Evidence

1. Choose information that you understand and can explain clearly.

Think about whether you understand each idea well enough to explain it in your own words. If you don't understand the information, you won't be able to write well about it and it will be better to omit it.

For example, based on one writer's research question and rough outline, she wrote the thesis statement:

> People become addicted to alcohol because of emotional distress, social pressure, and physical causes.

However, as she began to select evidence to support the idea of "physical causes," she realized that many physical causes of alcoholism were based on complex chemical processes that she did not completely understand. She decided to limit her discussion of physical causes to genetic predisposition. She revised her thesis statement:

> People become addicted to alcohol because of emotional distress, social pressure, and genetic predisposition.

2. Choose ideas that are directly related to the point you are making.

Sometimes it's tempting to include interesting details that are related to your topic in a general way but don't help to explain your specific supporting points.

For example, if your focus is a comparison of the cost, nutritional value, and availability of fast food and health food, you need evidence that illustrates the differences in these two kinds of food. Information about the history of tofu, a common health food, will not be useful in this paper.

Now You Try

Working with a partner or a small group, decide which pieces of evidence would effectively explain the underlined supporting point in the following thesis statement. Circle Yes or No and explain the problem, if there is one.

Thesis statement:

Using the Internet gives young people increased literacy but also leads to health problems and isolation from other people.

Evidence:

A. Asked their preferences for spending free time, 19% of the student body at the high school chose playing sports; 24%, watching TV; 22%, listening to music; and 34%, surfing the Internet.

Is the evidence effective?   Yes   No

If not, what is the problem? _____

B. In Waltham's study, business people between the ages of 35 and 50 reported spending 10 to 12 hours a day online, thus severely impacting the time they spent with colleagues and family.

Is the evidence effective?   Yes   No

If not, what is the problem? _____

C. Feeling isolated, many teenagers turn to drugs or gang membership to solve their problems, according to interviews conducted by Smith and Paget at the Outsiders Café.

Is the evidence effective?   Yes   No

If not, what is the problem? _____

D. "The problem of feeling estranged from society is much more severe among young people who spend more than four hours a day online," states Martha DePriau, psychologist at Vanderbilt University

Is the evidence effective?   Yes   No

If not, what is the problem? _____

E. Sixty percent of Internet users between the ages of 12 and 25 reported that they spend more time online than with family or friends.

Is this evidence effective?   Yes   No

If not, what is the problem? _____

3. Select a variety of types of evidence.

Writers can support their ideas with several kinds of information. The following are three common types of evidence that you may find as you look through your focused reading notes. In each example paragraph, the paraphrased evidence is underlined.

Einstein Evidence

Einstein evidence shows that other scholars or thinkers on the topic have come to the same conclusion as you have.

When using this kind of evidence, provide as much information as you can about the expert. For example, you might include where you found the information, the research the expert has done, or the university or institution where he or she works.

Example:

It has been argued that the reason why some terminally ill patients wish to commit suicide is that they are depressed. Patients suffering from terminal illness might tend to feel negative and hopeless. Edward Marlough, an associate professor of clinical psychology at Columbia Presbyterian Medical Center in New York, argues that <u>in many cases, a dying patient is simply occupied by negative reactions to their critical condition</u> ("When Patients Want to Die," 1999).

Example Evidence

Example evidence consists of specific examples that illustrate the point you are making.

Example:

The direct and independent connections through the Internet create new relationships among people, relationships that can change the way we think and act. To illustrate this point of view, Brian Belsie, in his article "The Electronic Village" (n.d.) showed how <u>a large number of people living in widely separated areas could form a community simply through electronic communication; in this case, the parents of children who suffered from a certain kind of psychological problem</u> formed an online support group.

Fact Evidence

Fact evidence includes statistics and other objective information. As you read your sources in Part Two, you may find specific facts that you can use to demonstrate the point you are making.

Example:

> First of all, many people become vegetarians to maintain good health. Vegetarianism can prevent people from getting diseases. Castleman (1995) writes that <u>many studies prove that meat, especially beef, pork, and lamb, likely increase the percentages of heart disease and cancer.</u> In his article, he points out that <u>the rate of vegetarians who die from these diseases is definitely lower than the rate of meat eaters. For example, 28% fewer vegetarians than omnivores die from heart disease, and 39% fewer die from cancer.</u> The National Cancer Research Institute found that <u>meat-eating women get breast cancer almost four times more often than women who do not eat meat or eat only a little.</u> ("Why Be a Vegetarian?" 1999)

Undocumented Evidence

Another kind of evidence, called undocumented evidence, comes not from written sources, but from your experience and things that you know or that are commonly understood to be true.

Suppose you are writing about the causes of alcohol abuse. An example of a personal experience that could be used as evidence would be a story, or anecdote, about a friend who began drinking to escape from the stress of her job.

An example of evidence that is commonly known to be true would be that many teenagers want to fit in with their peer group and will feel pressure to behave like the teenagers around them. This information could be used as evidence in a discussion on social pressure as a cause of alcohol abuse. The point that teenagers feel pressure from their peers would not have to be documented; however, linking this pressure to alcohol abuse would.

In academic writing, most evidence is from documented sources, but anecdotal or undocumented evidence can be an effective addition to your paper.

Now You Try

Work in pairs or small groups with the following thesis statement.

Thesis statement:

Being forced into a sedentary lifestyle by the demands of their jobs is making young professionals more conscious about their health, <u>increasing the popularity of risky sports,</u> and leading to the development of more health foods. . . .

Here are some excerpts from several articles on taking risks. Decide whether each excerpt would support the underlined supporting point in the thesis statement above as Einstein evidence, example evidence, or fact evidence.

1. "The number of people who dive out of planes, for instance, has risen about 5 percent a year since 1990."—*Bowers, Joe, "Going Over the Top," 1995*

   Type of evidence _____

2. "'Five–four–three–two–one–see ya!' And Chance McGuire, 25, is airborne off a 650-foot concrete dam in northern California. In one second he falls 16 feet, in two seconds 63 feet, and after three seconds and 137 feet, he is flying at 65 mph. . . . McGuire is a practitioner of what he calls the king of all extreme sports, BASE— an acronym for building, antenna, span (bridges) and earth (cliffs) jumping."—*Greenfield, Karl, "Life on the Edge," 1998*

Type of evidence _____

3. "Michael Apter, a Georgetown University visiting scholar and the author of *The Dangerous Edge: The Psychology of Excitement* explains, 'The safer you make life, the more people feel the need for excitement.'"—*Bowers, Joe, "Going Over the Top," 1995*

Type of evidence _____

Activities to Practice Selecting Evidence

To practice selecting evidence, do one or more of the following activities.

ACTIVITY **1**   *Finding Documented and Undocumented Evidence*

To get an idea of the percentage of documented and undocumented evidence that is appropriate in a well-written paper, analyze one of the student papers in the Appendix, page 205. Highlight all the documented evidence in one color. Documented evidence is any information that begins or ends with the name of an author or title of a source. Highlight the undocumented, or anecdotal and common knowledge, evidence in another color.

ACTIVITY **2**   *Choosing Effective Evidence*

With several classmates, look at each piece of evidence and decide whether it would be effective to support the underlined supporting point in the thesis statement. Effective evidence should be:

- Information you understand and can explain clearly
- Ideas directly related to the point you're making

For each piece of evidence, circle Yes or No and explain the problem, if there is one.

Thesis Statement:

Ships and planes often vanish in the Bermuda Triangle because of <u>environmental reasons,</u> supernatural causes, or unexplained phenomena.

Evidence:

1. Christopher Columbus observed a huge ball that looked like a meteor falling into the sea as he first sailed near the Triangle on his way to the West Indies in 1492.

Is this evidence effective?   Yes   No

If no, what is the problem? _____

2. One hundred miles north of Puerto Rico is the deepest part of the Atlantic Ocean, estimated to be 30,100 feet deep; it is here that most of the accidents between Miami and the Bahama Islands have happened.

   Is this evidence effective?   Yes   No

   If no, what is the problem? _____

3. According to Angelina Campo in "Mysteries from the Realms of Outer Space," highly developed beings from outer space have created their own society under the Atlantic Ocean in the area of the Bermuda Triangle and it is they who abduct the travelers.

   Is this evidence effective?   Yes   No

   If no, what is the problem? _____

4. Roy Hutchins, a retired Coast Guard Captain, said, "Weather within the Triangle where warm tropical breezes meet cold air masses from the Arctic is notoriously unpredictable."

   Is this evidence effective?   Yes   No

   If no, what is the problem? _____

5. The Bermuda Triangle is one of the few places on earth where the compass points to the true north instead of the magnetic north. Because of this, sailors must adjust their direction carefully and the inexperienced may fail to do this, thus losing their way.

   Is this evidence effective?   Yes   No

   If no, what is the problem? _____

ACTIVITY 3 *Working with Expert Groups*

To complete this activity, select a supporting point from a thesis statement on a topic that your class is working on.

1. Divide into small groups. Each group is responsible for one source (these are the expert groups).
2. In your group, identify pieces of information from your source that you think would be useful evidence for the idea you support. Discuss why the information would be convincing to a reader.
3. After you identify the useful evidence, break up and reform into new groups (the sharing groups). Have one member from each expert group in each sharing group.
4. In your sharing group, take turns discussing the evidence each expert group selected.
5. As a group, decide whether the evidence selected is appropriate for the point.

   • Is the evidence easy to understand and explain?
   • Is the evidence appropriate for the point?
   • Does more than one source contain the same idea?
   • Does your group have any questions about specific pieces of evidence?

BUILDING YOUR PAPER

Select Evidence

Create a list of evidence for each supporting point in the rough outline you wrote.

- As you search for potential evidence in your sources, remember to choose information that you understand and can explain and that is directly related to the points you want to make.
- Try to select a variety of types of information.
- Try to find two to three pieces of evidence for each supporting point.

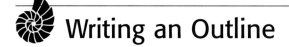

Writing an Outline

You can now put together a detailed plan for writing your paper that includes both the supporting points you want to discuss and the evidence you will use to help explain each point. If you plan to use undocumented evidence, you need to include that in your outline too.

NOTE: The organization of argumentation papers needs special consideration. For information on organization and a sample argumentation paper see the *Sourcework* website at http://esl.college.hmco.com/students.

You want a plan that is detailed enough to provide a guide as you write. Think of it as a lifeline to hold onto if you get lost. With an outline to return to, you can put your paper aside and not lose track of what you are going to say next. You may discover as you begin to write that you will discard some of the information or that you need to look for more evidence to support certain points.

As you work, you may change the outline, rearranging the order or adding or deleting sections. Since the outline is a tool for your own use, write it in any way that works for you. The following are three methods that other writers have found useful.

Three Outlining Methods

Traditional Outline

In this outline, the notations, such as Markoff, p. 1 and NPR, p. 14 refer to the sources the writer plans to use. The note "personal" in parenthesis reminds the writer she will use a personal anecdote, a kind of undocumented evidence. The note "summarize article" means that the writer will use a brief summary of this whole article as evidence here, rather than just paraphrasing a sentence or two. Notes like these help make your outline more effective by reminding you in detail how you plan to use your notes.

I. *Thesis Statement:* Compared with other inventions, the Internet has changed our styles of communication and led to more freedom for individuals.

II. Comparison with other inventions

    A. TV

        My friends and I often discuss TV (personal example)

    B. Phone

        My family used to use the phone to keep in touch (personal example)

III. Styles of communication

    A. Less time than with old methods of communicating

        1. Less time with people

            a. Markoff, p. 1 (evidence from source)

            b. My family uses phone less (personal example)

        2. Less time with TV

            a. Markoff, p. 2 (evidence from source)

    B. New ways of communicating

        1. Chat rooms

            a. NPR, p. 14 (evidence from source)

            b. My experience in chat rooms (personal example)

        2. Helps with some jobs

            a. NPR, p. 6 (evidence from source)

            b. Economist, p. 2 (evidence from source)

IV. More freedom for individuals

    A. Ordinary people have opportunities

        Romero (summarize whole article)

    B. More democracy

        Economist, p. 1 (evidence from source)

Cluster Outline

A cluster outline includes all the same information that a traditional outline does, but is written as connected circles rather than the linear form of the traditional outline.

Cluster Outline

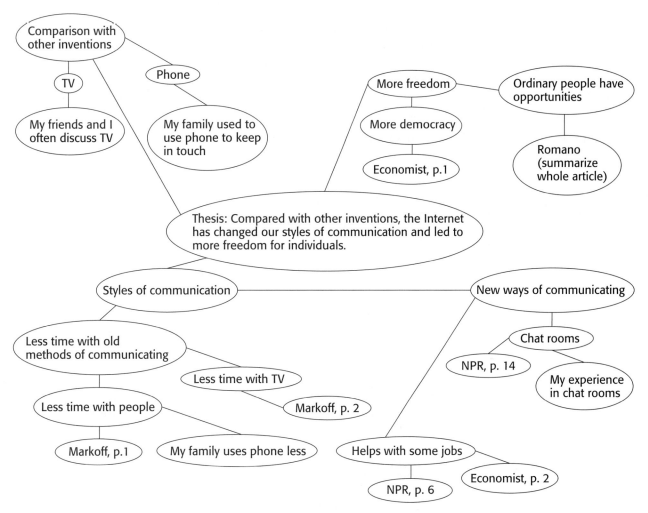

Grid Outline

Like the other outlining methods, a grid outline includes the thesis, supporting points, sub-points, and evidence. Information is organized as a chart, which offers a visual perspective of your ideas, just as a cluster does, while keeping some of the more structured elements of a traditional outline.

Thesis: Maintaining a strong family identity and promoting cross-generational communication are two reasons why heritage language programs should be encouraged.

Supporting Points	Sub-points	Evidence
1. Encourage young people to learn about their family's culture and history.	**A.** culture **B.** family	Wilson p. 56 Tam p. 12 grandpa story Tam p.13
2. Better communication between generations	**A.** communication in family Hiang p. 35 **B.** stronger family connection	Peterson p. 8 Wilson p. 51 family trip

Activities to Practice Outlining

To practice outlining, do one or both of the following activities. Blank outlining grids are available on the *Sourcework* website at http://esl.college.hmco.com/students.

ACTIVITY 1   *Outlining a Paper*

Work with a partner to read one of the student research papers in the Appendix, page 205, or on the *Sourcework* website. Use one of the methods described and prepare an outline of the paper.

ACTIVITY 2   *Filling in a Detailed Outline*

To complete this activity, select a representative thesis statement created by one of your classmates or by the whole class.

1. Focusing on one supporting point at a time from the thesis statement, look through your sources or notes to identify two to three pieces of evidence you could use to support each main idea in the thesis.
2. Using an overhead transparency or large sheet of paper, write the evidence you have selected for each supporting point.
3. Share your list of evidence with the class.
4. Discuss problems you had or questions that came up in your group.
5. With this information, you can create an outline following one of the methods discussed in this section.

BUILDING YOUR PAPER

Write a Detailed Outline

Select an outline format and create a more detailed plan for your paper. In this outline include:

- Your thesis statement
- A phrase that explains each supporting point
- A plan for where you will use each piece of evidence

Getting Feedback

Provide a copy of your research paper outline for each person.

1. Take turns reading each person's outline.
2. Discuss each outline using the following critique questions and jot comments on your copy of your classmate's outline.
3. When you finish, give all the copies back to the persons who wrote them.

Critique Questions:

1. In the thesis statement, circle the topic, underline the focus once, and underline the supporting points twice.
2. Does each major section of the outline logically connect to the thesis statement? If not, what changes could be made?
3. Do two or three details support each topic sentence? Is each detail supported with specific evidence from the sources?
4. Is any part of the thesis statement omitted from the outline?
5. Does the outline include any major new ideas that should be added to the thesis?
6. Other comments? Questions left unanswered? Confusing parts?

CHAPTER

4

Building a Paper:
Create

Now it's time to actually write the whole research paper. There is no best way to do this. You can skip the beginning and start in the middle, or faithfully follow your outline from start to finish. You may choose to write the easiest part first to encourage yourself or to write the hardest part first because then it seems like "the worst is over." You may use a computer or write by hand. You can write it all in one sitting, or you can write a few sentences at a time and then get up and wander around.

As you begin your work, make yourself comfortable. Allow enough time; don't be impatient with yourself for taking a long time. Write everything that comes to mind; you can always cross it out later. If you can't think of a good idea, leave space and go back to it. Plan on correcting mistakes later.

No matter how you decide to write, a big part of putting this paper together is combining ideas from your reading notes with what you yourself want to say. Using your detailed outline as a guide, you can work paragraph by paragraph to explain each point and support it with the evidence you've chosen. The more smoothly you can make the connection between the ideas you are using from other writers and your own ideas, the more effective your paper will be.

The point is to keep at it until you complete a first draft. You can always change it later by adding, deleting, or rearranging your words. But, once you have written a first draft, you have something to work with.

In this chapter you will practice:

- Writing topic sentences
- Preparing evidence from sources
- Integrating evidence into paragraphs

By the end of this chapter you will have written a topic sentence for each paragraph in your paper. You will have prepared evidence from your sources in Part Two and integrated evidence into a paragraph. Finally, you will write the first draft of your research paper.

Sourcework: Academic Writing From Sources

Well-Constructed Paragraphs

With your outline, supporting evidence, and thesis statement prepared, you are ready to write your guided research paper. While your paragraphs may vary in the amount of evidence from sources they contain and their purpose, the basic structure will be similar. The three qualities listed offer a simple guideline of what your paragraphs should include.

Three Qualities of a Well-Constructed Paragraph

1. A topic sentence written in the writer's own words.
2. Evidence to support the topic sentence, usually taken from an outside source.
3. A brief conclusion and/or transition to the next paragraph.

Example of a Well-Constructed Paragraph

Topic sentence ⟶	The value of independence is one reason why young and old people become isolated from each other.
Explanation of topic sentence with supporting evidence ⟶	Being independent is an important quality of life for most Americans. Since childhood, people have been taught to be independent. The notion continues through their lives until they become old. Margaret Mead (1971) an American anthropologist writes in her article, "Grandparents Have Copped Out," that old people don't want to be a burden to their children so they try to live their lives independently. That is, old people do not want to interfere with their children's lives. Young people also believe their lives will be better without their parents as constant companions.
Concluding sentence ⟶	Consequently, communication between the generations is limited and isolation gradually occurs.

NOTE: The sentences in this example paragraph have been separated for clarity. The sentences in your paragraphs should flow together, without separation.

To write a well-constructed paragraph, we must pay special attention to the topic sentence, prepare evidence for the paragraph, and smoothly integrate the evidence into our writing. These three aspects of writing a paragraph are discussed in the following sections.

Writing Topic Sentences for Paragraphs

Topic sentences for your paragraphs come from the supporting points in your thesis and outline. A good topic sentence has three characteristics.

Characteristics of an Effective Topic Sentence

- It has a logical connection to the focus in the thesis statement.
- It repeats the focus idea.
- It repeats one of the supporting points in the thesis but says it differently.

To study these characteristics in detail, look at the thesis statement for the example paragraph above about communication problems between young and old people.

Thesis statement: Emphasis on individualism, loss of focus on extended families, and overscheduled lifestyles are three reasons for the generation gap between young and old people.

First Supporting Point

The supporting points we can extract from the thesis tell us that the first part of this paper will be about how individualism can create distance between young and old people. Therefore, the topic sentence for the first section might be something like this:

The value of independence is one reason why young and old people become isolated from each other.

- Note that the topic sentence is connected to a supporting point, but does not repeat the same words. In the example above, "the value of independence" is another way of saying "emphasis on individualism," and "young and old people become isolated from each other" is another way to say the "generation gap."

There are many ways to write a good topic sentence that expresses the idea in the supporting point without being repetitious. Equally good topic sentences for the first point in the example thesis would be:

Fear of appearing too dependent can cause older people to limit their interaction with their children.

Valuing their independent lifestyles causes adult children and their parents to lose contact with each other.

Second Supporting Point

A topic sentence for the second section of the paper on the loss of extended families might be:

The change in family structure from extended families to nuclear families has resulted in less connection between generations.

Third Supporting Point

For the third section of the paper—overscheduled lifestyles—the topic sentence could be:

> A third cause of the generation gap is the lack of time that family members have to spend with each other.

Now You Try

For each thesis statement, decide whether the topic sentences contain the characteristics of an effective topic sentence:

- Does it have a logical connection to the focus?
- Does it repeat the focus of the thesis?
- Does it repeat the supporting point idea using a different way of saying it?

1. *Thesis statement:* The negative effects of the Internet can be defined as a deterioration in courtesy while communicating and an isolation from other people.

   Topic sentences:

   a. The decrease in politeness is common knowledge to those who work in network communication.

   Is this topic sentence appropriate? If not, what is the problem?

   _____

   b. People who use the Internet are lacking one of the most important things human beings need: connection to other people.

   Is this topic sentence appropriate? If not, what is the problem?

   _____

2. *Thesis statement:* Exposure to violence, an inadequate rating system, and too little parental supervision are three reasons why children shouldn't play video games.

   Topic sentences:

   a. Children in the United States love to play video games.

   Is this topic sentence appropriate? If not, what is the problem?

   _____

   b. Unclear standards for evaluating video games is another reason why children should avoid video games.

   Is this topic sentence appropriate? If not, what is the problem?

   _____

   c. Too little parental supervision is a third reason children shouldn't play video games.

   Is this topic sentence appropriate? If not, what is the problem?

   _____

Activities to Practice Writing Topic Sentences

To practice writing topic sentences, do one or more of the following activities.

ACTIVITY 1   *Identifying Topic Sentences*

1. Select one of the model essays in the Appendix, page 205.
2. Find the thesis statement in the introduction of the essay. Highlight the focus of the thesis with one color. Highlight the overview of supporting points using a different color for each point.
3. In the body of the essay, highlight the topic sentence for each supporting point using the same color you used in the thesis statement.
4. Analyze these topic sentences by answering the following questions:

   - Are the topic sentences for supporting points organized in the same order as they appear in the thesis statement?
   - Do the topic sentences repeat the focus idea from the thesis statement?
   - Does each topic sentence repeat a supporting point idea? If yes, does the writer say the idea differently?

ACTIVITY 2   *Writing Topic Sentences*

For each thesis statement, write topic sentences to introduce the main sections of the paper. Use separate paper.

1. Alcohol addiction can lead to mental, physical, and social problems.
2. Social expectations, moral beliefs, and consideration of alcohol as a drug are three differences between American and Japanese attitudes toward alcohol.
3. Drinking behavior can be divided into three categories: social drinking, problem drinking, and alcoholism.
4. Quitting a bad habit requires four steps: acknowledging the problem, brainstorming solutions, devising a plan to quit, and, most difficult of all, monitoring yourself as you follow the plan.
5. Although some people worry that lowering the drinking age will result in alcohol abuse and increased traffic accidents, the legal drinking age should be 18 because it is consistent with other adult rights and responsibilities.

BUILDING YOUR PAPER

Write Topic Sentences

Working from your detailed outline, write a topic sentence for each supporting point you will include in your guided research paper. Be sure each topic sentence has a logical connection to the focus in your thesis. Remember that while it is important to repeat the ideas from the thesis, you need a different way of saying each point.

Preparing Evidence to Use in Paragraphs

As you begin to write the first draft of your guided research paper, you will decide how to use each piece of evidence listed in the detailed outline you made in Chapter 3, page 68. Evidence used to support ideas in an academic essay is usually paraphrased. As discussed in Chapter 1, page 6, a paraphrase uses your own words to restate what the author said. Less frequently, evidence is presented in a direct quotation, using the exact words of the original source with quotation marks around the author's words.

Using Quotations and Paraphrases

The examples here show how a quotation and a paraphrase of the same piece of evidence differ.

Examples:

Original excerpt from source to be used as evidence:

> To behave aggressively is no longer considered unfeminine and unattractive. Girl characters are expected to be assertive and achievement-oriented.
> —*Hopkins, Susan, "Bam! Crash! Kapow! Girls are Heroes Now"*

Quotation of this excerpt:

> According to Hopkins (n.d., p. 13), "To behave aggressively is no longer considered unfeminine and unattractive. Girl characters are expected to be assertive and achievement-oriented."

Paraphrase of this excerpt:

> According to Hopkins (n.d.), females in movies and books today are often hard-driving and ambitious; unlike in the past, it is now socially acceptable for women to act boldly and forcefully.

Using Quotations

We use direct quotations in only a few circumstances:

- When the original is written in poetic language or provides a unique image as in this description of the differences between a woman and her Chinese grandmother:

  "The difference between (my grandmother's and my) feet reminds me of the incredible history we hold between us like living bookends. We stand like sentries at either side of a vast gulf."
  —*Wu, Janet, "Homework Bound"*

- When the original was spoken or written by a famous person and is generally recognizable as a famous saying. For example, we would never try to paraphrase the beginning of President Abraham Lincoln's Gettysburg Address:

  "Fourscore and seven years ago our nation brought forth on this continent, a new nation, conceived in Liberty, and dedicated to the proposition that all men are created equal."

Using Paraphrases

Much more often, we paraphrase evidence from sources. In some cultures, it's considered acceptable or even good taste to copy from the writings of experts or classical authors. However, in Western academic culture, writing someone else's ideas or words as if they were your own without acknowledging the original author is called *plagiarism* and is considered very dishonorable behavior. In the academic environment at colleges and universities, copying someone else's work can result in a failing grade and possible expulsion. In public life too, plagiarism is a serious offense; people have lost jobs or have had to pay thousands of dollars in damages when they were convicted of plagiarism.

You'll need to paraphrase almost all the pieces of evidence you plan to use. You will also need to document, or acknowledge, the original author. This means that you include the author's name and/or the article's name when you mention the piece in your paper. This is not difficult to do, but it is very important. It lets the reader know you are presenting someone else's information. Referring to the original author helps to establish your honesty and reliability as a writer and is expected in academic writing in American universities. Documenting is discussed in detail in Chapter 5, page 116.

Using the techniques described in Chapter 1, page 6, you can paraphrase the information you plan to use as supporting evidence. Recall that a good paraphrase meets these criteria:

- It means the same as the original
    no new ideas are added
    no important ideas are deleted
- It differs enough from the original to be considered your own writing
- It refers to the original

BUILDING YOUR PAPER

Paraphrase Evidence

Choose one section of the detailed outline of your guided research paper and prepare all the evidence for that section. In most cases, you'll paraphrase, rather than quote, each piece of evidence.

: OPTIONAL Paraphrasing Challenges

Paraphrasing can present some special challenges. Paraphrasing well requires you to truly understand the original and to present this information as clearly and accurately as possible. Below are six challenges you may encounter as you paraphrase your evidence.

1. Paraphrasing Word-by-Word

It's tempting to simply use synonym substitutions or grammatical changes without considering the overall context of the sentence. Here are two examples of problems this can cause.

Problems with Synonym Substitution

Example:

Original: A hero has a story of adventure to tell and a community who will listen. —*Tollefson, Ted, "Is a Hero Really Nothing But a Sandwich?" 1993*

Weak Paraphrase: A hero has a tale of experience to share and a community who will hear (Tollefson, 1993).

- Because this paraphrase relies only on synonym substitution, it is not really a paraphrase; it's too similar to the original. Also, the substituted vocabulary doesn't have exactly the same meaning as the original. For example, "experience" is broader in meaning than "adventure," and "hear" is more passive than "listen."

Stronger Paraphrase: Heroes have both a unique experience to share and a community that is eager to listen to it (Tollefson, 1993).

Now You Try

Write a stronger paraphrase of this original sentence after you study the weak paraphrase.

Original:	The process by which sunglasses have gained worldwide popularity is a fascinating one that began, surprisingly, in the justice system of medieval China. —*"How Sunglasses Spanned the World," n.d.*
Weak Paraphrase:	The procedure by which sunglasses have earned global fame is a very interesting one that started, amazingly, in the fairness system of middle China ("How Sunglasses Spanned the World," n.d.).

Stronger Paraphrase:

_____

_____

Problems With Incorrect Grammar

Example:

Original:	Without Ghandi, India might still be a part of the British Empire. —*Sudo, Phil, "Larger Than Life," 1990*
Weak Paraphrase:	Without Ghandi, India could stay a part of the British Empire until now (Sudo, 1990).

- This paraphrase is grammatically incorrect. The new adverb phrase, *until now,* although similar in meaning to *still,* requires a different verb tense.

Stronger Paraphrase:	England might still be governing India if Ghandi hadn't been there (Sudo, 1990).

Now You Try

Write a stronger paraphrase of this original sentence after you study the weak paraphrase.

Original:	Opponents of standardized testing believe tests are a limited way of assessing students. —*MacDonald, Moira, "Does Province-Wide Testing Distort Reality?" 2001*
Weak Paraphrase:	MacDonald (2001) thinks that people who want to use standardized testing to know the students' ability or knowledge is very limited.

Stronger Paraphrase:

_____

_____

2. Dealing with Poetic or Idiomatic Language

When you're paraphrasing sentences from sources that are poetic or that use idiomatic language, it's best to focus on the overall meaning of the sentence and use the Tell a Friend technique (Chapter 1, p. 8).

> You can run into problems if you try to use the Grammar Toolbox method (see the *Sourcework* website at **http://esl.college.hmco.com/students**) with these kinds of sentences.

Example:

Original:	Like serpents, we keep shedding the skins of our heroes as we move toward new phases in our lives. —*Tollefson, Ted, "Is a Hero Really Nothing But a Sandwich?" 1993*
Weak Paraphrase:	We never stop changing our heroes when we face different stages of our lives, as if we were snakes (Tollefson, 1993).

- The phrase, "like serpents" in the original sentence is poetic or a "figure of speech." It means that people are flexible or changeable, which is also a characteristic of snakes. In the weak paraphrase, the reference to a snake has no meaning because the image of "shedding our skin" has not been included.

Stronger Paraphrase:	Because we face different challenges at each stage of our lives, whom we consider a hero also changes (Tollefson, 1993).

Now You Try

Write a stronger paraphrase of this original sentence after you study the weak paraphrase.

Original:	Medical science, focused on curing the ills of the body, has often treated the mind like an annoying younger brother: a presence to be ignored whenever possible. —*Goode, Erica, "Your Mind May Ease What's Ailing You," 1999*
Weak Paraphrase:	Goode (1999) writes that in medicine, the mind is like a little brother and doctors are interested only in the body.

Stronger Paraphrase:

_____

_____

3. Managing Passages with Statistics

The information in a source that contains several statistics can be dense and thus tricky to paraphrase. Sometimes, drawing a picture or making a chart of the original information will help you to understand it and provide a way to present it clearly.

Example:

Original:	In the most comprehensive national survey on driving behavior so far, a Michigan firm, EPIC-MRA, found that an astounding 80% of drivers are angry most or all of the time while driving. Simple traffic congestion is one cause of irritation, but these days just about anything can get the average driver to tap his horn. More than one-third of respondents to the Michigan survey said they get impatient at stoplights or when waiting for a parking space; an additional 25% can't stand waiting for passengers to get in the car. And 22% said they get mad when a multi-lane highway narrows. —*Ferguson, Andrew, "Road Rage," 1998*
Traditional Paraphrase:	A national survey about driving attitudes by EPIC-MRA, a business in Michigan, was the most extensive ever done. According to the survey, about four fifths of drivers are mad a lot of the time while they are driving. There are many reasons, such as too much traffic. Waiting at traffic lights or for a chance to park makes more than 33% of people angry, and waiting for people to enter the car makes about one fourth of drivers mad. Finally, almost one fourth of the drivers get cross when a wide highway becomes narrower (Ferguson, 1998).

Paraphrase presented as a chart:

80% of drivers get angry:	
33%	Waiting at traffic lights
25%	Waiting for passengers to get in cars
22%	When highway narrows

Now You Try

Create a chart that presents the information in this thesis sentence.

Original:	In the most sprawling cities in the United States, 49 of every 100,000 residents die each year in traffic crashes. The least sprawling cities have fewer than 20 people per 100,000 die in fatal crashes each year. —*Ewing, Reid, "Measuring Sprawl and Its Impact"*

4. Handling Passages With Opinion or Bias

When the author of the original passage expresses an opinion or bias, your paraphrase must include the point of view along with the facts he or she states.

Example:

Original: I think it's a very simple deduction that the music is Negro music to begin with; and for these guys (critics) to write about the music as though it's an American music, that everybody plays equally, and that we all love one another and we're all brothers—to me, really, that's a lot of horseshit. —*Lott, Tommy Lee, "The 1960s Avant-Garde Movement in Jazz," 2001*

Weak Paraphrase: Lott (2001) thinks that it's easy to see that this is really black American music and the critics say all Americans play this music the same way and love each other like family.

- This paraphrase does not include the author's strong disagreement with the critics, which he voices in the phrase "that's a lot of horseshit." This opinion must be included in the paraphrase.

Stronger Paraphrase: Lott (2001) says that it's clear that this music is uniquely black American music, not music appreciated by all in the United States, and he strongly disagrees with critics who say that all Americans love the same music like a big happy family.

Now You Try

Write a stronger paraphrase of this original sentence after you study the weak paraphrase.

Original: "It is inappropriate and simplistic to treat cohabitation as the major cause of divorce," says Larry Bumpass, a sociologist at the University of Wisconsin. —*Labi, Nadya, "A Bad Start? Living Together May Be the Road to Divorce," 1999*

Weak Paraphrase: Larry Bumpass (cited in Labi, 1999) says that cohabitation might be a major cause of divorce.

Stronger Paraphrase:

_____

_____

5. Providing Necessary Background Information

In some cases, the source idea you want to paraphrase refers to an earlier section of the passage. In this situation it is necessary to briefly explain the background information leading up to the part you are interested in. In other words, a paraphrase must include enough of the original so that it is meaningful.

The following original sentence is from paragraph 3 of "The Deadly Noodle" in Part Two, page 169.

Example:

Original:	But the trend has turned out to be more insidious and more widespread than previously thought. —*Hastings, Michael, 2003*
Weak Paraphrase:	The fad is even more common and difficult to get rid of than expected (Hastings, 2003).

- It isn't enough to simply paraphrase this short passage; you must begin by explaining what *the trend* is. Looking at the context in the original article on page 169, we can see that the paragraph discusses how more and more people all over the world are becoming overweight by eating American fast food. A good paraphrase will explain this.

Stronger Paraphrase:	The tendency for people everywhere to gain weight by eating American fast food is more prevalent and more difficult to stop than expected (Hastings, 2003).

Now You Try

Write a stronger paraphrase of this original passage after you study the weak paraphrase.

Original:	"Road-rage experts have come up with various solutions to the anarchy of our streets and highways. We could legislate it (lower speed limits, build more roads to relieve congestion), adjudicate it (more highway cops, stiffer penalties), regulate it (more elaborate licensing procedures) or educate it away (mandatory driver's ed). *Others suggest an option perhaps more typical of America circa 1998: therapize it.*" —*Ferguson, Andrew, "Road Rage," 1998*
Weak Paraphrase (of idea in italics):	Others say a likely possibility for Americans in the 1990s would be to see a counselor (Ferguson, 1998).
Stronger Paraphrase:	

_____

_____

6. Dealing with Long Passages

When you want to use the evidence in a long passage from a source, you can paraphrase by summarizing it, mentioning only the key ideas (underlined here), and summarizing others (italicized here).

Example:

Original: Alleging that whaling is inherently cruel, as the British do, often comes with the further claim that whales are somehow "special": they are *extraordinarily intelligent, perhaps, or spiritual, noble or peaceful, or they have some mixture of these qualities that makes killing them more reprehensible than, say, killing cows or pigs.* Science has little to say about this sort of speculation. Whales look peaceful enough, though bull whales of some species bear the scars of fierce fighting with other males.
—*"A Bloody War," 2004*

Strong Paraphrase: Many, such as the British, say that whaling is brutal because whales are more unique and human-like than other, domestic animals. However, there is no scientific proof of this and, in fact, male whales often fight among themselves, as shown by their scars ("A Bloody War," 2004).

Now You Try

Practice paraphrasing this longer passage

- identify the key ideas to paraphrase by underlining them once
- select the ideas to summarize and underline them twice
- write a short paraphrase of the passage

Original: Scientific research on reproductive cloning in other mammals shows that there is a markedly higher than normal incidence of fetal disorders and loss throughout pregnancy, and of malformation and death among newborns. There is no reason to suppose that the outcome would be different in humans. There would thus be a serious threat to the health of the cloned individual, not just at birth, but potentially at all stages of life—without obvious compensating benefit to the individual bearing this threat. —*White, J. "Science, Cloning and Morality," 2003*

Paraphrase:

_____

_____

_____

_____

Activities to Practice Paraphrasing

To practice paraphrasing, do one or more of the following activities.

Paraphrasing Challenging Passages

Working with a partner or small group:

1. Choose one of the following excerpts from articles in Part Two.
2. Identify the challenge in the excerpt you selected. In some cases, you may need to look at the original article in order to understand the context of the excerpt.
3. On separate paper, write a paraphrase of your excerpt and share it with your class. You may want to write it on the board or on an overhead transparency.
4. As a class, critique the paraphrase of each student pair or small group according to the criteria for a good paraphrase:

   - Has the same meaning as the original
     Includes all main ideas
     Adds no new ideas
   - Is different enough from the original to be considered your own writing
     Has no more than four or five words in a row from the original source
   - Grammar and vocabulary changed as much as possible
   - Refers directly to original source
     Includes name of author and/or name of source

Excerpts from Part Two articles

Excerpt 1 (p. 161)

   Since heroes and heroines live in the minds and hearts of people other than themselves, their existence as heroic figures depends on the communication that makes them known. In historical times, the medium that carried their fame was oral tradition. Later it was print—newspapers, books, and magazines. Now, of course, the medium is primarily television, the most widespread and effective creator and popularizer of heroes and heroines ever known. What we see in the television hero and heroine represents the changed tastes and needs of the receiving public, and consequently the changed heroic role. In newscasts, game shows, soap operas—in all the many faces worn by television—we see people who may illustrate the qualities that we think our society needs. —*Browne, Ray, "Contemporary Heroes and Heroines," 1990*

Challenge with excerpt 1: _____

_____

Excerpt 2 (p. 163)

It may be possible for large-scale change to occur without charismatic leaders, but the pace of change would be glacial, the vision uncertain, and the committee meetings endless. —*Tollefson, Ted, "Is a Hero Really Nothing But a Sandwich?" 1993*

Challenge with excerpt 2: _____

_____

Excerpt 3 (p. 198)

This comparison is *inflammatory* and unfair, and could make a desperate situation even worse. —*Ho, David, "It's AIDS, Not Tuskegee," 1997*

Challenge with excerpt 3: _____

_____

Excerpt 4 (p. 173)

One in every three Americans uses the Internet; only one in every 10,000 people in India, Pakistan and Bangladesh do. —*Dixit, Kunda, "Exiled to Cyberia"*

Challenge with excerpt 4: _____

_____

Excerpt 5 (p. 175)

Take extending First World labor standards to Third World countries. This is a major issue for most protesters, who have, of course, the best of intentions. But it is naive economics and is opposed by India and just about every other developing country. —*"Confronting Anti-Globalism," 2001*

Challenge with excerpt 5: _____

_____

ACTIVITY 2

Trading Paraphrases

Working with a partner or small group:

1. Select two to three passages from an article you are reading in Part Two for the research paper you're building.
2. Using the "Tell a Friend" technique (p. 8), the "Chunking" technique (p. 9), or a combination of the two, paraphrase the passages you have selected.
3. Evaluate your paraphrases using the criteria for a good paraphrase from Activity 1.
4. Trade your paraphrases with another pair or group.
5. Read the other students' paraphrases and see if you can identify the original passages in the article.

Sharing Paraphrases

1. Choose a paraphrase that you have worked on, either for a current or past writing assignment, but found particularly difficult to write. Bring both your paraphrase and the original passage to class.
2. Write both the original passage and your paraphrase on the board or on an overhead transparency.
3. With a small group or with the class, discuss the challenges in the paraphrase. In your discussion, consider the six paraphrasing challenges listed.

Integrating Evidence into Paragraphs

Whatever evidence we use to support our ideas, we still need to make the paper read smoothly and logically. In other words, to effectively use information from outside sources, we need to incorporate it gracefully into our work; we must fit quotations and paraphrases into our own well-written paragraphs.

To help accomplish this, we need to explain why we're using the evidence from sources. We do this by framing the evidence—introducing the paraphrase or quote—and then explaining what links the evidence to the topic sentence of the paragraph.

Two Steps for Integrating Evidence

1. Introduce the Evidence.

Provide the author's name and/or the title of the source.

- Include the author's name every time you use evidence from sources.
- Include the title of the source only the first time you use it.
- If available, include information about the author if he or she is an expert on the topic. Do this only the first time you use a source.

A description of how to formally document and cite your sources is given in Chapter 5, pages 116–122.

Example:

Here is an example of paraphrased evidence with an introduction:

> In "Leaving the Boys Behind," Jacqueline Thompson (2002), a professor of education at the University of Texas, writes that if current trends continue, fewer than 65% of boys will graduate from high school in 2010.

- This example includes both the title of the source, "Leaving the Boys Behind," and the author, Jacqueline Thompson. In addition, Thompson's professional status, a university professor, shows readers that she is an expert on the topic. If this source is used again later in the paper, only the author's last name needs to be given.

2. Connect the Evidence to the Topic Sentence.

Provide an explanation that helps the reader see how the evidence is related to the topic sentence or point you are making. This can be done before the evidence, after the evidence, or in both places.

Example:

The following example shows a section of a paragraph that includes the topic sentence, a piece of evidence, and connecting explanations that occur both before and after the evidence.

Topic sentence ⟶	The traditional structure of American high schools is clearly not meeting the needs of boys.
Connecting explanation ⟶	They drop out of high school at a higher rate than girls, and the number of boys who do not graduate from high school is increasing.
Evidence ⟶	In "Leaving the Boys Behind," Jacqueline Thompson (2002), a professor of education at the University of Texas, writes that if current trends continue fewer than 65% of boys will graduate from high school in 2010.
Connecting explanation ⟶	Educators have struggled to understand what has caused this disturbing trend and identified several possible factors related to how schools are organized.

- Note in this example that the writer has carefully linked the evidence to the topic of the paragraph. The connecting explanations occur both before and after the evidence.

A More Careful Look at Integrating Evidence

A more careful look at the example paragraph on why young and old people lose contact with each other (p. 73) reveals the writer's effort to smoothly integrate the supporting evidence into her writing.

Topic sentence ⟶	The value of independence is one reason why young and old people become isolated from each other.
Connecting explanation ⟶	Being independent is an important quality of life for most Americans. Since childhood, people have been taught to be independent and the notion continues through their old age.
Evidence ⟶	Margaret Mead (1971), an anthropologist, writes in her article, "Grandparents Have Copped Out," that old people don't want to be a burden to their children so they try to live their lives independently.
Connecting explanation ⟶	In other words, old people do not want to interfere with their children's lives. Young people also believe their lives will be better without their parents as constant companions and advisors.
Concluding sentence ⟶	Consequently, communication between the generations is limited and isolation gradually occurs.

- The connecting explanation that comes before the evidence in this paragraph explains how the idea of independence connects to old age.
- The evidence is given as a paraphrase and includes the author's name, the article title, and some information about the author. In paragraphs that follow, the writer will include only the author's last name—Mead—when she introduces this source.
- The connecting explanation after the evidence provides further information that relates the value of independence to the relationship between young and old.

Now You Try

Here is a well-constructed paragraph in which the evidence has been smoothly integrated into the writing.

The first characteristic of risk is that the outcome of the activity is uncertain. When the person begins the activity, he is not sure whether or not he will be successful. In her article "Taking the Bungee Plunge," Ginia Bellefonte (1992) writes about this uncertainty. "We build sustainable confidence not by taking life-threatening risks but by gradually working at things we never thought we could achieve." In other words, a risky activity does not have to be dangerous, but it must involve trying to accomplish something we are not sure we are capable of doing. The key here is that we try and succeed in doing something that is not easy for us to do. This also points to a second characteristic of risk; a risky activity must be challenging.

1. Put brackets around the topic sentence.
2. Underline once any sentences or phrases that provide connecting information before the evidence.
3. Circle the title of the article and the name of the author.
4. Put parentheses around the quote that is used as evidence and double parentheses around the paraphrase of that quote.
5. Underline twice the connecting explanation after the evidence.
6. Underline with a wavy line the conclusion and/or transition to the next paragraph.

Dumping Evidence

Dumping a piece of evidence from a source into your writing means inserting the quotation or paraphrase without a proper introduction or explanation. When this occurs, the reader is left to figure out the purpose of the quote or paraphrase. In the example, the writer has simply dumped the quote into the paragraph with no supporting information.

Example:

Weak Integration: An uncertain outcome is one characteristic of risk. In her article "Taking the Bungee Plunge," Bellafonte (1992) writes that "we build sustainable confidence not by taking life-threatening risks, but by gradually working at things we never thought we could achieve." Another characteristic of risk is that the activity must be challenging.

- Notice in this example how the writer simply included a quotation with no explanation of its relationship to the topic sentence either before or after.

NOTE: Good writers avoid dumping evidence into their papers.

Now You Try

Considering the qualities of a well constructed paragraph as well as the information on how to integrate evidence, identify two or more problems with dumped evidence in this paragraph.

Young and old people are segregated in American culture according to one article. In other words, the young and old do not communicate or interact enough with each other. This problem is caused by a lack of contact between them. The article says that old people don't want to be a burden to the young.

Problem _____

Problem _____

Problem _____

Activities to Practice Integrating Evidence

To practice integrating evidence, do one or both of the following activities.

Identifying Evidence in Paragraphs

1. With a small group, read the two paragraphs. Underline each piece of outside evidence.
2. Discuss the following questions about each paragraph:
   a. What is this paragraph about?
   b. How many pieces of outside evidence are used?
   c. Look at each piece of evidence. Does each one support the topic sentence?
   d. Is each piece of evidence well-integrated? Circle the words that introduce each piece of evidence. Put each connecting explanation in parentheses.
   e. Does the paragraph flow logically and smoothly?
3. Discuss your answers with the class.

Paragraph 1

The selling of human eggs raises a legal problem. In fact, U.S. law does not allow people to trade in human organs, except for sperm and eggs ("Millions Check In," 1999). Dr. Jeffery Kahn, Director of the Center for Bioethics at the University of Minnesota, confirms that it is an offense against federal law to deal in human parts, aside from human blood and tissue. On the other hand, he also argues that there are many important ways in which eggs should be considered more like tissue than like organs (Kahn, 1999). Meanwhile, in attempts to circumvent the law, several entrepreneurs are offering human eggs from beautiful women for sale on the Internet ("Eggs for Sale," 1999). And so far, such on-line commerce seems to be beyond the reach of the law. Objecting to these egg auctions in cyberspace, Ron Wyden, the Democratic senator from Oregon who wrote the 1992 federal law regulating fertility clinics, has called the operation "crass commercialism" (Lemonick, 1999).

Paragraph 2

As people around the world become more affluent, their diets get worse. According to Ted Wilcox (1999), a writer for the "New York Times," Japanese immigrating from the high-carbohydrate Pacific to high-fat America have a greater risk of heart disease the more westernized their diets become. Carolyn Henderson, a high school student in Tennessee, says that Mexican restaurants are becoming more popular everywhere. What is a safe level of cholesterol? Scientists in a laboratory in Texas wrote an article saying that as a country's food gets richer, infectious disease and malnutrition are replaced by heart disease, certain cancers, and obesity (Russo, 2000). People are eating more meat and dairy products in countries such as Cuba, Mauritius, and Hungary. Not surprisingly, the disease rates in these countries are changing along with the change in diet (Martinez, 2001). The American Heart Association National Cholesterol Education Program (1999) says that fat should be no more than 30% of our diet.

ACTIVITY **2**   *Grading Paragraphs*

1. With your group, read each of the three paragraphs. As you read, consider the following:

   * Does the paragraph meet the criteria for a well-constructed paragraph? (see p. 73)
   * Is the outside evidence carefully integrated? (see pp. 88–91)

2. Rate each paragraph according to this scale:

   A = Excellent. Meets all criteria for a paragraph with well-integrated evidence.

   C = OK, but needs work. Has some, but not all, characteristics of a good paragraph using outside evidence.

   F = Unacceptable. Doesn't have any characteristics of a good paragraph using outside evidence.

3. After completing your analysis of the paragraphs, discuss your ratings with the class and compare to the teacher's rating.

NOTE: Source evidence is indicated by a dotted underline.

Paragraph 1

Gender roles come from social factors such as culture and family as well as from biological factors such as age and physical characteristics. Because men have more testosterone, they have more physical energy and are more aggressive. This makes them like sports which makes them more competitive. Therefore, men are more interested in dominating others than in helping them. In social life, man is less nurturing because when he gets a promotion in his job, he gets less time to spend with his family (Farrell, 1986). Also, Houston (1973) mentions that she knows about Asian gender roles because her family taught her. Houston writes, "It would have embarrassed me to see my brothers doing the dishes."

Grade _____

Paragraph 2

One group of people who oppose xenotransplantation,* are animal rights advocates. These people state that the new science causes misuse and exploitation of animals' lives (Cassidy, 1994). To develop a new medical practice requires lots of precise and complicated testing. During the process, if scientists make some small errors, then they need other healthy animals to start the experiment over. Consequently the "old" animals are deserted and need to be killed. Animal rights activists wonder how many animals need to die due to the mistakes in experiments. They suggest that there must be an alternative way that could replace animals for testing (Cassidy, 1994). Sacrificing animals without considering the great pain and torture which the animals suffer as well as their right to live, is, according to these activists, selfish and immoral.

   *Xenotransplantation is the transfer of an organ from one species to another, for example, transferring a pig's heart to a human.

Grade _____

Paragraph 3

First of all, many people become vegetarians to maintain good health. Vegetarianism can prevent people from getting diseases. Castelman (1995) writes that many studies prove that meat, especially beef, pork, and lamb likely increase the percentages of heart disease and cancers. In his article, it is proved that the number of vegetarian deaths is definitely lower than meat eaters. For example, from heart disease, 28% fewer vegetarians die than omnivores do, and 39% fewer die from cancer. The National Cancer Research Institute also found that meat-eating women get breast cancer almost four times more than women who do not eat meat or eat little meat. ("Why be Vegetarian?", 1999). Hypertension, gallstones, constipation, and diabetes are also problems (Cerrato, 1991). Dworkin (1999) cites a Loma Linda University study that says vegetarians can live seven years longer than people who eat meat. Another positive health point of vegetarianism, according to Dworkin, is that vegetarians are generally slim and have stronger bones. Knowing these health benefits, many people are becoming vegetarians.

Grade _____

BUILDING YOUR PAPER

Write a Paragraph With Integrated Evidence

Choose one of the topic sentences you wrote for the Building Your Paper on page 77 and write one paragraph of that section. Do not choose the introduction or the conclusion because those paragraphs follow a different format and will be discussed in Chapter 5, pages 99–104. As you write your paragraph:

- Consider the qualities of a well-constructed paragraph on page 73.
- Prepare your evidence, paying special attention to paraphrasing.
- Integrate each piece of evidence carefully so that your paragraph flows smoothly and logically.

Getting Feedback

1. Bring the paragraph you wrote to class. Bring enough copies so that each member of your group can have a copy.
2. Take turns reading the paragraphs aloud while the others read along silently.
3. After you read your paragraph, listen to your classmates' comments and make notes about possible changes to your paragraph.
4. After you listen to each paragraph, give the writer feedback answering these questions:

   - Does the paragraph meet the criteria for a well-constructed paragraph on page 73?
   - Is the outside evidence introduced and explained following the steps for integrating evidence on pages 88–89?

Writer's Block

Writer's block happens when your mind goes blank and you have no ideas. You may think that you'll never be able to write again, that you don't have anything to say about your topic, or that you would rather do anything than write. This feeling strikes all writers from time to time. Some people say it is actually a healthy sign that the brain is working on ideas and has simply gotten stuck in one place.

Getting Out of Writer's Block

Here are some ideas that may help you to get out of writer's block.

1. Start with what you have accomplished and continue into new ideas from there.

   * Read over what you have written—your notes, outlines, and so on—and, without thinking in depth about what you've just read, immediately start your draft with whatever comes to mind.
   * Copy over sections of what you have written. New ideas may come to you while you do this, and if they do, write them down even if they are only one word at a time.
   * Whenever you stop, leave yourself a note about what you will write next so you won't have to wonder what to say when you get back to work.

2. Talk to yourself or someone else about your paper. Once you describe your ideas informally, writing the paper will just expand the same ideas in more formal language.

   * Write a paragraph telling what you think your finished paper will be about.
   * Pretend you are writing a letter to a good friend about your topic instead of an academic paper.
   * Call up a friend and talk about your paper. Tell him or her what you plan to write.

3. Start with something easy. Seeing certain sections finished will encourage you so that it won't be hard to go on to more challenging parts.

   * If you are stuck on one section of your paper, set that aside and work on another part for a while. You can return to the more difficult section later.
   * Do something that doesn't take a lot of thought, such as working on your reference list or proofreading what you have already written.

4. Take regular breaks the whole time you're working on the paper.

   * Take a walk around the block. Promise yourself that you will take a 10 minute walk every hour.

Another way to help yourself with your writing is to get assistance from a friend, a professional tutor, or an editor. However, it's important to keep in mind that working through the writing process yourself will give you the skills and confidence you need to write academic papers on your own. If you get too much help, too much advice from a friend or tutor, or if you copy (plagiarize) a paper, you miss the valuable practice in the writing process and you won't be able to apply what you have learned to later writing.

BUILDING YOUR PAPER

Write a Draft of Your Paper

It is at last time to write the first full draft of your guided research paper.

* Use your detailed outline and tentative thesis statement that you created in Chapter 3 to provide the framework for your essay.
* Review the information in this chapter on paraphrasing, constructing paragraphs, and integrating evidence. Use these strategies to integrate the information you have chosen as evidence for each of your supporting points.

Remember that your goal in a first draft is not to create a perfect paper. This draft is your first effort at expressing your ideas and ideas from sources in the form of a research paper.

Getting Feedback on Your First Draft

The following are two methods for getting feedback on your first draft. Both methods focus on the ideas, or content, of your paper. Writing to or talking with your readers (your teacher and classmates) can help you think about how another person might understand the ideas in your paper.

Write a Letter to Your Teacher

* Quickly read through your research paper draft.
* As you read, mark your favorite and least favorite sections.
* In a letter to your teacher, explain why you like your favorite section and why you're having difficulties with the sections you've marked as trouble spots.
* Give your letter to your teacher with the marked copy of your paper.

Discuss Your Paper with a Classmate

Exchange your paper with a partner or a small group of classmates and take turns as reader and writer.

Directions for the Reader

- Quickly read through your partner's paper.
- Select the section you think is the most impressive or interesting. This may be a single sentence or an entire paragraph. Mark this section and explain to your partner why you chose it.
- Select no more than two or three sections of the paper that you found the most difficult to understand. Mark these sections with a question mark. Ask your partner to explain what she wants to say in the marked sections. Don't let her give up until you really understand her points.

Directions for the Writer

Discuss with your partner the two sections of your paper that you found the most difficult to write. Explain the difficulty you were having while you were trying to write these sections. Discussing these difficult sections with another person can often help you clarify your thoughts about what you want to write.

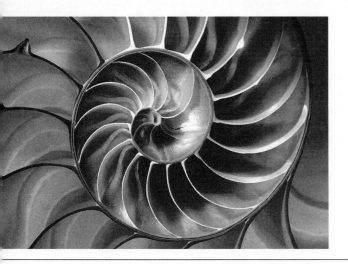

CHAPTER

5

Building a Paper:

Refine

When you began writing your guided research paper, you were working to understand the issues involved with your topic and deciding what you wanted to say about it. That part of the writing process can be called the writer focus stage when you, as the writer, are concerned with making sense out of the ideas.

Now that you've written your first draft, your goal is to make sure you've presented your ideas so they are clear to the reader. Your job is to create a reader friendly paper that smoothly guides the reader from one idea to the next. To help you identify strengths and weaknesses in your paper, it is useful to communicate directly with your reader. Your readers for this paper are your teacher and classmates because they understand the ideas you are writing about. By talking with or writing to your reader, you can think about how another person might understand your paper.

To refine your paper, you will add some finishing touches to your introduction and conclusion and to the language you use to clearly link ideas. You will also formally document your evidence. Based on your readers' comments and your own editing, you can polish your paper so it is cohesive and rich in detail.

In this chapter you will practice:

- Revising your introduction and conclusion
- Revising your use of guiding language for cohesion
- Documenting your evidence
- Getting feedback on your paper.

By the end of this chapter, you will have written an effective introduction and conclusion to your paper and used guiding language to make it cohesive. You will have documented your evidence and received feedback from your classmates on your whole draft. Finally, you'll write the final version of your research paper.

Writing Introductions and Conclusions

Because introductions and conclusions form the first and last impression of your paper, they deserve special attention. Often, in writing the body of the paper, the introduction and conclusion are hurriedly written and not very effective. Now is the time to revise these two sections with the reader in mind. Revising your introduction and conclusion at the same time can ensure that the beginning and ending of your paper link together smoothly.

Elements of an Effective Introduction

The introduction of the paper is your first contact with your reader. It is an opportunity to establish a clear and engaging connection to your topic for the reader. An effective introduction accomplishes three things:

* Focuses the reader's attention on the topic.
* Arouses the reader's curiosity.
* States your thesis.

Example 1:

Celebrating the revolution, French citizens sent King Louie XVI to the guillotine. Every Halloween day in ancient Rome, the most evil criminals were executed at the city square. In the 1800s, in an effort to deter crime in the United States, hundreds of bank robbers, killers, and horse thieves were hanged in front of the public. Capital punishment has been a useful and powerful tool to protect justice and deter crime. However, in the last half of the 20th century, the death penalty has faced increasing opposition. Many people, especially members of churches, are against capital punishment. Most advanced countries have eliminated the death penalty ("Down With the Death Penalty," 1998). While it is true that the death penalty has some negative points, it is still a powerful and useful tool. Therefore, so as to deter crime, to give fairness to victims and their families, and to punish inhumane criminals, our society should keep the death penalty.

* This introduction begins with three historical references to execution as a punishment in order to focus the reader's attention on the topic of capital punishment.

Example 2:

> Two years ago, my brother was killed in a bicycle accident. He was very important to me and losing him was a terrible experience. Since his death, I have thought a lot about the value of life. I have come to realize that life does not have any price. We can never be compensated for the loss of someone we love. People who support the death penalty feel that through the death of another person, they can pay for the life of a person who has been murdered. They believe that the death penalty will offer justice to the victim's family. However, the death penalty is not a good way to resolve problems of crime because the judicial system can make irreparable mistakes and the moral cost is too high.

> • In this introduction, the writer describes her experience with her brother's death as a way of presenting her opinion about capital punishment.

Introduction Techniques

The following techniques can be used to help create an effective introduction. Your introduction can include more than one of these techniques.

1. Use a quotation or a surprising fact or statistic from your sources that relates to the focus of your topic.
   For example, the introduction to a paper on male violence could provide statistics on the percentage of violent crimes committed by males.
2. Ask a question or describe a problem, dilemma, or controversy associated with your topic.
   For instance, the introduction to a paper on assisted suicide could discuss the dilemma of balancing the rights of individuals with the medical obligation of doctors.
3. Tell a story or relate a personal reason for your interest in the topic.
   See Example 2 above.
4. Define a word that is central to your topic.
   An argument paper on genetically modified food could begin with a brief definition of the term "genetically modified."
5. Make a historical comparison or contrast.
   See Example 1 above.

Now You Try

Read the introduction that follows. With a partner or a small group, discuss which of the five techniques the writer uses in this introduction.

Introduction

I was eating breakfast in a restaurant in Portland when Mike came in and sat at a table beside mine. He wore new jeans and a jacket, but what caught my attention more was that he had short hair and looked clean. Was he the same man I had seen a couple of times before coming into the restaurant looking like a homeless person and asking for empty cans and bottles in order to get some money? Yes, he was Mike. After finishing his breakfast, Mike asked for the check and paid as a normal customer. I was wondering how he had changed, so I asked the waiter about him. The waiter told me that Mike is a veteran, and he had just received his pension from the government after years of waiting. Due to bureaucratic problems, he had not gotten his pension for many years and had become homeless. Like Mike, there are a lot of homeless people that you see on the streets. According to the National Survey of Homeless Assistance Providers and Clients (NSHAPC), 23% of the total homeless population are veterans (Homelessness, 1999). The causes of homelessness are numerous and complex. The lack of both affordable housing and public assistance as well as the breakdown of the families are some of the principal causes of homelessness in the United States.

What technique(s) did this student use? _____

Elements of an Effective Conclusion

Just as an introduction is your first opportunity to connect with your reader, so the conclusion is an opportunity to guide your reader to the close of your research paper. A strongly written conclusion leaves your reader not only with a clear understanding of the central point in your paper, but also with a final comment that provides an interesting closing thought. An effective conclusion has two components:

1. A final analysis or interpretation of the main point of your paper.
   Avoid restating your thesis or simply repeating topic sentences.
2. An ending comment
   Include an interesting idea that inspires your reader to continue thinking about your topic.

Example:

This introduction and conclusion are from a research paper about the effects of globalization.

Introduction: What do we do when we have a problem? Leave it alone? Or try to solve it? Most people say that globalization creates more and more problems, such as increasing the gap between the rich and the poor. However, this difference between people who have a lot and those who have only a little is not the result of an intention to increase the income gap in the world; instead, it is a result of how well the first world nations have been managing their economies. In truth, the developed countries have been supporting developing countries, especially by providing jobs and other opportunities so that starving people can survive with dignity. There is an expression that says, if you give a man a fish, you feed him for a day; if you teach a man how to fish, you feed him for a lifetime. This saying illustrates how globalization is a positive force because it supports the lives of the poor with jobs, education, and access to improved technology.

Conclusion: ***[Summary of main points]*** Globalization is essential for people in Third World countries to rise from their present state of poverty. Because of globalization, more people than ever before have employment in meaningful jobs and literacy at all levels is spreading throughout the world. Technology such as the Internet, cell phones, and chances to travel connect people in all countries and help decrease the income gap between "haves" and "have-nots." ***[Ending comment]*** I refer the reader back to the expression about teaching a man to fish; globalization provides the necessary tools for the poor to "eat for a lifetime."

In this conclusion, the writer has provided a final analysis of the main points in her essay. Notice that the analysis includes the thesis ideas, but expresses these ideas in a new way. The final sentence of the conclusion links back to a proverb mentioned in the introduction. This strategy provides a strong connection between the beginning and ending of the essay.

Conclusion Techniques

1. Echo the approach used in the introduction, using different wording. See the conclusion example on globalization.
2. Use a quotation.
   For example, in a conclusion for a paper supporting capital punishment, you could include a quote from a victim's family on why they believe in the death penalty.
3. End with a powerful fact or other detail related to the topic of the paper.
   In a paper arguing for stronger recycling programs, you could conclude with a statistic that shows the amount of garbage produced each year.
4. Recommend a course of action, if called for in the material you present.
   To conclude a paper discussing reasons for male violence, you could offer a few suggestions for overcoming these causes.

Now You Try

Read the following introduction. Identify the thesis statement. Underline the focus of the thesis and circle the overview of supporting points. Then read each of the possible conclusions. With a partner or a small group, discuss the questions that follow, circle Effective or Ineffective, and give your reasons.

Introduction:

In the state of Oregon it is legal for a doctor to help a terminally ill patient to commit suicide. A doctor can prescribe a pill or injection to complete the process of assisting the patient to die peacefully and with less pain. Some people say they would rather accept the terminally-ill patient's wish to die because they feel that it is a kind of torture to see them suffering from intolerable pain. Others say they can't agree with assisting patients who want to die because there are some obvious problems which lead these patients to this decision. Problems in regulating assisted suicide and difficulties for patients making the choice to end their lives are two reasons why assisted suicide should not be legalized.

Conclusion 1:

In conclusion, problems in regulating assisted suicide and difficulties for patients making the choice to end their lives are two important reasons why assisted suicide should not be legalized. In Oregon, a very small number of people have used the assisted suicide program ("Insight on the News," 1999). However, rather than thinking that this means that legalized assisted suicide is a good idea, it should motivate the medical community to overcome the remaining problems that cause that small number of people to feel that dying is better than living.

Discussion:

Does the conclusion restate the focus and supporting points of the paper in a new way?

What, if any, conclusion technique does the writer use?

Effective / Ineffective

Reasons:

_____

_____

Conclusion 2:

Assisted suicide causes many problems. The process is easy to abuse. The boundaries of when assisted suicide is appropriate means that it is difficult to control. For example, it is not always easy to determine if and when a patient will die. Moreover, emotional factors and underlying problems, such as intolerable pain, influence many patients to decide that they want to die. A Korean proverb says "when a person falls in the water, he will grab even straws to pull himself out." I'm sure many terminally ill patients feel the same way. When faced with such pain, death seems to be the best way to escape. Society needs to find ways to improve the end of life for people so that the choice to live is more hopeful than the decision to die.

Discussion:

Does the conclusion restate the focus and supporting points of the paper in a new way?

What, if any, conclusion technique does the writer use?

Effective / Ineffective

Reasons:

_____

_____

Conclusion 3:

Even though many people agree with physician-assisted suicide, few people choose it in their own lives. In Oregon, only a few people have followed through on their request for assisted suicide. Many doctors think it is hard to determine when patients will die. In addition, the difficulty in distinguishing between a patient's rational thought and emotional depression as well as the fact that the medical community has not been successful at finding ways to ease people's pain, raise more problems.

Discussion:

Does the conclusion restate the focus and supporting points of the paper in a new way?

What, if any, conclusion technique does the writer use?

Effective / Ineffective

Reasons:

_____

_____

Activities to Practice Evaluating Introductions and Conclusions

To practice evaluating introductions, do the following activity.

ACTIVITY 1 *Evaluating Introductions*

With your group, read and discuss the following three introductions for their effectiveness. Then make notes in the chart to evaluate and compare them.

Introduction 1:

She wakes up in Japan and eats toast and sausage made in Germany for breakfast with her father, who checks the movement of the yen rate in the daily paper. She works at a Chinese pharmaceutical company and usually eats fast food like MacDonald's for lunch before she goes to English conversation school. She is a typical young person in the world today. Nowadays, our life itself is globalized. But the problem of globalization is still controversial. Although some people worry that it aggravates the problem of obesity all over the world, globalization is good because we can benefit from it in three ways: economics, health, and culture.

Introduction 2:

Have you ever taken standardized tests? Many people around the world have participated in standardized tests as a way to enter a new higher level of school or to prove that they have learned in school. Some people think standardized tests help improve education; however, some people disagree with standardized tests. Although standardized testing is a controversy around the world, national and local governments will continue to use standardized tests to measure schools and students. Standardized tests improve the quality of education in two ways: motivating students and providing an effective measurement of how schools are doing.

Introduction 3:

It is wonderful for people all over the world to communicate with each other through the Internet, or to enjoy foods from the opposite side of the globe. On the other hand, finding a case of mad cow disease in the United States makes beef disappear from the Japanese marketplace. These are both sides of the coin. In the article, "Globalization: Good or Bad?" Keith Porter (2004) writes "Globalization is much like fire. Fire itself is neither good nor bad. Used properly, it can cook food, sterilize equipment, form iron, and heat our homes. Used carelessly, fire can destroy lives, towns, and forests in an instant." While many people debate this issue, globalization has also influenced women's expectations of marriage recently.

	Introduction 1	**Introduction 2**	**Introduction 3**
1. Which technique(s) did the writer use?			
2. Does the introduction have a thesis? If yes, does the thesis appear at or near the end of the introduction?			
3. Is the writer's thesis clearly focused? Can you easily identify both the focus and overview of supporting points?			
4. Overall rating of the introduction? 4 3 2 1 excellent good fair weak			

ACTIVITY **2**

Evaluating Conclusions

With a partner or small group, read the introductions and conclusions for each example essay in the Appendix. Identify the thesis and underline the focus and supporting points in each introduction. Then make notes in the chart to analyze the conclusions.

	Conclusion "Risky Business"	Conclusion "Expectations of Marriage"	Conclusion "Vegetarianism"
1. Does the conclusion restate the focus and supporting points of the paper in a new way?			
2. What, if any, conclusion technique(s) does the writer use?			
3. Overall rating of the conclusion? 4 3 2 1 excellent good fair weak			

BUILDING YOUR PAPER

Revise Your Introduction and Conclusion

Revise the introduction and conclusion of your research paper draft. As you revise, consider the following:

- Does your introduction open with a strategy that will attract and engage the reader?
- Does your introduction guide the reader to the focus of your paper?
- Does your conclusion offer a final analysis of the central points in your paper? Does your conclusion have a final comment that leaves the reader with a thoughtful idea?

Getting Feedback

Make copies of your introduction and conclusion from the draft you wrote in Chapter 4. Bring enough copies for several classmates to read. Work in groups of three or four.

1. Decide how much time to spend on each person's paper.
2. Have the first person read his introduction and conclusion aloud while the others read along silently.
3. After the reading, discuss the introduction and conclusion:

   - Identify the technique(s) the writer uses in the introduction.
   - Identify the thesis.
   - On the basis of the introduction, discuss what you think the paper will be about. What questions will the paper answer?
   - What technique(s) does the conclusion use? Does it connect clearly to the introduction?
   - Tell the writer about any parts of the introduction and conclusion that are unclear to you.

4. When the first person's time is up, repeat the process with the next person until everyone in the group has had a turn.

Building Cohesion in Your Paper

When you created the outline for your paper and wrote the first draft, you had to decide how to organize each section so that the ideas would flow logically from one point to the next. Now, as you focus on creating a reader-friendly paper, you need to examine the language you have used. Your words should help the reader:

- see the relationship between your thesis and supporting points;
- understand how the paragraphs relate to each other;
- follow ideas easily within each paragraph.

When you logically organize and clearly connect your ideas in these ways, we say that the paper is **cohesive**.

Using Guiding Language

Guiding language is specific language that helps your reader see how your ideas are related. These words and phrases carefully lead your reader from one idea to the next within your paper.

Guiding Language to Connect Thesis and Supporting Points

A reader-friendly paper uses language that clearly links the main idea of each supporting point to the thesis. This helps the reader remember the larger goal of the paper and directs her to the specific focus of each section. Two simple techniques can help create strong, clear topic sentences to introduce each supporting point.

1. Repeat key words.

To emphasize the link between your thesis statement and each supporting point, you can repeat important words from your thesis.

For example, if your paper discusses reasons for an event, each topic sentence can include phrases such as "one reason, a second reason, another important reason." Repeating a key word in this way guides the reader to see how you have organized your ideas.

2. Restate the main point of the thesis.

Often it is useful to repeat the focus of your thesis, using different words. Referring to your thesis statement helps the reader recognize the connection between your thesis statement and supporting point.

Example (guiding language is underlined):

Thesis statement:

<u>Three major factors</u> lead to the <u>prevalence of child labor in Latin America</u>: family values, the dependent relationship many Latin nations have with developed countries, and economic globalization.

Topic sentence for the first supporting point:

The first factor is the belief by many Latin American people that expecting all family members, including children, to work is acceptable or needed for their living.

Topic sentence for the second supporting point:

Another factor involves the international relationship among developed and developing nations, which intensifies the need for children to work.

Topic sentence for the third supporting point:

The third factor that results in child labor is the influence of multinational corporations in Latin America.

- In this example, the writer repeats the word "factor" in each of her topic sentences. This signals to the reader each shift to a new point and that the point is directly related to the thesis statement.
- The writer also restates the focus of her thesis, "prevalence of child labor," in each topic sentence. Notice how she repeats the idea, but not the exact words. In this way, she expresses her main point in new ways while still carefully guiding her reader.
- Each topic sentence also includes the focus of the supporting point. These ideas are directly linked to the overview of supporting points in the thesis but are stated in a different way to guide the reader to the connection between the two.

Now You Try

Below is an example of a thesis statement and two topic sentences. Working with a partner or a small group, follow the directions to identify the guiding language provided by the writer.

1. Read the thesis statement. Then underline the focus of the paper and circle each of the three supporting points.

   Thesis statement: Although some people worry that globalization aggravates the problem of obesity all over the world, globalization is positive because of its health, economic, and social benefits.

2. Read topic sentence a.

   - *Topic Sentence a:* In addition to protecting our health, globalization is also good because it stimulates our economy and creates jobs.

   - Does it restate the focus of the thesis?

   - Which supporting point does it introduce? _____

   Underline the guiding language that links this paragraph to the previous paragraph.

3. Read topic sentence b.

   - *Topic Sentence b:* Not only can globalization positively affect health and economy, but it can also improve the social status of women.

   - Does this topic sentence restate the focus of the thesis?

   - What is the focus of this paragraph? _____

Guiding Language in Transitions Between Paragraphs

Carefully leading the reader from one paragraph to the next is another way to create a reader-friendly paper. When you write sentences or phrases that directly link the end of one paragraph to the beginning of another, you provide the reader with a smooth transition from one idea to the next.
(Guiding language is underlined in the examples.)

Example 1:

This section of an essay on overpopulation focuses on increasing the educational level of girls, so the writer must provide a transition between the statistical statement of the problem in one paragraph and the causes of the problem in the next.

End of paragraph:

In 1995, girls (mostly from poor rural families) comprised about 60% of the 130 million third-world children who failed to go to school.

Topic sentence of next paragraph:

There are several reasons why so many girls do not receive school education.

- Notice in this example, how the idea "girls fail to go to school" is brought into the topic sentence of the next paragraph, "so many girls do not receive school education," providing a clear link from one paragraph to the next.

Example 2:

In this section of a paper on juvenile violence, the writer is transitioning from a definition of the problem of media violence and children to the ways that the violence can influence children's behavior.

End of paragraph:

Some researchers say the violence portrayed in the media can contribute to causing children to commit murder (Waldron, 1999). How does media influence juveniles and encourage teenage violence?

Topic sentence of next paragraph:

First, sometimes movies and television dramas glamorize murderers.

- To create a smooth transition between one supporting point and the next, the writer used a question as a conclusion and then answered this question—the underlined guiding language—in the topic sentence of his next supporting point.

Example 3:

In this example from an essay on transplanting organs from animals to humans for medical purposes (xenotransplantation), the writer is making a transition from medical problems to social problems associated with xenotransplantation.

End of paragraph:

Will xenotransplantation be ready after scientists solve the medical difficulties? In fact, when the media presents a new science, <u>it always causes both positive and negative reactions</u> from the public. Likewise, xenotransplantation is not an exception.

Topic sentence of next paragraph:

In spite of opinions that support xenotransplantation, scientists must still overcome <u>the negative social reaction</u> that prevents them from succeeding in studying the new science.

- Here the student used both a question and linking phrases as guiding language to create a clear transition.

Now You Try

In the following two examples, underline the guiding language in the concluding and topic sentences that link the two paragraphs.

1. *Concluding sentences of the preceding paragraph:*

Basically, heroes live for ideals and their principles function as a catalyst that motivates society. However, sometimes a hero's ideals conflict with some members of society.

Topic sentence of the next paragraph:

Because heroes often must face some opposition to their ideals and their effort to change society, they must also be brave, a second characteristic of heroes.

2. *Concluding sentences of the preceding paragraph:*

Haggarty (1999) asserts that heredity studies prove that human bodyweight is influenced by genetic factors. Research on adopted children shows that most of the adopted children followed the pattern of weight gain of their biological parents rather than their adopted parents.

Topic sentence of the next paragraph:

Having a genetic makeup to gain weight does not, however, mean that somebody is automatically obese. The environment, a person's eating habits, and the amount of physical activity play a significant role in the amount of weight a person gains.

Guiding Language Within Paragraphs: Transition Words, Phrases, and Sentences

You have learned that you need to be sure your reader can easily understand how each supporting point is related to your thesis and how individual paragraphs are related to each other. In addition, you need to guide your reader smoothly from one idea to the next *within* each paragraph. This includes using clear transition words and phrases to signal a switch to new ideas and carefully introducing and explaining outside evidence.

Often, when writing first drafts, we focus on trying to understand and explain each idea we are including. In our minds, the relationship between ideas in a paragraph is clear, but this relationship is not always as clear in our writing. Notice in the example how much easier it is to understand the ideas in the revised paragraph after the writer uses transition words and phrases to carefully connect them. The added guiding language is underlined in the revised paragraph.

First Draft: It has been argued that standardized testing causes students and teachers to work harder. It may be true that teachers teach hard and students study hard to pass these tests. In "A Self Fulfilling Prophecy," Rotbert (2001) notes that teachers and students feel an obligation to improve standardized test scores. Under the pressure of test scores, they may work harder, but they don't work deeply. In "Standardized Testing: A Defense," Ashworth (1990, p. 71) admits that "when it comes to figuring out the system, most students learn to be con artists." They study to learn test-taking strategies; they focus on patterns of test questions. Their goal is to get high scores on tests and they don't care where their answers come from. They don't focus on subjects that are not covered by tests such as art and current events (Kohn, 2000). Standardized testing may motivate students to study intensely, but the quality of education doesn't improve because students' efforts reflect only a shallow approach to learning.

Revised Paragraph: It has been argued that standardized testing causes students and teachers to work harder. It may be true that teachers teach hard and students study hard to pass the test. In "A Self Fulfilling Prophecy," Rotbert (2001) notes that teachers and students feel an obligation to improve standardized test scores. However, under the pressure of test scores, they may work harder, but they don't work deeply. For example, in "Standardized Testing: A Defense," Ashworth (1990, p. 71) admits that "when it comes to figuring out the system, most students learn to be con artists." In other words, they study to learn test-taking strategies; they focus on patterns of test questions. Their goal is to get high scores on tests and they don't care where their answers come from. In addition, they don't focus on subjects that are not covered by tests such as art and current events (Kohn, 2000). Thus, standardized testing may motivate students to study intensely, but the quality of education doesn't improve because students' efforts reflect only a shallow approach to learning.

- The transition signals in this revised paragraph help guide the reader through the many different ideas the student wants to express.

  —<u>However</u> signals that the writer is about to disagree with the information presented in the preceding sentences.
  —<u>For example</u> lets the reader know that what comes next is an example of how studying for standardized tests does not encourage deep thinking.
  —<u>In other words</u> signals that the writer is going to explain how the source evidence is related to her point.
  —<u>In addition</u> signals that the writer is providing a second example.
  —<u>Thus</u> lets the reader know that a conclusion for this point is next.

More Guiding Language Methods Within Paragraphs

An important part of creating a reader-friendly paper is using appropriate words, phrases, and sentences to signal to your reader how your ideas are organized. Here are two methods for providing strong signals within a paragraph.

> For further discussion and more examples see
> **Transition Signals** on the *Sourcework* website at
> **http://esl.college.hmco.com/students**.

1. Using sentences to signal the structure of a paragraph

Sometimes including a sentence that indicates the organization of ideas in your paragraph can help guide the reader.

Example:

> Although the perception is that homeless people are usually single men, the reality is much different. *There are three main groups of homeless people.*

- The italicized signal sentence lets the reader know that the paragraph will be organized according to the three main categories of homeless people.

2. Using signals that guide readers through a sequence

If the ideas in your paragraph are part of a sequence, it is helpful to use signal words to alert readers to each transition to a new idea in the sequence.

- First, second, etc.
- Last(ly), finally

Example:

> Scientists have provided several reasons why hearts from a pig are more suitable for transplanting to humans than hearts from other animals. <u>First</u>, a pig's heart is most compatible in size and function. <u>Second</u>, a pig's heart is more easily accepted by the human body and is more likely to work properly once it has been transplanted. <u>Lastly</u>, because pigs are able to produce many litters, life-saving organs can be provided quickly and therefore can decrease the need for people to spend such a long time waiting for a transplant.

Now You Try

In the following paragraph, the writer uses guiding language in several places to make the relationship between her ideas clear. In some instances, she uses full sentences to help her reader see how her ideas are organized. In other places, she uses transition words and phrases. Underline each use of guiding language.

One reason young people commit suicide is because of pressures from their daily lives. According to Merritt (2000), growing up is more stressful today than it's ever been before. Merritt writes that "the cumulative weight of life's stresses makes growing up a difficult experience for many young people, one that can seem overwhelming to some." Family conflict and school pressures are two examples of issues young people often find difficult to deal with. A person who grows up in a single parent household or in a home where family members spend little time together can feel he or she does not get enough support. One study found that 90% of suicidal teenagers believed that their families did not understand them (American Academy of Pediatrics, 2001). Pressure from school is another source of stress for young people. Competition for good grades and college admission is stiff. Moreover, parents' high expectations of their children's academic performance increases the pressure young people feel. This pressure to succeed in school is one reason why young people commit suicide (Merritt, 2000). In one example, a 19-year-old college sophomore finished his term paper, asked his roommate to hand it in, and then killed himself. He left a note that asked his parents for forgiveness because he "could not succeed in college" (Smith, 2002). The kinds of pressures that young people experience in their lives can seem impossible to overcome. For some, suicide offers a way to escape.

Activities to Practice Building Cohesion

To practice building cohesion, do one or both of the following activities.

ACTIVITY 1 *Analyze Guiding Language in a Paper*

Select and read one of the research papers in the Appendix, page 205. Alone or with a partner, analyze the writer's use of guiding language.

1. Highlight the thesis statement. Identify the focus and overview of supporting points.
2. Highlight the topic sentence for each supporting point in the body paragraphs of the essay.

   - Does the writer repeat key words from the thesis statement?
   - Does the writer restate main ideas using different language?

3. Analyze the transitions between paragraphs in the body of the essay.

  * Does the writer use guiding language (at least some of the time) that links the ending of one paragraph to the beginning of the next?
  * Do you notice any transitions between paragraphs that seem especially smooth or abrupt? Can you identify any guiding language?

ACTIVITY **2**   *Identify Supporting Points*

With a partner, exchange copies of the research paper drafts you wrote in Chapter 4.

1. Read your partner's paper. Highlight the thesis statement and the topic sentences in body paragraphs.
2. On a separate sheet of paper, write an outline of your partner's paper.

  * Use your own words to describe the thesis and supporting points. Don't simply copy your partner's sentences. As you work on the outline, notice whether it is easy or difficult to find where new supporting points begin.

3. Discuss the outlines together.

  * Were you able to easily describe the focus and overview of supporting points in the thesis statement?
  * Were the topic sentences easy to identify?
  * Did the writer repeat key words from the thesis?
  * Were the ideas in each topic sentence clear enough that you were able to paraphrase them?

BUILDING YOUR PAPER

Revise Your Use of Guiding Language for Cohesion

Take some time now to analyze and revise your research paper draft for the use of guiding language between supporting points, and individual paragraphs, and within paragraphs.

  * Rewrite supporting point topic sentences if they don't use guiding language that clearly links the topic sentence to the thesis statement.
  * Analyze your transitions between paragraphs. Revise endings and/or beginnings of paragraphs if the transition is abrupt or unclear.
  * Consider how your ideas are organized within paragraphs. Add appropriate signal words, phrases, or sentences to make your ideas flow more clearly.

Documenting Evidence

You must properly document all the evidence from sources that you use in your research paper. Whether you use direct quotes or paraphrases, it is essential to identify the original source so that your reader knows where the information came from. The process of acknowledging your sources is called **documentation.** When you document a source, you tell the reader exactly where you found the information.

> **NOTE:** For more comprehensive coverage of APA conventions, see these Houghton Mifflin books: *Universal Keys for Writers* by Ann Raimes or *Pocket Guide to APA Style* by Robert Perrin.

Three Reasons to Document Sources

1. To let the reader know that you have carefully researched your ideas.
2. To tell the reader where to find the original source if she wants to learn more about your topic.
3. To avoid plagiarism, a serious offense in American academic writing.

Each field of study uses a particular system of documentation. The system presented in *Sourcework* is APA, which stands for American Psychological Association. APA documentation is commonly used in business, engineering, and the social sciences. Other documentation formats include MLA (Modern Language Association) used in the humanities, CBE (Council of Biology Editors) used in the life sciences, and Chicago (follows the *Chicago Manual of Style)* for humanities and social sciences.

> For links to documentation systems not presented in *Sourcework* go to the website at **http://esl.college.hmco.com/students**.

As with most documentation systems, APA documentation occurs in two places in your research paper:

- Within the text of your paper (in-text citations)
- At the end of your paper in a reference list

Here are examples of how the documentation for the same source looks in these two places.

Example of documentation within a paper (in-text citation):

In "Birth Order and Adult Personality," Elaine Harper (2001) writes that later born children are more likely to pursue nontraditional careers.

Example of documentation at the end of a paper (reference list entry):

Harper, E. (2001). *Birth order and adult personality.* New York: Collins Inc.

The citations in your paper and on the reference page at the end of your paper work together as a formal documentation system. As you document your sources, keep in mind that your goal is to help the reader identify the source of your information. To this end, be consistent in the format you use.

In-Text Citations

When you include a paraphrase or quotation in your writing, you will need to acknowledge the source. In other words, you will need to *cite your source.* In the APA system, a citation includes the following four pieces of information.

- The name of the author
- The name of the source
- The year of the source
- The page number (required only for quotations)

Citations occur in one of two places: within the sentence or at the end of the sentence. Usually, the first time you use evidence from a source, you will cite it within the sentence rather than at the end.

Citing Your Source Within the Sentence

Information to include	Name of the author	Date	Title
First time	First and last name	• Include the year only • Place in parentheses • No extra punctuation	• Full title • Use quotation marks • Capitalize all words four letters or longer
All other times	Last name only	Year only	Do not include the title

Examples:

First time a source is cited:

> In "Taking the Bungee Plunge," Ginia Bellafonte (1992) argues
>
> **source title**   **1st name last name**   **year**
>
> that extreme sports provide only a short-term superficial sense of
>
> **paraphrase**
>
> satisfaction.

Subsequent citation of the source:

> Bellafonte (1992) argues that genetic factors have played a role in
>
> **last name**   **year**   **paraphrase**
>
> people's need to take risks.

Citing Your Source at the End of a Sentence

In general, this method is used *after* you have already mentioned the source once in your paper. End of sentence citations can be used when you want to emphasize the information rather than the source of the information; when you refer to the source many times throughout the paper; or when including the source information within the sentence causes the sentence structure to be awkward. This can occur, for example, when a source has more than one author.

	Name of the author	**Date**	**Title**
Author and date are placed together in parentheses.	• Last name only • Place in parentheses. • Put a comma directly after the name.	• Year only • Place in parentheses after the comma after author's name. • Put a period after the parenthesis mark.	Not included

Example:

> Extreme sports provide only a short-term superficial sense of satisfaction (Bellafonte, 1992).

Now You Try

Practice writing in-text citations using the information below.

Author: Ann Fishburn

Date: May 3, 2000

Article Title: "Analyzing Art Programs"

Paraphrase: Freedom to explore, a caring community, and exciting art projects are three important characteristics of an art program.

Citation within the sentence: _____

_____ freedom to explore, a caring community and

exciting art projects are three important characteristics of an art program.

Citation at the end of the sentence:

Freedom to explore, a caring community, and exciting art projects are three

important characteristics of an art program _____

Special Citation Situations

Here are several common situations that occur when you write from sources that require special citation formats.

Idea Taken From More Than One Source

Sometimes you will want to include an idea that is mentioned by more than one of your sources. In this case, you'll need to include all the sources in your citation.

- Use the end-of-sentence format.
- List the authors alphabetically.
- Separate sources with a semicolon.

Example:

We cannot rely on technology to solve our problems (Feisk, 1995; Punon, 1995).

Now You Try

Write an in-text citation for this paraphrase of an idea taken from two different sources.

Author: Daniel Birge   *Date:* 2001

Author: Kate Spoon   *Date:* 2000

Paraphrase: Critical thinking must be a central part of university studies.

In-text citation: _____

Unknown Author

If the author's name is not given, you will need to use the title of the source instead.

- Use quotation marks around the source title.
- Include the date.
- Use the full title in the first citation. In later citations, use only the first two to four words of the title.

Example 1 (citation within the sentence):

"Choosing Your Friends Wisely: How to Develop Lasting Friendships" (2004) describes three common mistakes that occur in new relationships.

Example 2 (end of sentence citation):

There are three common mistakes that occur in new relationships ("Choosing Your Friends Wisely: How to Develop Lasting Friendships," 2004).

Example 3 (subsequent citation):

"Choosing Your Friends" (2004) presents results from a survey on long term friendships suggesting that learning how to argue respectfully is a key to making friendships last.

Now You Try

Write an in-text citation for this paraphrase of an idea taken from a source without an author listed.

Source Title: "Study Skills for University Success"

Source Date: June 2002

Paraphrase: Success in college depends on effective study habits.

In-text citation: _____

Source With More Than One Author

If a source is written by two authors or by three or more authors, you will need to use slightly different citation formats.

Example 1 (source with two authors):

- List the authors in the order they appear in the source
- Use an ampersand (&) when using the end of sentence format

Cited within the sentence:

Blackburn and Little (2005) note that exposure to secondhand smoke can increase the risk of lung cancer by over 30%.

Cited at the end of the sentence:

Exposure to secondhand smoke can increase the risk of lung cancer by over 30% (Blackburn & Little, 2005).

Example 2 (source with three or more authors):

- When citing the source the first time, list the name of all the authors in the order they appear in the source.
- In subsequent citings, use the end of sentence format. List the first author only followed by the phrase "et al."

Cited within the sentence:

Kapline, South and Findel (2003) write that dark chocolate contains four times more antioxidants than green tea.

Cited at the end of the sentence:

Dark chocolate contains four times more antioxidants than green tea (Kapline et al., 2003).

Now You Try

A. Write an in-text citation for this source written by two authors.

  Authors: Jenny Pope and Marge Green

  Date: 2003

Paraphrase: Most students change their major at least once during their undergraduate studies.

B. Write an end of sentence citation for this source written by three authors.

  Authors: Gene Jones, Richard Letham and Wendall Brout

  Date: 2004

Paraphrase: The primary difference between a digital camera and a traditional film camera is how they capture the image.

Indirect Source

Often sources include paraphrases and quotes from experts on the topic. You may want to use this information that is included in the source but comes from someone other than the author.

- Include background information about the person whose idea you are using.
- Use an end of sentence format.
- Write "cited in" and then the last name of the author(s) of your source.
- No extra punctuation is needed.

Example:

According to Joan Sinker, a San Francisco psychologist, increasing wealth does not result in greater happiness (cited in Hamblen, 2001).

- In this case, Hamblen wrote the article and, in her article, she included a quote from the psychologist Joan Sinker. The student writer wanted to use Sinker's idea so this is how she documented her information.

Now You Try

Write an in-text citation for this paraphrase of a quote by Patricia Manning in an article by Matt Simms.

Source Author:	Matt Simms
Source Date:	January 21, 2003
Evidence Author:	Patricia Manning
Paraphrase:	The health effects of secondhand smoke are still being studied.

In-text citation: _____

Quotations

Occasionally, you will use a direct quotation from your source.

- Within parentheses following author's last name, first write the date followed by a comma. Then write the page number, using a small *p* followed by a period. Include the page number inside the parentheses.

  NOTE: When you are working with articles from Part Two, use the *Sourcework* page numbers.

- Place quotation marks around any part of the original sentence that you include.

Example:

Souza (1997, p. 31) writes that "these spiraling human demands for resources are beginning to outgrow the earth's natural resources."

Now You Try

Write an in-text citation for this direct quotation.

Source Author:	Jane Donner
Source Date:	March 15, 2000
Quotation:	"Volunteering in our community helps both the community and ourselves." Page 112

In-text citation: _____

Writing the Reference Page

As discussed on pages 116–117, documenting your sources includes both citing sources within your paper and on a reference page. The list of your references (your sources) is the second of the two-part documentation process. Include the references at the end of your essay on a separate piece of paper. The format of information in the reference list corresponds to the citations within your paper. For example, the author's last name occurs in both the citations within your paper and in the reference list:

Example:

In-text citation:

> Harper (2001) writes that later-born children are more likely to pursue nontraditional careers.

Reference list entry:

> Harper, E. (2001). *Birth order and adult personality.* New York: Collins Inc.

Example Reference List

book

References

Copstead, L. & Banasik, J. (2000). *Pathophysiology.* Pennsylvannia:
      authors   **date**   **book title**   **state/city of publication**

W.B. Saunders Company.
     publishing company

on-line article from database

Hudd, S. (2000, March 15). Stress at college: Effects on health habits,
    author   **date**   **article title**

health status, and self-esteem. *College Student, 34,* 217. Retrieved
                  periodical title

March 8, 2001 from EBSCO.
   retrieval date   **database**

periodical

Kowalski, L. (2000, September 15). Coping with stress. *Current Health,*
    author   **date**   **article title**   **periodical title**

27, 16–17.

on-line article available in print

Sellman, S. (2000, June). The physiology of hormones [electronic
    author   **date**   **article title**

version]. *Healthy and Natural, 16,* 53–58.
       periodical title

on-line article not available in print

Sklare, J. (2001). Stress-eating: A hard habit to break but one you can
    author   **date**   **article title**

overcome. Retrieved March 3, 2001 from http://www.ediets.com
        retrieval date   **website**

article with unknown author

The influence of stress-eating on behavior. (2000, December).
        article title   **date**

Newsweek, 194, 81–82.
periodical title

Guidelines for APA Reference Lists

1. Double-space all entries.
2. Have the first line of each entry at the left margin; indent subsequent lines five spaces.
3. Use the author's full last name and only the initial of his or her first name.
4. If there is more than one author, separate the names by a comma and put an ampersand (&) before the last author's name.
5. If the author's name is unknown, write the title of the article first.
6. Organize the entries alphabetically by the author's name, if known, or the title of the article.
7. At the end of each item in an entry, type a period, unless the entry ends with a URL address.

Now You Try

Identify the five general formatting mistakes in the reference list below. Use the **Guidelines for APA Reference Lists** to help you.

References

Nancy Merrit. (1997). *Teen suicide: Light in the shadows.* Sacramento: Full House Press.

Brook, S. (1998, February). Some things you should know about preventing teen suicide. *Psychology Today,* 51, 20–25.

Author Unknown. (1997). Youth suicide. Retrieved March 6, 1999 from http://www.juring.my/befrienders/youth

Mulrine, A (1999, December) Preventing teen suicide: It starts with straight talk *U.S. News and World Report 68,* 55–57.

Problem 1 _____

Problem 2 _____

Problem 3 _____

Problem 4 _____

Problem 5 _____

Reference List Formats for Specific Types of Sources

Each type of source has specific rules for how it should appear on a reference page. Here are guidelines for five common types of sources that students use.

> Links to additional types of sources can be found on the *Sourcework* website at **http://esl.college.hmco.com/students**.

Periodical and Newspaper Articles

This includes both scholarly journals and general interest magazines. Information you will need:

- Author
- Date of the periodical
- Title of article
- Title of periodical
- Volume number of magazine (also include issue number if available)
- Page numbers of the evidence you use

Example (reference entry for periodical):

Corpet, F. (2002, September 3). Global warming revisited. *Science*

    author   **date**   **article title**   **periodical title**

Today, 52, 24.

    volume   **page**
      #   **number**

Specific Guidelines for Periodical and Newspaper Articles

- Capitalize only the first word of the article title, the first word of the subtitle, and any proper nouns.
- Do not underline the title or enclose it in quotation marks.
- Capitalize all important words of the periodical or newspaper title.
- Italicize the periodical title and volume number.
- Include the page numbers after the volume number.

Now You Try

Write a reference list entry for this periodical:

Author:	Martha Summer
Title of Article:	Five Steps to Success in College
Title of Magazine:	American Survey
Date and Volume:	September 21, 2000 Volume number 36
Page Numbers:	14–15

Reference list entry: _____

On-Line Articles Available in Print

Articles accessed electronically, but also available in print follow the same format as print articles with one exception. After the title of the article, type [electronic version].

Example reference entry for on-line article available in print:

Motavalli, J. (2000, November/December). Coming to America
 author   **date**   **article title**

[electronic version]. *Newsweek, 31,* 47–53.
 periodical volume page
 title   #   #s

Now You Try

Write a reference list entry for this on-line article available in print:

Author:	Georgia Brown
Article Title:	Down With the Death Penalty
Magazine Title:	The Economist
Date and Volume:	May 15, 1999 Volume 351
Page Number:	20

Reference list entry: _____

Article Retrieved From an Electronic Database

Libraries often provide several databases that can be used to search for sources of information. EBSCO, InfoTrac, PsychINFO, and WilsonWeb are examples of a few. Sources found via a database require the following information:

- Retrieval date
- The name of the database

Example of article retrieved from a database:

Marcus, D. & Hartigan, R. (2000, November 27). They're coming to

        authors   **date**   **article title**

American schools. *U.S. News & World Report, 129,* 68. Retrieved on

                  periodical title   **vol. #, page #**

August 22, 2002 from EBSCO.

      retrieval date   **database name**

Now You Try

Write a reference list entry for this article retrieved from an electronic database:

Author:	Bernard Gert
Title of Article:	Genetic Engineering: Is it Morally Acceptable?
Title of Source:	USA Today Magazine
Date of Source:	March 31, 1999
Retrieval Date:	January 1, 2001
Database:	Britannica.com

Reference list entry: _____

Information Retrieved From a Website

For information retrieved from a website with no available print source, it is important to include the following information:

- The date the information was retrieved.
- The web address used to retrieve the information.
- If no date is given for the website, write "n.d."

Example of article retrieved from a website:

Collins, K. (n.d.). A mission to educate. Retrieved on April 22, 1998

      author   **date**   **title of source**   **retrieval date**

from http://www.americanlandinstitute.org

               web address

Now You Try

Write a reference list entry for this information retrieved from a website:

Website Title:	Career Browser: What do you want to be?
Date:	None given
Retrieval Date:	June 15, 2001
Web Address:	http://www.collegeboard.com

Reference list entry: _____

Books

In addition to the author, date, and title, reference list entries for books also require the city of publication and the name of the publishing company.

Example of a reference for a book:

Caplan, A. (1998). *Due consideration: Controversy in the age of medical*
author   **date**   **book title**

miracles. New York: John Wiley & Sons.
         city of publication/publishing company

Specific guidelines for books

- Italicize the title of the book
- Capitalize the first word of the title, the first word in a subtitle, and proper nouns only.
- List the first city of publication only.

Now You Try

Write a reference list entry for this book.

Author:	Richard Rodriguez
Date:	1982
Title:	Hunger of memory: The education of Richard Rodriguez
City of Publication:	New York
Publishing Company:	Bantam Books

Reference list entry: _____

Reference Page Conventions and Punctuation

What Gets Capitalized?

- The first word in book titles and article titles
- The first word in a subtitle that comes after a colon
- All important words and words four letters or longer in the title of a magazine

What Gets Italicized?

- Titles of books
- Titles of periodicals
- Volume numbers for periodicals

NOTE: Do not italicize titles of articles and chapters of books.

Where Do Periods Go?

- After each piece of information:
  —author
  —date
  —name of article
  —page number in information about a periodical
  —initial of an author's first name

NOTE: Do not place a period at the end of retrieval information for an electronic source (e.g., a web address).

Where Do Commas Go?

- In between the last name and the initial of the author's first name
- After each author's name when listing two or more authors
- After the title of a periodical
- After a volume number
- After the year in a date that includes a month
- Before a web address

Activities to Practice Documenting Sources

To practice documentation, do one or more of the following activities.

ACTIVITY 1

Correcting Documentation Mistakes

Practice with in-text citations. With a partner, find the six mistakes in the following citations. One of the citations is correct and one has two errors.

1. Brown suggests that we have the ability to develop a sustainable society (1996).
2. Human population will grow in relation to technology's ability to support it (1995, Weiskel).
3. Urban centers are often associated with ecological destruction. (Weiskel, 1995)
4. Cohen (1995) believes that organized religion is not always the cause of increased population growth.
5. "There is no single numerical answer to the question of how many people the earth can support (Cohen, 1995)
6. People tend to see heroes as role models (Lark, 1992 and Sudo, 1997).

ACTIVITY 2

Charting Information to Document

1. Fill in the charts with information from the sources you are working with for your research paper.
2. Use the information in the chart to help you create a reference page. Remember that different sources require different kinds of information; therefore, you will not need to fill in every cell for every source.

For more blank charts, go to the *Sourcework* website at
http://esl.college.hmco.com/students.

Author	
Date	
Title of article	
Title of book or magazine	
Volume & page number	
City of publication	
Name of publication company	
Retrieval date and web address	

ACTIVITY **3**

Peer-Editing for Documentation

1. For homework, insert an in-text citation for each piece of outside evidence in one or more paragraphs of your research paper draft.
2. Bring a copy of your draft to class.
3. Trade papers with a partner.
4. Read your partner's paper, checking the format for each citation.

   • Circle any citations that are not correctly formatted.
   • Circle any pieces of outside evidence that have not been cited.

5. Discuss your suggestions with your partner.

BUILDING YOUR PAPER

Document Your Evidence

Check your research paper draft for each piece of paraphrased and quoted evidence from sources in Part 2 of *Sourcework*.

- Complete an in-text citation for each piece of evidence within your paper.
- Create a reference page that lists all the sources you used in your paper.

Getting Feedback on Your Whole Draft

As a writer, you have a sense of some of the strengths and weaknesses of your paper, so you can decide which parts of your rough draft you would like to get a reader's opinion about.

Using a Checklist

The following is a checklist of many of the issues you must consider as you write your research paper.

If you would like to use a rubric, or system, to evaluate each part of your paper, see the *Sourcework* website at **http://esl.college.hmco.com/students**.

Checklist for an Academic Paper

1. Thesis statement and topic sentences

- Does the thesis statement include the topic, focus, and supporting points?
- Is the thesis written in language that is formal, yet easy to understand?
- Is the topic sentence in each paragraph logically connected to the thesis statement?
- Is each topic sentence written in the writer's own words?

See Chapter 3, pages 49–57, for a review of thesis statements. See Chapter 4, pages 74–75, for a review of topic sentences.

2. Well-constructed paragraphs

- Does each paragraph include a topic sentence in the writer's words, at least one piece of evidence, and some form of conclusion?

See Chapter 4, page 73, or a review of well-constructed paragraphs.

3. Paraphrases of evidence

- Are the paraphrased ideas in the writer's own words and easy to understand?
- Did the writer provide enough background information to explain the idea presented in the paraphrase?

See Chapter 1, pages 6–7, and Chapter 4, pages 77–85, for a review of paraphrasing.

4. Using evidence

- Is each piece of evidence appropriate for the point the writer is making?

See Chapter 3, pages 61–64, for a review of using evidence.

5. Integration of evidence

- Is each piece of evidence introduced with the name of the author or name of the source?
- Is the evidence carefully explained and connected to the point that is being made?
- Has the writer avoided dumping the evidence?

See Chapter 4, pages 88–91, for a review of integrating evidence.

6. Introduction and conclusion

- Does the introduction clearly introduce the topic of the research paper?
- Does the introduction include an interesting hook?
- Does the conclusion provide a comment about the focus of the paper as well as an interesting closing idea?

See pages 99–102 in this chapter about introductions and conclusions.

7. Documentation

- Has the writer correctly documented each piece of evidence?

See pages 116–129 on documentation in this chapter.

8. Cohesion within paragraphs

- Has the writer used guiding language to provide clear transitions from one idea to the next within paragraphs?

See pages 108–114 on cohesion in this chapter.

9. Sentence level editing

- Does each sentence have a subject and verb that agree in number?
- Are verb tenses consistent?
- Are there other grammatical problems?

For more information on editing your paper, see links on the *Sourcework* website at **http://esl.college.hmco.com/students**.

Sequence for Giving and Getting Feedback

To complete a focused discussion of your paper with your classmates, follow these steps:

1. For homework, before your discussion, choose two issues from the **Checklist for an Academic Paper** about which you most want feedback.
2. Bring enough copies of your paper so that each person in your small group can have a copy.
3. In your group, decide how much time you will spend on each person's paper.
4. Ask the first person which two parts of his paper he wants feedback about. Then read only those parts and discuss them. Jot brief suggestions for changes on your copy of your classmate's paper. (When it is your turn to hear feedback on your paper, listen carefully and make changes on your own copy.)
5. When the time is up for the first person's paper, move to the second.
6. After all the papers have been discussed, return all the copies to each writer.

As you talk with your classmates, keep in mind that you can help each other most by speaking honestly and respectfully about each other's work. The purpose of getting feedback from a reader is to improve the written paper, not to comment on the writer as a person. As a reader, don't be afraid to tell a classmate that her paper is weak in one area, but phrase your comments tactfully. As a writer, try not to be overly modest; recognize the good parts as well as the weaker parts of your own paper.

BUILDING YOUR PAPER

Write the Final Paper

Using the revised introduction and conclusion, the guiding language, and the documented evidence you have worked on in this chapter, write the final version of your paper. Be sure to consider the feedback your classmates have given you.

6

Building a Paper:

Independent Research

After you've written a guided research paper, you may have the chance to undertake a research and writing project on your own. In that case, you have some interesting work ahead of you.

The first step is to determine a topic that appeals to you and will fit the time and resources you have. Research and writing are more fun if the subject interests you enough to spend time on it. A good topic has enough information so that you can write a paper about it, but not so much that you can't cover it all in the time you have.

Once you settle on a topic, you will search for sources related to your idea. As you sift through the information, you must decide what to use. Set aside whatever is too opinionated, complicated, unreliable, unrelated, or unsuitable in some other way.

Finally, with a clear focus for your paper and with the sources you want, you are ready to write your research paper, following the same writing process you practiced in Chapters 1 through 5. You may review those chapters to remind yourself of the steps in writing an effective paper.

In this chapter you will practice:

- Choosing a topic and writing a research proposal
- Finding and evaluating sources
- Writing a working references list
- Managing complex assignments

By the end of this chapter, you will have chosen a suitable topic and written a research proposal. You'll have learned how to locate and evaluate sources and written a list of references. You'll be ready to begin writing your independent research paper.

Choosing a Topic

For some writing assignments, your teacher will select the topic. In other cases, you will choose your topic, do the research to find appropriate sources, and write a paper incorporating the evidence you gather from your reading. Although the writing process is much the same as that for more structured assignments, you must first take the preliminary steps of clarifying your topic and finding your own sources.

You may be given a general topic, as in this assignment:

Research Paper Topic: Select a topic in psychology that you find interesting and use the research paper to learn as much as possible about the subject.

In this case, it's up to you to decide what to write about, how to focus your ideas, and what questions to address. As you think about your topic, look for a subject that:

1. interests you.

 * It's not easy to write a good research paper if the topic bores you.

2. is covered in a number of sources.

 * You will need a variety of sources to give your paper depth.

3. can be written in the time you have available.

 * Realistically assess how long it will take you to find your information, organize your paper, and write it.

4. is appropriate for your level of knowledge.

 * Choosing a subject that is too technical or that requires specialized knowledge you don't have will take a lot of extra time.

Developing Ideas for Topics

Here are some places where you may find good ideas for topics:

Classes

 * Look over your class syllabus and readings. Do you see any topics you would like to explore in more depth?
 * Think about issues you have studied in previous classes. What more could you learn about these?

On-line Databases

 * When you decide on a possible topic, you can use a computerized index like EBSCO, InfoTrac or ProQuest at the library. Enter your topic as a search term and get more ideas by reading the abstracts of articles that interest you.

The Web

- Use a search engine such as Google, Alta Vista, or Yahoo to see what other people are saying about your topic.

Newspapers and Magazines

- Go to the library and skim national newspapers and magazines (e.g., *Time, Newsweek, The Smithsonian, Discover, The Economist*) to learn about interesting subjects or current topics in the news.

Your Experience

- Is there an issue that has affected your family, your community, or your country that you'd like to learn more about?
- Do you have a special interest that you'd like to research?

Narrowing a Topic

When you find a subject you want to explore further, think about the time you have available. The subject of a research paper should be specific; it should be limited to the amount of information you can reasonably expect to include in the time you have.

Here are some topics that other students have considered. In each case, the writer began with a general topic, then moved to a more focused idea, and finally narrowed the idea to a suitable topic for a research paper.

General Topic	Focused Topic	Narrowed Topic
1. Dogs	Dogs and humans	Use of dogs in psychotherapy
2. Architecture	Japanese architecture	Influence of Buddhism on Japanese Architecture
3. Sports	Snowboarding	Reasons for popularity of snowboarding
4. Family	Korean families	Cultural conflicts in raising Korean children in the United States
5. Genetic engineering	Help for infertility	Selling human eggs on the Internet
6. China and WTO	Effects of WTO on Chinese economy	Effect of WTO on unemployment in China

Some Common Problems With Topics

Some topics don't work well for research papers because:

1. There isn't enough information available.

- An example of this might be topic 3 on the previous page. While you may like snowboarding and have ideas about its popularity, you may not be able to find much written evidence about why people enjoy it.

2. Information is available, but the sources contain too much jargon or are too technical for your level of knowledge.

- Some aspects of "genetic engineering," topic 5 on the previous page, require a great deal of background knowledge of chemistry and biology. However, the writer in this case was able to find an area of genetic engineering, "selling human eggs on the Internet," that was interesting to her but did not involve a detailed knowledge of science.

3. The topic is too broad; that is, the topic requires more pages to explain than is expected.

- All the focused topics listed would probably fall into this category; whereas, the narrowed topics are all subjects of suitable scope for research papers.

Activities to Practice Developing Topics

To practice developing topics, do one or more of the following activities.

ACTIVITY 1 *Brainstorming Topics*

1. For five minutes, brainstorm a list of things you know something about or might even be an authority on. List everything.
2. Now, for five more minutes, brainstorm a list of things you'd like to learn more about. Be as specific as possible. Don't worry if something appears on both lists.
3. Now look at both lists. Circle one item from either list that you want to research more closely. For five minutes, brainstorm a list of questions about this topic that you would like to learn the answers to.
4. Share your topic and questions with a partner or group of classmates. They may have more questions to suggest.

ACTIVITY 2 *Answering Questions*

1. On one side of the room, your teacher will post these three questions about global issues:

- What events in the twentieth century had the greatest impact on the way we live?
- What are the five most pressing global issues of today?
- What changes have you noticed in your own country in the last five years?

On the other side of the room, your teacher will post these three questions about a personal view of history:

- What historical figure do you admire and why?
- What scientific discovery would you like to know more about?
- What historical event in your own country or elsewhere would you like to know more about?

2. Sitting in a circle, each person in the room, including the teacher, briefly answers one question from each side of the room.

3. After each person speaks, discuss whether the response would make a good topic for a paper, considering questions such as:

- Would you be interested enough in the topic to spend many hours, from a few to several weeks, investigating and writing about it?
- Would you be able to find enough information about it?
- Is the topic something you and your readers can understand or is it too technical to explain easily?
- Is the topic broad enough so that it can be explored in some depth?

ACTIVITY 3   *Writing Questions on the Walls*

1. Write a topic you're considering for a research paper at the top of a large sheet of newsprint and post the sheet on the classroom wall. Each class member will do the same, covering the walls with sheets, each with a topic at the top and plenty of blank space below.

2. Walk around the room, jotting questions you have about each topic on the sheets. Everyone else, including the teacher, will be doing the same.

3. After everyone has had a chance to write questions on each posted topic, sit together and spend a couple of minutes clarifying the questions.

4. At the end of class, take your sheet home and use the questions from others to help you focus on your topic.

***Example of a posted topic with some questions
generated by classmates and teacher:***

Topic:　Food

Questions:　How do food taboos develop in different cultures?
　　　　　What role does food play in social rituals?
　　　　　Why do people become vegetarians?
　　　　　What are the causes of eating disorders?
　　　　　Who discovered chocolate?

Writing a Research Proposal

When you're writing on a topic of your own choice, creating a research proposal is one of the best ways to clarify what you will write about. A good research proposal:

1. Is about 75 to 100 words long
2. Is written in informal language
3. Includes the topic you will research
4. Gives an explanation of why the topic interests you
5. Mentions several questions you hope to answer about the topic

The research proposal may help you think about how you will approach your topic; it's a place to define your focus as well as to express doubts or mention problems you anticipate.

Sample Research Proposals

Here are some research proposals others have written.

Proposal 1:

At first I thought of writing about bilingual education, but that topic is too broad, so I will narrow it to one example in California, of how bilingual education is actually not working very well. I will write about Proposition 227, a law passed in California but which many people now don't want. To begin with, I will have to define some terms. I will explain both bilingual education and Proposition 227. Then I will explain why some people do not like Proposition 227.

Proposal 2:

My original idea was to write about a comparison of Swiss and U.S. schools, but since it is impossible to get references on Swiss schools in such a short time, I will concentrate on U.S. schools, with a few references to Swiss schools. In particular, I will discuss whether rules for classroom behavior encourage a humanistic school climate and/or self-discipline.

Proposal 3:

This paper will be about how joining the World Trade Organization (WTO) will affect unemployment in China. Most people think that joining WTO will totally benefit China, but there probably will be some negative results. One problem about writing on this topic is that it is something that has not yet happened. Therefore, I will look for information about China's present unemployment and the effects the WTO has had on employment in other countries similar to China. Then I will put the information together to make a prediction about what will happen in China.

- In proposal 1, the writer reminds herself that she must narrow her topic and define terms.
- The writer of proposal 2 notes that some information will be too hard to access quickly.
- In proposal 3, the writer acknowledges that his topic will be a challenge, so he comments on how he will solve the problem of writing about a future event.

BUILDING YOUR INDEPENDENT PAPER

Choose a Topic and Write a Research Proposal

Choose a topic and write a research proposal about it that includes an explanation of your interest in the topic, and possible questions you might answer in your paper.

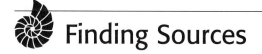

Finding Sources

Now that you've chosen your topic, you have a clearer idea of what you are writing about. You're ready to look for suitable sources.

Searching for Information

Searching for your sources can lead you in many new and interesting directions. Because you have a deadline for completing your assignment, you will have to balance the fun of exploring new ideas with the need to find a useful collection of sources for your assignment.

As you search, you may even change or revise your topic. You may find sources that interest you more than your original topic and decide to pursue a new subject. Or, a topic may sound great at the beginning, but a lack of suitable sources may force you in a different direction. For example, the writer of Research Proposal 3 (the WTO and unemployment in China) found, when he began his search for sources, that before China joined the WTO, there was no solid information about how joining would affect unemployment in China. He decided to change his topic to the effect the WTO had on unemployment in other countries that had already joined.

You will probably want to include information from several different kinds of sources to give your paper more depth. Here are some common places to find information for a research paper.

The Internet

The Internet is one place where information is easy to access and read. But be careful—many sites contain unreliable information and hidden biases. When you use a search engine to scan for key words that match your search term, you will probably find numerous sites, but many will not fit your needs. Some tips for conducting an efficient search online are:

1. Get to know the various search engines. Although different search engines may uncover some of the same sites, you will find that each also offers some unique sources. Google and Alta Vista are two of the most popular search engines, but there are many others.
2. The "hit list" of many search engines is organized according to the sites most frequently requested rather than the date published. This means you may find a good source buried deep within your list of potential sources.
3. When you type in your search term:

   * List the most important key word first (e.g., *stress and health effects*)
   * Use lowercase letters (e.g., *falconry* rather than *Falconry*)
   * Enter phrases in quotation marks (e.g., "assisted suicide")
   * Use AND when looking for combined subjects (e.g., marijuana AND "medical use")
   * Use AND NOT when excluding a subject (e.g., marijuana AND NOT legislation)

Electronic Databases

Another good place to look for sources is in electronic databases, usually available through libraries. These provide full or partial texts of articles in periodicals, newspapers, encyclopedias, and other reference works. Articles found in databases are usually a short, manageable length.

EBSCO Host, InfoTrac and ProQuest are three examples of electronic databases that are commonly available in libraries. They focus on articles in periodicals and newspapers and provide reliable sources for academic work.

Books

Books are a good source for general background information on a topic, as well as for reliable, in-depth information, but you may not have time to read a whole book. The introduction of a book often provides a useful overview of the subject. Using the table of contents and index can help you find specific information.

Newspapers

Newspapers are a good place to look for short articles, but be aware that the information may be focused too specifically on their place of publication.

Interviews

If you find the right person to talk to, an interview can provide information directly related to your research. Sometimes, it's difficult to find an appropriate person to interview, and it may take time to set up an interview. But if you can arrange it, an interview is an excellent primary source of information.

Evaluating Sources

As you assemble a list of sources, you may find that your problem is not finding enough information, but deciding which information to use. You can save time and effort by briefly evaluating the sources before you read each article in detail.

Guidelines for Evaluating Sources

1. Is the source about the topic?

Looking at the title and related notes can often give you a sense of the main idea of the article. Notice whether it is likely to be too general or too specific for your topic. Some articles may be very scientific and technical; others may concentrate on only one aspect of the topic while you plan to write about it in a more general way.

For example, if you plan to write about the effects of smoking on college students, but you find an article about the chemical composition of tobacco smoke, that article is probably too technical for your purposes.

2. Is it enough information or too much?

To judge this, look at the number of pages. A one-page article may give you a little bit of information and may be worth looking at if its title sounds good. On the other hand, it probably won't give you much substance, so you'll need other sources to supplement it. On the other hand, a 10-page article will keep you busy reading for a long time and may be more information than you really need.

3. What kind of information does it offer?

Some articles provide statistics and the results of scientific studies about the issue. Other anecdotal articles tell personal experiences related to the topic. Look for the kind of information that you plan to focus on in your paper.

4. Is it up-to-date?

Look at the publication date. If your topic is a current problem, you probably don't want to use articles that are more than 6–8 years old. But, if you're writing about historical trends that led to a current problem, you will want sources that go back a number of years.

5. How is the information biased?

Every article is written with an audience in mind, but some are written with the intent to present only one point of view or to persuade the reader to the writer's opinion. It is fine to use such an article as a source as long as you are aware of the opinion, or bias. Look at who the writer is and what organization she or he represents. Read carefully. Look for words with positive or negative connotations or statements that make unrealistic claims.

Some Special Considerations in Evaluating Websites

Websites are perhaps the easiest sources of information to access and yet may be among the most biased. Anyone can create a website about any topic. This means that a website with information about your topic may be written by an expert or simply be the ideas of someone who wants to share them. For most university assignments, you are expected to support your ideas with evidence from people or organizations that have carefully researched the topic and are generally accepted as reliable. Before you use a website as a source for an academic paper, consider these factors.

Guidelines for Evaluating Websites

1. Look at the web address to see where it comes from.

- Government sites (.gov) are often reliable sources of facts and statistics.
- Educational sites (.edu) are usually dependable places to find reliable information.
- Nonprofit organizations (.org) may be objective or may be promoting a social cause and, therefore, may be biased in favor of or against a certain point of view.
- Commercial providers (.com) charge for use of the site and thus have control over content. These are not considered objective sources.

2. Determine who wrote the page.

- Is it a personal website? If so, the opinions may be solely those of the writer and you need to find out more about the writer in order to evaluate the site.
- Is there a place on the website to find out more about the author? Are the author's credentials provided? If the author has done research or published in her field, then she has expertise in the subject and you can safely assume the information is reliable.
- If the site is written by an organization, is the purpose of the organization provided? If the organization is selling a service or product, the information it provides is not objective. Sometimes you can learn something about the author or organization by truncating the URL to locate the website, For example, (e.g., www.religioustolerance.org/euthanas.htm can be truncated to www.religioustolerance.org to find information about the Religious Tolerance organization)

3. Consider whether the information is up-to-date.

- If your topic is one that changes rapidly, you need a site that is updated frequently.
- Check the links on the site to see if they are current.

4. Notice whether the format is easy to access.

- Is the information easy to find and understand? If the source is confusing to navigate, you may be better off looking elsewhere.
- Is the site free? If you must pay for information, you know that the site is created to make a profit and may not be objective. Some information, such as that in newspaper archives also requires a fee but is entirely reliable.

Activities to Practice Finding Sources

To practice finding sources, do one or more of the following activities.

ACTIVITY 1   *Evaluating Sources From a Database*

For this activity, you need access to a computer lab.

1. Go to the website for any large library; it can be academic or public. Follow the links to the databases and choose EBSCO Host, which is a collection of many databases.
2. As a class, select a topic to search for (e.g., causes of stress or gun control) and enter the key phrase into the EBSCO Host database.
3. Working with a partner, print out the first few pages of the list of articles about the topic generated by EBSCO Host.
4. Using Guidelines for Evaluating Sources on page 143, decide which articles might be useful. Write *Y* on sources you think will be useful, *N* on sources you know won't be useful, and *M* on sources that might be useful.
5. Discuss your evaluations with the class.

ACTIVITY 2   *Evaluating Websites*

For this activity, you need access to a computer lab.

1. As a class, select any search engine. Use "birth order" as a search term.
2. With a partner, evaluate the reliability of the first five websites that your search engine generates. Use Guidelines for Evaluating Websites on page 144.
3. As a class, discuss which sources you believe are reliable and which are not. Give reasons for your opinions.

ACTIVITY 3   *Comparing Search Engines*

For this activity, you need access to a computer lab.

1. With a partner, explore several common search engines. Use the same search term for each engine, for example, "genetically modified food."
2. Take notes on these questions: What did you notice about the different hit lists? Did any of the search engines have useful qualities or ones that made them difficult to use?
3. After you compare the search engines, share your observations with the class.

ACTIVITY 4   *Conferencing With Your Teacher*

For this activity, you need access to a computer lab.

1. Schedule a time to meet with your teacher for 20 to 30 minutes. Bring your research proposal with you.
2. Discuss possible search terms and type one of these terms into EBSCO.
3. With your teacher, evaluate the usefulness of the sources. Remember to keep a list of new search terms as you skim titles and articles.
4. Print or mark any potentially useful sources.
5. If your search is not generating the information you want, consider how you might modify your topic based on the information you are getting.
6. You will not find all your sources during this conference, but you will begin to get an idea of whether your topic will be manageable.

Writing a Working Reference List

After you have evaluated a number of sources, you can write a rough list of the ones you think will be useful. This is your "working reference list." It will probably not include all your final sources and it may include some sources that look promising now but you'll end up not using. However, at this point, the working reference list will provide a good start on finding information for your paper.

BUILDING YOUR INDEPENDENT PAPER

Create a Working References List

Write a working references list of the sources you have found. Your list should include 10 to 15 sources and have the following information for each:

- Title, author, and date
- Where you found the source

Remember not to rely only on the Internet for your sources. Consider books, periodicals, and electronic databases as well. Take time to evaluate each source before including it in your working reference list.

Managing Complex Assignments

Some writing assignments may include so many details that you must first clarify what you are going to write about before you can even begin to explore your subject. For example, in the following writing assignment from an introductory sociology course, the teacher devotes the first half of the paragraph to a description of the issue before he introduces the assignment topic. Finally, he gives some advice about how to focus the paper.

Internet and Social Change Research Paper Assignment

Description of Issue ⟶ The Internet has fostered communication between people who never before could have communicated directly, and it has brought about an unprecedented democratization of publishing. Anyone who has access to the Internet can potentially communicate with millions of people worldwide and can publish virtually anything he or she desires. These new forms of communication and publication—particularly through list serves, web pages, and newsgroups—have brought together people of practically every conceivable interest or concern, creating an enormous range of "virtual communities." While the nature and significance of these virtual communities vary greatly and are the subject of considerable academic debate, it is clear that the Internet has made possible forms of cooperation, sharing, and collective action never before possible on this scale.

Topic of Assignment ⟶ What I want you to do in this research project is to explore how people are using the Internet to bring about social change, the new possibilities for collective action that the Internet is making available, and the social significance of these new forms of computer-mediated communication.

Suggestions for Focus ⟶ Start by choosing a social issue that you care about and/or would find interesting to study. However, your objective will not be to study the issue per se, but rather to study how people who care about this issue are attempting to use the Internet to change the world in some way.

When you read a complicated writing assignment like this, your first task is to determine the teacher's expectations for the focus and content of the paper. Below are several methods for identifying a general focus in complex writing assignments.

Techniques for Identifying the Focus of an Assignment

Technique 1: Identifying Key Phrases

By identifying some of the main ideas in the teacher's instruction, you can decide on a tentative focus and pinpoint some central questions for your paper. Identifying key phrases is one technique to use in reading a complicated writing assignment.

Key phrases that signal the teacher's expectations for the focus of your paper are often verbs that describe ways of discussing ideas: *compare, contrast, argue, define, persuade, explain* causes or effects. Look for these words or synonyms for them, such as *take a stand, give an opinion, defend your ideas, show how this has led to these results.* Look at Focus of Thesis Statements, Chapter 3, page 54 for examples of how various kinds of focus are commonly described.

Here is an example of a complex assignment from an undergraduate university course that we will study for key phrases and focus.

Relevance of a New Medical Technology

Topic: The social and ethical relevance of a new genetic or medical technology we have discussed this quarter, which includes the following list of possible topics:

- Biotechnology and food
- Ownership of the body and its genetic material
- Manipulating our genes, as in somatic cell manipulations or germline gene therapy
- Genes for sale
- Genetic discrimination
- DNA- based identification systems
- Groups working to stop the genetic altering of foods or animals
- Eugenics

Suggested Focus ——→ Write a 7–10 page research paper on one of the topics listed in which <u>you take a stand</u> (probably this will be your thesis) based on your research <u>as to what limitations or restrictions, if any, should be placed on scientists working in that field</u>. If such measures were put in place, what role should the scientific community play? The government? Private citizens? It is also possible that you will conclude that no restrictions are necessary. If so, why not?

Your paper should address most of the following questions:

More About Focus ——→ 1. Include a discussion of <u>why this technology was developed. What problem was it developed to solve? How is it currently being used</u>?
2. <u>How does this technology work</u>? Explain the principles involved.
3. <u>What are the moral and ethical issues involved in using this technology? What possible consequences will it have? What groups or individuals are against the use of this technology? What are their concerns</u>?
4. <u>How is this technology transforming fundamental aspects of our society</u>?

- The challenge in this assignment is choosing one of the eight topics and then figuring out how to answer so many questions in one paper, while still finding a focus to bring it all together.
- To decide which topic to select, you might ask yourself these questions:
  —Which topic interests me?
  —Which one do I already know the most about or want to learn more about?
- To find a focus, try rereading the assignment, specifically looking for words that signal a focus. Although the usual focus words, such as "compare" or "define," do not appear, the teacher does give some suggestions for the focus in the words that are underlined in the assignment:

  ". . . <u>take a stand</u> . . . based on your research as <u>to what limitations or restrictions, if any, should be placed on scientists working in that field</u>."

- The phrase "take a stand" indicates that this will be an argument paper. The underlined parts of the questions at the end of the assignment give further information about the focus, telling the student what questions need to be answered.

Now You Try

In the assignment that follows, identify the intended focus by underlining it once. Underline twice the questions to be addressed.

Social Responsibilities of Scientists

Choose one of these topics, which we have discussed this term:

- Cloning
- Genetically modified foods
- Genetically altered animals
- Reproductive technologies, for example, choosing the sex of a baby

Write a research paper explaining what responsibilities scientists have when they are working in their field. You should consider these issues: How can this science advance our society? What harm might this technology do? How should the government be involved in regulating research on this subject? What is the social responsibility of scientists with knowledge in this field?

Technique 2: Paraphrasing

Some assignments don't provide any clear statement of the expected focus. Here is a complex assignment that requires paraphrasing to understand the focus.

A Stereotyped Social Group

Select a social group who are underserved or negatively stereotyped by the dominant culture in America and research the problems they experience as a result of their social status. Also, select and research a group who are acting as allies and advocates of the underserved group to effect a positive social change on their behalf. Consider the advocate group's goals and effectiveness in improving the situation. In researching this paper, you should at least consider the following questions:

- Who is the underserved group?
- What is the negative stereotype held by the dominant culture group(s)? This may involve some historical framework.
- Who are the allies or advocates? What are their goals? How are they organized? What changes have they effected and by what strategies?
- What impact have those changes had and what are the future implications and possibilities for the underserved group?

This assignment does not include a central question, so the focus for the paper is up to the writer. However, by reading the questions, you can get some clues as to the teacher's expectations. Notice these phrases used:

- "some historical framework"
- "What changes have they effected . . . "
- "by what strategies?"
- "What impact have those changes had . . . "
- ". . . what are the future implications and possibilities for the underserved group?"

Based on these questions, you would probably choose a cause focus for the paper (see Chapter 2, p. 37).

A good way to understand longer instructions like this is to paraphrase them and then check with your teacher to see if your understanding is accurate. In your paraphrase, include your understanding of the focus. See more information about paraphrasing in Chapter 1, pages 6–11 and Chapter 4, pages 77–85.

A possible paraphrase of this assignment is:

> Choose a group that is viewed in a negative way in U.S. society and find out about the difficulties the members face. Also, choose at least one group who is supporting the disadvantaged group and find out what that group is doing to help them cope with prejudice. Some questions to address are who the disadvantaged group is, the background of their difficulties with the mainstream U.S. culture, who their friends are, and what may happen to them next. The focus of the paper will be the causes of the negative stereotyping.

Now You Try

Read the following assignment. Write a paraphrase of the instructions that includes the focus for the paper.

Changes in a Social Institution

This paper is focused on social change. You should consider how social change happens, what impact a change in one part of society may have on other parts, and what implications for future social structures such changes may present.

Select a social institution, such as the family, public schools, distance learning, the media, consumerism, working at home, or any other area of society that has shown a change. Research the nature and impact of the changes in this institution over the last 50 years. Include the causes for the changes, the effects these changes have had on other parts of society, and predicted related changes in the future.

Paraphrase: _____

_____

_____

Technique 3: Writing a Research Proposal

Another useful tool for organizing your thoughts when you're writing about a complex topic is a research proposal. See page 140 in this chapter for a description of a research proposal.

A research proposal helps because when you write out or state the focus of your paper and the main questions you'll answer, you are already forming a rough outline (see Chapter 2, page 44).

For example, a research proposal for the assignment "Relevance of a New Medical Technology" on page 148 might be:

> I am going to write about biotechnology and food. I think that genetically modified food is important for feeding people suffering from famine but that it should be labeled and that certain kinds should not even be allowed. I am going to write about why GM foods were developed and where they are being used now. I will explain the basics of how GM foods are produced. Then I'll discuss why GM food has some problems, what groups are against it, and why. I'm not sure how GM foods are transforming society so I'll have to wait until I've done some research to answer that question.

- This proposal states which topic the writer has chosen from the list provided—genetically modified food. It gives the writer's opinion about restrictions on her topic and mentions that she will answer most of the teacher's questions. Finally, it says she has some doubts about how to answer part of the assignment. By jotting down these ideas, the writer has begun the process of understanding the assignment and exploring what she will write about.

Now You Try

Choose a suggested topic and write a research proposal for this assignment:

An Issue in Epidemiology

This paper should focus on a topic relevant to a developing country. It must be an issue that significantly impacts the health and well-being of the population. The following are suggested topics:

- Diseases: cholera, plague, hepatitis
- Disasters: earthquake, chemical accident, famine
- Social Change: land ownership, urbanization, child labor

Your paper should cover the following points:

1. A description of the population in the country you are writing about
2. The distribution of the problem, how widespread it is, how long it has been a problem, and the geographic and social factors involved
3. The solutions that have been attempted and their success or failure in solving the problem
4. Your recommendation for solving the problem, including difficulties to be overcome and why your suggestion is likely to be successful.

Write your research proposal here:

_____

_____

_____

_____

_____

_____

_____

Activities to Practice Managing Complex Assignments

To practice complex assignments, do one or both of the following activities.

Activity 1 *Analyze a Complex Assignment*

For each complex assignment given, use one or more of the techniques discussed to identify what you are supposed to write about.

- Identify key phrases
- Paraphrase the instructions
- Write a research proposal about how you would write the paper.

Use separate paper.

1. Power of Place

Since the theme of this course is landscape, any topic related to this idea is appropriate. Here is a list of ideas to get you thinking, but these are suggestive, not directive. Some topics:

- Comparison of Chinese and Japanese gardens
- Pilgrimages in Buddhism, Islam, Christianity, or any other religion
- Frank Lloyd Wright and organic architecture
- Famous bridges
- Native American sacred sites
- The Nile River in history, myth, and the modern period
- Machu Picchu in Peru
- The meaning of the "Pacific Rim"
- The significance of the capital city in any nation

In writing your paper, your task is to define the importance of the place you have chosen. You may do this by reviewing its history, comparing it with other similar places, and/or explaining how the place of your choice connects with the culture of which it is a part.

2. Controlling Scientific Information

In our readings and discussions this term, we have considered a number of scientific discoveries and the technological inventions that have come about through those discoveries. In almost every case, the knowledge gained from science can be used in both beneficial and destructive ways. Therefore, the question arises: how should the use of scientific information be controlled and, if so, by whom?

Write an essay that explores the responsibility for scientific knowledge. Consider these questions, although you do not need to answer them all in your paper: Who should pay for the research, keeping in mind that whoever pays will probably have some control over the results? What role should international bodies, national governments, scientists themselves, technicians and inventors, and the public play in the control of how the knowledge is used? How can the general public be well-informed to make good decisions about using new technology?

This paper should not simply summarize the ideas from the articles we have read; it is your opinion about the question of who is responsible for the wise use of scientific information. To support your opinion, give specific examples of cases when science has been used in positive and negative ways and explain how the knowledge has been controlled or not controlled in each case.

3. The Internet

Our history is full of inventions that have changed the way we live, inventions that have revolutionized food production, medical care, communication, warfare, and many other aspects of human life. In this paper, you have an opportunity to explore how one of our recent inventions is changing and will change our lives, especially our psychology and our behavior.

Write a research paper that explores these questions: Compared with other inventions throughout history, how has the Internet influenced our thinking about ourselves and our ways of relating to each other. How will it change us in the future? In other words, is the Internet simply another tool for our convenience, or is it something that will transform our lives in a lasting way? Is it more or less influential than paper, the phone, the car, the compass, or other inventions? How is it the same or different from these earlier inventions?

This paper should not simply synthesize ideas from the articles we have read; it is your opinion about the significance that the Internet will have in our social lives as human beings.

ACTIVITY 2

Analyze a Current Assignment

1. Bring in a writing assignment in any discipline from a current or previous class.
2. With a partner or small group, use one or more of the techniques discussed in this section to identify the focus:

- Identify key phrases
- Paraphrase the instructions
- Write a research proposal about how you could write the paper.

BUILDING YOUR INDEPENDENT PAPER

Write Your Research Paper

Now that you've chosen a topic, written a research proposal, learned how to collect and evaluate your sources, and written a working references list, it is time to retrace the steps in the writing process. Use Chapters 1–5 in this book to guide you through the process of writing a research paper.

Sources for Research

 ## Introduction to Part Two

The articles in this part of *Sourcework* provide the sources of information for your guided research paper. Your teacher will choose one of the themes in this section and work with you through the process of writing a research paper using the articles in that unit.

You will begin by doing the Getting Started activity about your theme. Then your teacher will assign one or more of the Questions About . . . the theme (following the articles) and several of the articles in the unit. You and your classmates will use those questions and articles to write a paper following the writing process in Part One, Chapters 1 through 5.

After you have written a guided research paper working on the same theme with your classmates, you can repeat the process to write a second research paper. This time you have a few choices.

- You can write about the same theme but expand it by using one of the ideas in More Writing About. . . . at the end of each unit or by looking at the additional resources listed on the *Sourcework* website at http://esl.college.hmco.com/students.
- You can write about one of the other themes in Part Two.
- You can do research on a topic of your own choosing. Chapter 6 Independent Research will help you get started on an independent research paper.

For additional resource lists on the themes in Part Two, and on the following additional themes, go to the *Sourcework* website at **http://esl.college.hmco.com/students**:

1 Birth Order and Personality
2 Standardized Testing
3 Expectations of Marriage
4 Taking Risks
5 Home Schooling

Heroes:

The People Who Inspire Us

"Heroism is idealism in action"—*Miriam Polster*

Getting Started

What does being a hero mean to you? Think of someone you consider a hero. Freewrite for 5 to 10 minutes about this person and why you think he or she is heroic. Then discuss your ideas with a partner, a small group, or the whole class.

Introduction to the Theme

There have always been a few people who have led the way into change, taking the first risks and setting the standards for others. Some people call them heroes.

Every society throughout history has had such heroes and heroines, people who stand out as ideals and inspirations for others to follow. They may be recognized leaders—politicians, warriors, scientists, or artists—

or they may be less conspicuous, so-called "ordinary" individuals thrust into leadership by circumstance. Some would say that they define us; the heroes we choose reveal our own values.

This unit examines the question of what it means to be a hero. The first two articles, "Cathy Freeman" and "Ray Anderson" offer profiles of people who some consider heroes. The third article, "Contemporary Heroes and Heroines," explores the role heroes play in society and how that role has changed over time. The last two articles "Is a Hero Nothing but a Sandwich?" and "Eve's Daughters: The Forbidden Heroism of Women," suggest some traits that most heroes have.

NOTE: For discussion questions on each article, go to the *Sourcework* website at http://esl.college.hmco.com/students.

Cathy Freeman

Claudia Herrera Hudson
My Hero Project, myhero.com

The bold tattoo on her right triceps reads: "Cos I'm Free." Her running shoes sport the bright red, black and yellow of her beloved Australian Aboriginal flag as she races across finish lines and receives award upon award.

Cathy Freeman is proud of being a star athlete and prouder of being a native Australian.

As Australia's first Aboriginal track and field athlete to represent Australia at the Olympics (in 1992), Cathy, born February 16, 1973, has broken boundaries no one believed possible in a country riddled with deep-rooted racism against its own natives.

Although her running career stats read like a page out of that of any historical world-class athlete, she has still been met with a mix of controversy and praise thanks to her unbridled overt passion towards her heritage.

In a both genuinely heartfelt and bold gesture, at the 1994 Commonwealth Games, Cathy took her victory lap with the Aboriginal flag draped over her shoulders and then later added the Australian flag. It was a public proclamation of Aboriginal rights and a powerful political statement.

Cathy told the *New York Times,* "The time will come when I can be more instrumental in politics and Aboriginal affairs. But now, I think I'm playing a big part doing what I'm doing."

She still remains the object of prejudice despite her talent and the glory her awards bring to Australia. She attracts both press criticism and public disapproval for a cultural pride many feel should be kept undercover. There was even an appeal for nominations as to whom the flag-bearer should be at the opening ceremony of the Sydney 2000 games and some wrote in saying it shouldn't be Cathy.

"I just wanted to show I am proud of who I am and where I come from. I would love to one day go out to the bush and spend time with the elders of my culture, and get back to my roots," she said.

After lighting the torch, Cathy was quoted as saying "Much is made about me being an Aboriginal. This fact should be celebrated, not abused. I love where I come from, but I am not at the Olympics to be political. I don't think to myself that I've got to make this next move for the Aboriginal cause." While some may take this as a hypocritical thought from someone thought to be a forerunner for Aboriginal rights, in reality it just proves that her actions are heartfelt, not planned. They are dictated from within without a thought to consequence, negative or positive. ●

Ray Anderson

Jennifer Beck
My Hero Project, myhero.com

Interface, Inc. CEO Ray C. Anderson has been called the "greenest chief executive in America." By combining environmentalism with dedication to his company's success, Anderson has proven that being green can also bring in the green for big business.

When Anderson started Interface, in Atlanta, Georgia, in 1973, he wasn't concerned about the environment. He'd earned a degree from Georgia Institute of Technology, worked for fourteen plus years in various positions at Deering-Milliken and Callaway Mills, and was out to make his own carpet business the biggest in the world. He succeeded, turning Interface into a billion-dollar-a-year company. But there was a price. Every year his factories produced hundreds of gallons of wastewater and nearly 900 pollutants.

"I just wanted to survive," Anderson recalled in an interview with Kate Jaimet of *The Ottowa Citizen.* "I never gave one thought to what we were doing to the earth."

Then Anderson read Paul Hawkens' book, *The Ecology of Commerce.* The book suggested that industry was systematically destroying the planet, and the only people in a position to stop the destruction were the industrialists themselves. The books' argument spun Anderson's perspective 180 degrees.

"It was like a spear to the chest," he said of Hawkens' book, in a speech before California's Waste Management Board. Almost immediately, he began to turn Interface, Inc. into an environmentally-friendly enterprise.

He began by taking steps to reduce the company's waste and conserve energy by recycling. At its plant in LaGrange, Georgia, Interface used to send six tons of carpet trimmings to the landfill every day. By June of 1997, it was sending none. At Guilford of Maine, a division of Interface, new computer controls installed on boilers not only reduced carbon monoxide emissions by 99.7%, but also improved the boilers' efficiency. The result? Waste decreased and profits increased.

Anderson also spread the word to other companies and to consumers worldwide. He funded the Alliance to Save Energy, helping children design energy-saving campaigns for their schools, and through his frequent speaking engagements and his book, *Mid Course Correction: Toward a Sustainable Enterprise: The Interface Model,* helped prove to other businesses they could protect the environment while increasing profits. Anderson explained his philosophy to Charles Fishman, of *Fastcompany.com Magazine:*

"The new course we're on at Interface . . . is to pioneer the next Industrial Revolution: one that is kinder and gentler to the earth."

Anderson's efforts have begun to pay off. Sunco, Bank of America, Polaroid, and General Motors now regularly consult with The Coalition for Environmentally Responsible Economics. Xerox Corporation now leases many of its business machines, recycling old equipment and parts instead of discarding them.

Anderson acknowledges there is still much work to be done, even within his own company. Interface, Inc. is only about a quarter of the way to its ultimate goal—a goal employees refer to as "the peak of Mount Sustainability." Still, Anderson believes the tide has turned irrevocably in his favor. As he told *Ottowa Citizen,* "It's a wave that's forming. I have no way of knowing how fast or how big the wave will be, but businesses that don't move in this direction won't survive." ●

Contemporary Heroes and Heroines

Ray Browne
Gale Research Inc., Detroit, 1990

Heroes and heroines serve as models and leaders of people and nations because they reflect the feelings, dreams, fantasies, and needs of individuals and of society itself. There is in society, writes Ernest Becker in *Denial of Death,* a constant hunger for heroes, a need for the power they give us, because we realize our own limitations and know that we all must die with our aspirations and hopes largely unfulfilled. To Becker, modern life is not full enough "to absorb and quicken man's hunger for self-perpetuation and heroism." So we continue to create heroes and heroines because they can concentrate the power of a people—of a nation—and serve as the driving force for the movement and development of individuals and society.

Heroes Perpetuate Society's Goals

In a simple society such as the Greeks' of three thousand years ago, the heroes' world was straightforward and uncomplicated. It was, in the words of Joseph Campbell, a world of "monomyths": it had single goals, definite and clear purposes. The heroes and heroines of that society spoke for and perpetuated mankind's goals and purposes. In more complicated societies, such as our own, heroes and heroines wear many faces because of their numerous responses to the varied needs of individuals, groups of people, and national purposes.

As a society's needs become more complicated, so too do the heroes and heroines; as people become more sophisticated the heroes and heroines become less modeled on the conventional demi-gods of the past, less clear-cut and obvious. In a swiftly moving society like America today, heroes and heroines undergo rapid transformation. They frequently develop in ways and for purposes that are not immediately apparent. Twentieth-century American heroes and heroines, existing in a highly technological society and driven by the electronics of mass communication, change quickly. They often are hailed as heroic today and forgotten tomorrow. But though they may disappear rapidly, they serve useful and needed purposes while they endure.

Today's Heroes Help Define Our World

Earlier societies did not demand much information about the reality of the heroes and heroines and their heroic actions because they accepted the stature of the hero or heroine on faith; they were less critical and analytical about the real accomplishments of those individuals. Our current civilization has little patience for the misty semi-divine heroes and heroines who were popular in the past. The kind of hero or heroine needed and created today—the down-to-earth, realistic role-model that demonstrates how a person can develop all of his or her potential—serves present-day society well. Yet they are no less genuine heroes and heroines and serve no less important purposes than did their counterparts of old. In fact, in their capacity as role models, modern-day heroes and heroines share the conventional body and soul of their predecessors. They still serve the mythological purpose of helping to explain ourselves to ourselves, of clarifying the meaning of life and eternity, of illustrating some of the purposes of our world. In doing so they help us maintain a personal stability and a social purpose. They assist us in making sense of the world and ourselves. Our sophisticated population likes its heroes and heroines more its own size, more believable. The heroes and heroines of contemporary life serve more as role models, less as spiritual leaders.

Heroic Diversity Reflects Our Culture

Heroes and heroines are also more numerous in kind now than they were in the past. In old societies the hero developed in several predictable roles, as explained by Joseph Campbell in his book *The Hero With a Thousand Faces.* That is, the similar kinds of heroes and heroines developed in similar kinds of societies to fulfill similar functions. In twentieth-century America, a richly diverse society of two hundred and fifty million people, the various heroic faces have grown into the many thousands, and the number is expanding all the time as the needs for heroes and heroines multiply and change. Thus the diversity of the more than one hundred heroes and heroines discussed in this book, and of the thousands of others known locally, regionally, nationally, and globally. They are *our* heroes and heroines, created to serve our world and ourselves. They continue to work with and for us.

Communication Fosters Fame

Since heroes and heroines live in the minds and hearts of people other than themselves, their existence as heroic figures depends on the communication that makes them known. In historical times, the medium that carried their fame was oral tradition. Later it was print—newspapers, books, and magazines. Now, of course, the medium is primarily television, the most widespread and effective creator and popularizer of heroes and heroines ever known. What we see in the television hero and heroine represents the changed tastes and needs of the receiving public, and consequently the changed heroic role. In newscasts, game shows, soap operas—in all the many faces worn by television—we see people who may illustrate the qualities that we think our society needs.

　　To many observers, the contemporary media create not heroes and heroines but celebrities, and therefore we live in a world in which there are no real heroes. "The hero," as Daniel Boorstin, ex-Librarian of Congress, phrases it, "was a big man, the celebrity is a big name." The celebrity, Boorstin feels, is *a person who is known for his well-knownness.* As such he or she cannot be a true hero or heroine. Yet even these heroes-for-a-day, if that is all they are, serve a purpose, or else they would not be elevated to the status. They incorporate the qualities that we wish we had or that many of us do in fact possess to some degree, qualities that we think society needs.

　　Take, for example, Lenny Skutnik. Not many of us today remember Skutnik. He was forced into being a hero by circumstances over which he had no control. On an afternoon in early 1982, Skutnik, a minor Federal Government employee, happened to be on a bridge outside Washington, D.C., when an Air Florida jetliner on take-off hit the bridge and crashed into the Potomac River. Skutnik dove into the freezing waters and rescued an injured and drowning crash survivor. His deed was recorded by television cameras and he was, for a couple of days, a national hero. Skutnik was lionized because the public saw themselves in his face and actions. We wanted to think that Skutnik was only one among the thousands of us who would have done the same—and possibly greater—deed under the circumstances. We somehow need to feel that, like Skutnik, we are prepared to risk life and limb in an unselfish willingness to aid, or even to die for, other people.

Heroes Can Embody Our Ideal Selves

We like to see in ourselves the qualities of Dag Hammarskjold, the one-time Secretary-General of the United Nations whose profile appears in this volume; he believed that "no life was more satisfactory than one of selfless service to your community—or humanity." Or, as another heroine whose career is outlined in this volume, Eleanor Roosevelt, demonstrated, "Our own success, to be real, must contribute to the successes of others." The ultimate and final unselfish act is, of course, death in the service of others. And many still feel the noble willingness to give their lives for others. Heroism probably provides no better example of such willingness than that of Martin Luther King, Jr., whose life is also traced in this book; he often said, "Certainly I don't want to die. But if anyone has to die, let it be me."

Many products of television heroism last much longer than Lenny Skutnik's fame. King's influences, for example, will never fade. More to the point, thousands of other heroes and heroines in our midst today are in their individual and usually unheralded ways, willingly or unwillingly, achieving heroic status and providing us with models of philosophy, behavior and actions that we want to emulate. The hundred-plus examples in this collection, a handful among thousands that could have been chosen, provide excellent examples of the qualities that make good modern-day world citizens and show us what we can do in order to become as great as our heroes and heroines. In their totality they help profile the wishes and accomplishments of the ideal contemporary citizen. ●

Is a Hero Really Nothing but a Sandwich?

Ted Tollefson
Utne Reader, May/June 1993

For several years a picture of Warren Spahn of the Milwaukee Braves hung on my closet door, one leg poised in mid-air before he delivered a smoking fastball. Time passed and Spahn's picture gave way to others: Elvis, John F. Kennedy, Carl Jung, Joseph Campbell, Ben Hogan. These heroic images have reflected back to me what I hoped to become: a man with good moves, a sex symbol, an electrifying orator, a plumber of depths, a teller of tales, a graceful golfer. Like serpents, we keep shedding the skins of our heroes as we move toward new phases in our lives.

Like many of my generation, I have a weakness for hero worship. At some point, however, we all begin to question our heroes and our need for them. This leads us to ask: What is a hero?

Despite immense differences in cultures, heroes around the world generally share a number of traits that instruct and inspire people.

A hero does something worth talking about. A hero has a story of adventure to tell and a community who will listen. But a hero goes beyond mere fame or celebrity.

Heroes serve powers or principles larger than themselves. Like high-voltage transformers, heroes take the energy of higher powers and step it down so that it can be used by ordinary mortals.

The hero lives a life worthy of imitation. Those who imitate a genuine hero experience life with new depth, zest, and meaning. A sure test for would-be heroes is what or whom do they serve? What are they willing to live and die for? If the answer or evidence suggests they serve only their own fame, they may be celebrities but not heroes. Madonna and Michael Jackson are famous, but who would claim that their adoring fans find life more abundant?

Heroes are catalysts for change. They have a vision from the mountaintop. They have the skill and the charm to move the masses. They create new possibilities. Without Gandhi, India might still be part of the British Empire. Without Rosa Parks and Martin Luther King Jr., we might still have segregated buses, restaurants, and parks. It may be possible for large-scale change to occur without charismatic leaders, but the pace of change would be glacial, the vision uncertain, and the committee meetings endless.

Though heroes aspire to universal values, most are bound to the culture from which they came. The heroes of the Homeric Greeks wept loudly for their lost comrades and exhibited their grief publicly. A later generation of Greeks under the tutelage of Plato disdained this display of grief as "unmanly."

Throughout most of the world, it is acknowledged that heroes need a community as much as a community needs them.

And most Americans seem to prefer their heroes flawless, innocent, forever wearing a white hat or airbrushed features. Character flaws—unbridled lust, political incorrectness—are held as proof that our heroes aren't really heroes. Several heroes on my own list have provided easy targets for the purveyors of heroic perfectionism.

The ancient Greeks and Hebrews were wiser on this count. ◉

Eve's Daughters

Miriam Polster
Gestalt Journal Press, 2001

When we move beyond the classic stereotype, we can see that many ordinary women and men are actually heroes. Furthermore, heroes are more numerous than we may have thought. Although heroes of the everyday may not receive the great acclaim accorded the classic hero, the value of private heroism may be greater precisely because we see everyday heroes up close; they are so near, so intimately connected. They are family, co-workers, neighbors, and their heroism takes place in commonplace settings and in response to everyday challenges.

Our images of heroes provide an inventory, if you will, of heroic characteristics. And while some of these characteristics may be basic to all heroism, others may be distinctly related to whether the hero is a woman or a man. A useful definition of heroism must include both types.

Five Shared Characteristics of Heroism

Heroism takes many forms. Out of the roster of qualities ascribed to heroes over the ages, I would like to focus on five.

1. All heroes are motivated by a profound respect for human life.
2. Heroes have a strong sense of personal choice and effectiveness.
3. Their perspective on the world is original, going beyond what other people think is possible.
4. They are individuals of great physical and mental courage.
5. Heroes are not measured by publicity. Whether a heroic act receives worldwide attention or occurs in an obscure setting with only a single witness, a heroic act is still heroic.

Respect for Human Life

The hero profoundly believes in the value and dignity of human life. The one act that most people would agree is heroic is risking one's life to save another. The annual Carnegie Hero Fund Commission endorses this opinion by giving medals and cash awards to women and men who have saved lives. In 1990, eight women won awards for acts ranging from saving people from assault to rescuing people from runaway automobiles or from drowning (Carnegie Hero Foundation, 1990). Mythology is full of hero tales about unfortunate victims apparently doomed if not for the intervention of the hero.

Valuing life can also mean preserving the dignity with which a life is to be lived. Many of the chores that women have quietly but heroically performed over the years have been the simple services that support the dignity and welfare of the people in their care, adults as well as children. Feeding, clothing, and keeping others clean are all humble tasks, but how quickly a life deteriorates when these basic needs go untended. Many women have faced overwhelming odds—and many continue to face them—on untamed and unpublicized frontiers: in the schools and clinics of our city slums, in wartime hospitals, collecting and distributing food and clothing to the homeless. All ways of preserving lives.

Faith in Her Effective Exercise of Choice

The hero has a profound faith in herself as an essential influential force. An unhappy circumstance is not simply to be endured. Personal action is called for, and she chooses to act. She balances her own energy against the opposition and moves to make changes.

One heroic woman who went beyond resignation is Betty Washington. She set herself and others to work toward their common goal. She singlehandedly recruited and organized people for a citizen's watch program to rid her Boston neighborhood of the drug dealing and crime that were threatening to take it over. This made her a publicly marked target, vulnerable to reprisal. But here is how a modern hero talks: "Either you speak out and take the risk, or you die in the cesspool" ("Heroes, Past and Present," 1987, p. 63).

The heroic woman believes, and reminds others, that common experience and accepted opinion can be changed, and she is willing to be the catalyst, even though she may confront opposition and criticism.

Original Perspective

The hero has an original perspective that distinguishes her from others who settle for agreement and conformity or are too beaten down to ask necessary questions. The relationship between the hero and the established order of things is fluid; she insists on her freedom to perceive, within the context of things-as-they-are, the way things *could* be.

Doubting the inevitable rightness of unquestioned assumptions has gotten women into trouble ever since Eve. It leads to unwelcome questions, but opens a new view of old behavior. Looking at voting privileges in an untraditional light, the suffragists began to question the historic restriction of the vote to white male property owners only. The trite answer—that there was a classic precedent, that this policy had been good enough for the ancient Athenians—did not satisfy. In our own times, the whistle-blower exposes wrongdoing, fraud, or inefficiency in his or her workplace, where one is not supposed to rock the boat. Rocking the boat, however leaky it may be, requires an original perspective and involves risk of reprisal, slander, ridicule, demotion and even loss of job.

Courage

It is almost redundant to say that heroism requires courage, both physical and mental; personal cost takes a backseat to getting the job done. The traditional hero often risks death or injury. In our sensationalistic age, the defiance of death has become one of the accepted signs of heroism. In disregarding her personal welfare, the hero may *appear* to be courting death. This is an oversimplification. In truth, she simply considers the risk of death or injury to be less important than her purpose.

Women unconcerned with personal sacrifice have often given years of devoted service to a cause or a person. They have persisted at unconventional efforts with little recognition or encouragement, willingly surrendering their personal comfort in order to pursue their goals. One example is Marie Curie, who persevered in her research in the face of the disrespect and open disapproval of women scientists that characterized her time (and that still taint our own). Mother Theresa, whose lifelong devotion to the victims of poverty and disease is known throughout the world, is another compelling example.

The mental courage of the hero permits her to be aware of accepted "truths" and yet not be restricted by them. When the child in the fairy tale says loudly that the emperor isn't wearing any clothes, that child speaks from innocence, not from courage. The heroic woman, however, knows the danger and nevertheless asserts an unwelcome truth. But she speaks from the integrity of the clearsighted. For her, it isn't enough merely to think the unorthodox; she chooses to espouse it publicly.

Since the heroic act may involve going against the habits and customs of the community, opposition is inevitable; supporters of the status quo do not happily welcome disagreement. The hero needs the mental and emotional stamina to sustain energy and intelligence in the face of personal loss, disapproval, or ostracism. Obviously, one of the most powerful sanctions a community can impose is the threat of ostracism or expulsion. This can be formal, as when a society executes, expels, or jails its dissidents, or informal, as in exclusion from social interactions, passing people over for promotions, or ridicule that isolates psychologically.

Public or Unpublic Heroism

Public heroes are what we usually think of when we think of heroes. They have great impact and are noble examples for a number of people. Drama, awe, and admiration accompany them, and recognition is underscored by ceremonies that accord them even more fame.

But the grandness of these celebrations can sometimes overshadow a far more pervasive and important factor in the lives of most people: the heroes of the intimate setting. The actions of parents, teachers, relatives, neighbors, and occasionally even strangers provide an immediacy that profoundly colors a person's life.

All heroism is characterized by these five basic traits I have just described: respect for human life, faith in one's ability to make a difference, original perspective, physical and mental courage, and public or unpublic impact. They are not all equally evident in every heroic life or act; sometimes one or another may dominate. These five characteristics do not constitute a hierarchy of heroism; they are not intended to provide a scale on which heroism can be rated. They are guidelines by which we can recognize the heroism that fills our everyday experience. They help us to appreciate heroism in its ordinary guise, unaccompanied by background music or special effects, and to find the heroic elements in our own lives. •

Questions for Writing About Heroes

1. Using evidence from at least three of the articles, define what it means to be a hero.
2. Select a hero profiled in this unit or on the *Sourcework* website, or choose your own personal hero and explain why this person is a hero. Use information from the sources in this section to support your position.
3. In what ways are cultural attitudes about heroes the same or different? Select two cultures and compare their beliefs about heroes. Use evidence from the articles and your experience to support your ideas.
4. What is the difference between a hero and a role model, celebrity, or icon? Use evidence from the articles to support your ideas.
5. How has the concept of heroes been used by political leaders?
6. Select a current public figure who is admired by some and disliked by others. Discuss whether or not this person should be considered a hero. Use evidence from the articles to support your ideas. You may also need to find additional articles on the person you choose to discuss.

More Questions for Writing About Heroes

Below are additional ideas for writing about heroes that can be developed into research papers. On the *Sourcework* website you will find a list of sources that may help you with these topics. You will also need to find some of your own sources.

- How have gender roles influenced the traditional concept of heroes?
- How has the concept of heroes been used by political leaders?
- Should whistle blowers be considered heroes? Analyze an example of a whistle blower in the current news and discuss whether or not this person matches the qualities of a hero.
- What is an anti-hero? How are anti-heroes similar or different from heroes?
- Consider a current or historical event involving social conflict or change. Analyze the people at the forefront of this change. In what ways could these people be considered heroes?

NOTE: For practice with in-class writing on the Heroes theme, see the *Sourcework* website at http://esl.college.hmco.com/students.

Globalization:

Changes That Draw Us Together

"The fact that free trade is now becoming truly global is one of the most important achievements in the history of mankind. If, in the end, it wins out over statism, global capitalism will bring about the greatest degree of prosperity and the greatest period of peaceful cooperation in world history." —*Edwin A Locke, behavioral psychologist in "Anti-Globalization: The Left's Violent Assault on Global Prosperity" in CapitalismMagazine.com. Available at* http://capitalismmagazine.com, *May 1, 2002.*

"The West has driven the globalization agenda, ensuring that it garners a disproportionate share of the benefits, at the expense of the developing world—. . . . The result was [sic] that some of the poorest countries in the world were [sic] actually made worse off." —*Joseph Stiglitz, Nobel Prize winner and former World Bank chief economist in* Globalization and Its Discontents.

"Many people, particularly in less developed countries, have been hurt by globalization without being supported by a social safety net; many others have been marginalized by global markets–. . . . The heedless pursuit of profit can hurt the environment and conflict with other social values."—*George Soros, money manager in* On Globalization.

Getting Started

The three statements above illustrate some of the many reactions to globalization. To begin thinking about the issues in this unit, choose one of the quotes. Explain to a small group or to the class what you think it means and whether you agree or disagree with it.

Introduction to the Theme

Humans have always been curious about each other and looked for ways to exchange things and ideas. With today's rapid systems of communication, this trading happens constantly and influences almost everyone in the world on a daily basis, changing how we think and behave.

Globalization, the term often applied to these economic and cultural transformations that are making all the world's citizens more closely connected, means different things to different people. For some, it is an exciting opportunity to meet new ideas, create new products, and blend traditions. For others, it divides more than it unites, widening a gap between rich and poor, between the "haves" and the "have-nots."

This unit introduces some of the issues involved in globalization. The first article, "The Deadly Noodle," describes an example of globalization in action, an instance in which the connection with the global economy is affecting individuals and small communities. The next reading, part of an introduction to a book, "Spiritual Perspectives on Globalization," briefly defines globalization. The third article, "If Poor Get Richer, Does World See Progress?" introduces some of the problems as well as some of the benefits brought about by globalization. The next, "Exiled To Cyberia," gives an example of positive change made possible by the global sharing of resources. "The Pew Global Attitudes Project," an excerpt from a public opinion survey, gives an overview of what people around the world think of globalization. The following article, "Confronting Anti-Globalism," summarizes the business point of view about why globalization is a good trend. Finally, the scholarly article, "Poverty and Environmental Degradation" discusses the connections between poverty and deterioration in the environment.

NOTE: For discussion questions on each article, go to the *Sourcework* website at http://esl.college.hmco.com/students.

The Deadly Noodle

Michael Hastings, Stefan Thiel, Dana Thomas
Newsweek January 20, 2003, Volume 141 Issue 3

Greasy burgers and processed food may be the most insidious forms of American cultural imperialism. They're making the world fat.

Of all the ways France has resisted the cultural imperialism of the United States, it has arguably achieved its greatest success in the realm of food. Not only is French cuisine the envy of the world, but culinary tradition has allowed the French to consume their sauce velouté and crème brûlée without succumbing to the ills of over consumption that plague the land of burgers, fries and angioplasty. In recent years, however, statistics have begun to reveal that France is vulnerable to America's junk-food influence after all. Although southern, rural France remains steadfastly healthy, its more urban neighbors to the north suffer more from eating-related problems, not least a rise in childhood obesity. "We can't point our finger at any one thing," says Mariette Gerber, a nutritional scientist at the National Institute for Medical Research and Health in Montpellier. "It's a modern way of life, very urban. And it has come from the United States."

France's growing fat problem underscores how inexorable the Americanization of food habits has become. The problem is even more acute in the developing world, where the taste for American fast-food products like McDonald's hamburgers and Coca-Cola has long been fashionable. Urbanization is leading to more sedentary lifestyles in many places. And more and more, even traditional foods are being prepared from processed flour and other ingredients that yield more calories and less healthy roughage. Nobody ever thought resisting the export of American diets would be easy. But the trend has turned out to be more insidious and more widespread than previously thought. "It's very easy to blame globalization, or the big brands like Coca-Cola or McDonald's," says Derek Yach, executive director of the World Health Organization's disease prevention, nutrition, diet and physical-fitness program. "But the problem goes much, much deeper."

Diet and exercise habits may be complex, but the basic recipe for health problems is simple: a rise in caloric intake and a decline in calorie-burning activities. The number of overweight people in the United States doubled in the past 20 years to 60 percent, and Europe and Asia are catching up. In some developing countries, obesity is increasing faster than in America—the rate is three times higher in Mexico and Egypt. Each year more new cases of diabetes arise in China and India than in all other countries combined.

Where are all the extra calories coming from? One surprising source is the raw grains and other ingredients used for cooking traditional—formerly healthy—dishes. When crops are grown in big farms and processed en masse, much of their nutrient value is taken out, and their "caloric density" rises. Even the noodle, a staple of many traditional diets, is no longer as healthy as it once was. In China, for instance, home-cooked noodles used to be made from whole-grains, ground by hand. Now, households use factory-made "refined" flour, from which the grain husks have been discarded along with nutrients like fiber and minerals. What remains are simple carbohydrates that the body more easily turns into fat.

Cooking oils have taken a similar turn for the worse. Back in the 1960s, Japanese and American researchers discovered an inexpensive way to extract oil from vegetables. Westerners and developing countries alike adopted vegetable oils as a cheaper alternative to butter, healthy if used in moderation. The problem is, the oil is so cheap that in places like India it's used to excess. It's not uncommon for Indian cooks to use vegetable oil for breakfast, lunch and supper, and to throw in an extra 10 or 20 grams to enhance a dish's flavor.

Sugar is another culprit. Diets in some developing countries contain on average about 300 more calories a day than they did 20 years ago, according to Barry Popkin, professor of nutrition at the University of North Carolina. Some of the extra sugar comes from soda, but a bigger factor is the growing adoption of Western manufacturing practices, which allow local companies to sweeten bread and other staples. Brazil now consumes more sugar per capita than even the United States.

No part of the world, no matter how remote, is immune from empty calories. Over the course of 30 years, the native population of Samoa has fallen victim to rampant weight gain—today more than half its residents are clinically obese. James Bindon, a biological anthropologist at Alabama University, traced one of the causes to a fondness for tins of corned beef imported from England. Similar trends have been observed in Fiji. "Where in the past they produced their own fruits and vegetables, now they're swamped with canned soda and mutton fat imported from New Zealand," says Yach of WHO. "Call it the Coca-Colafication of the Pacific islands."

People in both developed and developing countries are also doing less and less physical activity. It's the couch-potato syndrome. Rather than riding their bicycles and working the fields, people sit on assembly lines, ride in cars and spend their free time watching television—95 percent of Chinese households now have a TV set. "We export our jobs, and our wage-labor patterns," says Bindon. "It's a culture-bound syndrome."

The syndrome is raising health-care costs—$100 billion for obese children in the United States, estimates the Centers for Disease Control. What about the 35 million overweight kids around the world, not to mention 300 million adults? "The cost of health care—to feed the hungry and pay for the medical bills of obesity—is staggering," says Weight Watchers International chief science officer Karen Miller-Kovach. Unfortunately, obesity and all the illnesses it entails hit the poor hardest of all. High-caloric junk food is cheap enough to afford even on a low income. And the well-heeled and well-educated tend to be better about hitting the gym. In developing countries, those leisure activities aren't even an option yet. The popularity of Western-style food has thus led to an alarming trend: obese parents and undernourished children living under the same roof. "It's a very attractive lifestyle," says Popkin. But it's killing people all the same. ●

Spiritual Perspectives on Globalization

Ira Rifkin
Skylight Paths Publishers, Woodstock, VT, 2003

What is globalization, and why do so many people—including many people of faith who see ultimate good, and even God's hand, in the process—share concerns about how it is unfolding, and, like the demonstrators, blame it for so much?

Abstract as it may be, globalization can be said to encompass certain elements. In the economic sphere, globalization refers to the recent decades' unprecedented flow of capital and commerce across national borders, leading to the hegemony gained by international financial markets and multinational corporations, abetted by transnational agencies and organizations such as the WEF, the World Bank, the World Trade Organization (WTO), and the International Monetary Fund (IMF).

On a cultural level, globalization refers to the spread of what has been pejoratively termed "McWorld"—shorthand for the Western-oriented (many say American) global mono-culture that is burying countless regional and even national cultural expressions in an avalanche of MTV, Disney, Michael Jordan endorsements, and, of course, McDonald's-style fast food.

On an individual level, globalization is about the promotion of consumer values that feed on the perception that happiness is rooted in material progress, that choice equals the highest freedom, and that being well connected is more important than being deeply connected. All of this has been pushed at a dizzying pace by the extraordinary recent advances in information and travel technology that seem to mock time and space. The end result is the transformation of human society to a degree and in ways not yet fully understood—but deeply disturbing nonetheless to many who worry about the growing divide between rich and poor nations, the commodification of life's basic resources, and consumerism's steady ascendancy.

In truth, though, the only things new about globalization are the phrase and the speed at which it is now occurring. Humans, in the parlance of the day, seem hardwired to seek the next valley and make it their own. We've been spreading around the globe and taking over since our ancient ancestors ventured out of Africa, perhaps as long as a hundred thousand years ago. Hunters and gatherers did it in their day. The early agriculturalists slashed and burned their way across the landscape, in some cases leaving it irrevocably changed. Greeks, Romans, Arabs, Chinese, Columbus, the conquistadors, and the Hudson Bay Company all pushed the globalization envelope, even if they did not always understand the globe's full breadth.

But globalization as we know it may be traced to a 1944 meeting in Bretton Woods, New Hampshire, at which representatives from forty-five nations sketched out a plan for post–World War II economic recovery. In doing so, they created the IMF and the International Bank for Reconstruction and Development, better known as the World Bank—institutions that critics charge are responsible in good measure for the economic, environmental, and cultural fiascos they cite as proof of globalization's systematic wrongs. International trade rules were liberalized and the flow of capital turned national borders into sieves. Soon, new media and new modes of transportation revolutionized the way we defined foreign and distant. A global village was upon us that more and more resembled an American buffet table—even if chilies, chutney, and kimchee were added to the mix. ●

If Poor Get Richer, Does World See Progress?

Brad Knickerbocker
Christian Science Monitor, January 22, 2004

In Shanghai this month, bicyclists found themselves banned from certain portions of main thoroughfares. By next year, this ubiquitous two-wheel mode of transportation will have been kicked off such roads altogether. Why? To make way for all the new cars—11,000 more every week—pouring onto Chinese streets and highways.

A sure sign of growing affluence in the developing world? Without a doubt. A consumer trend portending a better world? That depends on one's point of view.

"Rising consumption has helped meet basic needs and create jobs," says Christopher Flavin, president of the Worldwatch Institute, a Washington, D.C., think tank. "But as we enter a new century, this unprecedented consumer appetite is undermining the natural systems we all depend on, and making it even harder for the world's poor to meet their basic needs."

That's the message underlying Worldwatch's annual "State of the World" report, an influential book-length collection of data-packed chapters that has been used by supporters as ammunition and by critics as a pincushion since 1984.

This year's report focuses on the growing global "consumer class"—defined as individuals whose "purchasing power parity" in local currency is more than $7,000 a year (roughly the poverty level in Western Europe). As economies expand—accelerated by globalization that has opened up markets, greater efficiency in manufacturing, and advancing technologies—that consumer class has grown rapidly. It's the main reason there are more than 1 billion cell phones in the world today.

The consumer class now includes more than 1.7 billion people. High percentages in North America, Western Europe, and Japan (85 to 90 percent) are no surprise.

But nearly half of all consumers now are in developing nations. China and India alone account for 362 million of those shoppers, more than in all of Western Europe. That can be a good thing to the extent that it improves health rates, education levels, and social conditions (like the status of women).

"The almost 3 billion people worldwide who barely survive on less than $2 a day will need to ramp up their consumption in order to satisfy basic needs for food, clean water, and sanitation," says Brian Halweil, codirector of Worldwatch's "State of the World 2004" project. "And in China, the rush to meet surging consumer demand is stimulating the economy, creating jobs, and attracting foreign investment."

But there are troubling indicators here as well, say Worldwatch researchers:

- Damage to forests, wetlands, ocean fisheries, and other natural areas as resources are used and pollution created.
- Higher levels of obesity, personal debt, and chronic time shortages as people work longer hours to satisfy the demand for consumer goods.
- Indications that increased consumption doesn't necessarily mean a better quality of life. In the United States, for example, average personal income more than doubled between 1957 and 2002. There now are more cars than licensed drivers, and the typical house is 38 percent bigger than it was in 1975, even though fewer people live in it. But when asked to rate how they feel about their lives, the same portion of Americans as a generation ago—only about one-third—describe themselves as "very happy."
- Growing disparities between rich and poor. More than 1 billion people still do not have reasonable access to safe drinking water. More than twice that number live without basic sanitation. (It's estimated that hunger and malnutrition could be eliminated globally for less than is spent on pet food in Europe and the U.S.; universal literacy could be achieved for one-third of what is spent annually on perfumes.)

On the other hand, critics argue, the swelling numbers of consumers reflect the improvement in material conditions that has paralleled the progress of nations since the dawn of civilization. And historically, when Malthus and other analysts pointed to factors that would limit future growth, human ingenuity has found ways around those obstacles, these critics point out.

"Rather than contributing to global destruction and third-world poverty, consumerism actually promotes technologies that serve to better environmental and human well-being," says Ezra Finkle of the Competitive Enterprise Institute in Washington, D.C.

The question is: Will the growing tide of new consumers in the developing world—joining an increasingly aware body of consumers who've known relative affluence all along—contribute to the solution or simply add to the problem? ●

Exiled to Cyberia

Kunda Dixit
Global Envision.org

As the "Knowledge Revolution" takes root, are developing countries at risk of sacrificing the wisdom of the ages?

A new buzzword has entered the development lexicon: "Knowledge Society"— the Information Age is the Age of Knowledge, we are told. There is a danger that the wisdom of the ages is now going to be another piece of jargon. And like all the extinct buzzwords that preceded it, "knowledge" will end up in that dusty shelf where all past development clichés are stored. Blaming underdevelopment on lack of knowledge has two other dangers. It may make us overlook the fundamental economic factors that keep the poor poor, widening disparities between and within nations.

Second, the knowledge hype may tempt us to regard only formal modern knowledge systems as worthy of attention. Mainstream economics tends to regard knowledge of the seasons, the different uses of roots and fruits, and evolved traditional wisdom as dispensable. Ironical, isn't it, that the so-called "information poor" may be sitting on a gold mine of information stored in the DNA of the plants they use daily.

Knowledge is not new—we have known it for millennia. We have also known that wisdom only comes about when knowledge is assimilated, internalised, when it changes existing behaviour patterns and makes things better. The wisdom of a monk meditating on a mountaintop is not much use because no one knows what is in his head. The knowledge to build a nuclear warhead is not wisdom, because atomic bombs fail an important test: they do not make the world a better place.

There is a similar lesson for the Information Age: the Internet does not necessarily spread knowledge. And even if it does distribute information widely and cheaply, what results is not necessarily greater wisdom.

The latest scientific information on tuberculosis is all over the Internet: how to prevent it, which therapies work, the antibiotics that bacilli have become resistant to. But this information needs to get where it is needed as cheaply as possible, it needs to be relevant to the needs of the people it is meant for, and it must be packaged so that it is easily understood. To be useful, information must help people communicate, participate and allow them and their rulers to make informed choices.

Recognition of the power of knowledge may be as old as civilisation, but what is different now is the speed and capacity to move that information. At present, this speed and capacity are concentrated in the same countries in which wealth and power are concentrated. And the gap between them and the rest shows signs of widening. One in every three Americans uses the Internet, only one in every 10,000 people in India, Pakistan and Bangladesh do. India's "teledensity" is 1.5 in every 100 people and narrow bandwidth in most places does not allow Internet use; only 13 percent of Nepal's population has access to electricity; and Sri Lanka has 3.3 personal computers for every 1000 people compared to 400 per 1000 in Switzerland. Alongside knowledge, another buzzword is "leapfrogging": bypassing obsolete and expensive copper cable for digital wireless signals, and using the Internet for distance learning and e-commerce. ●

The Pew Global Attitudes Project

The Pew Research Center for the People and the Press
people-press.org

"Yes" to a Smaller World

Beyond their common desire for democracy and free markets, people in emerging nations also generally acknowledge and accept globalization. People worldwide have become aware of the impact of increasing interconnectedness on their countries and their own lives. Majorities in 41 of 44 countries surveyed say that international trade and business contacts have increased in the past 5 years.

The survey finds broad acceptance of the increasing interconnectedness of the world. Three-quarters or more of those interviewed in almost every country think children need to learn English to succeed in the world today. People generally view the growth in foreign trade, global communication and international popular culture as good for them and their families as well as their countries. For most of the world's people, however, this approval is guarded. Increased trade and business ties and other changes are viewed as somewhat positive, not very positive.

Despite the widespread support for the globalization process, people around the world think many aspects of their lives—including some affected by globalization—are getting worse. Majorities in 34 of 44 countries surveyed say the availability of good-paying jobs has gotten worse compared with five years ago. They also see the gap between rich and poor, the affordability of health care and the ability to save for one's old age as getting worse. But people do not blame a more interconnected world for these problems—they mostly point to domestic factors. This is especially true in economically faltering countries in Africa and Latin America, such as Kenya and Argentina.

People around the world are more inclined to credit globalization for conditions they see as improving, such as increased availability of food in stores and more modern medicines and treatments.

While anti-globalization forces have not convinced the public that globalization is the root cause of their economic struggles, the public does share the critics' concerns about eroding national sovereignty and a loss of cultural identity. Large majorities in 42 of 44 countries believe that their traditional way of life is getting lost, and most people feel that their way of life has to be protected against foreign influence. There is less agreement that consumerism and commercialism represent a threat to one's culture. However, that point of view is prevalent in Western Europe and Latin America.

The polling finds, however, that the idea of "global" forces is something of a red flag to people around the world. "Global economy" is seen as more threatening than "trade with other countries." People worry about the impact of global trade on themselves and their families even though they believe that global trade is probably a good thing for their country as a whole.

Globalization Foes Fail to Get Through

People around the world generally have a positive view of the symbols of globalization. Large corporations from other countries get a favorable review in much of the world, as do international organizations.

In Africa, people express highly favorable opinions of foreign corporations, while the Middle East is more divided. Dislike of foreign firms is mostly limited to people in the major advanced economies of Western Europe, the U.S. and Canada. Even in these countries, however, positive evaluations of multinationals outweigh negative assessments.

Similarly, the impact of international financial organizations such as the World Bank, the IMF and the World Trade Organization is seen as much more positive than negative in most parts of the world. This is overwhelmingly the case in Africa. Argentina, Brazil, Jordan and Turkey stand out for their highly critical view of these institutions.

In contrast, people generally have a negative view of anti-globalization protesters. The French give higher ratings to multinational corporations than to the protesters. And in Italy, site of a major clash in 2001 between police and anti-globalization forces in Genoa, the public by nearly two-to-one (51%–27%) says the protesters are having a bad influence on the country. It should be noted that majorities in many countries declined to give an opinion of anti-globalization protesters. This is mostly the case in developing countries, but also in more advanced nations like South Korea (61%) and Japan (55%). ●

Confronting Anti-Globalism

Business Week, August 6, 2001, Issue 3744

The bloody Group of Eight summit meeting in Genoa is a watershed event. The violence that has been intensifying since the first Seattle demonstrations finally split the anti-globalization movement, with reformers of the international capitalist economy distancing themselves from the anarchists who simply want to destroy it. This could open an opportunity for corporations to sit down and negotiate compromises with groups willing to reason. But the task may be forbidding. The anti-globalization movement, as it stands now, is an inchoate collection of nongovernmental organizations and individuals that often hold mutually contradictory beliefs and promote clashing agendas.

Take extending First World labor standards to Third World countries. This is a major issue for most protesters, who have, of course, the best of intentions. But it is naive economics and is opposed by India and just about every other developing country. Why? The competitive advantage of many developing countries lies precisely in their lower costs of doing business. As Japan, Korea, and Taiwan have shown, the road to prosperity often begins with low wages and cheap exports. As skills increase, the sophistication and value of goods produced rise, allowing wages and income to move higher. West Germany's attempt to impose its higher wages on East Germany after the fall of communism led to an economic disaster, with little growth and high unemployment in the east. It's one thing for corporations to pay decent local wages and follow local laws protecting workers. But buckling under to pressure to extend U.S. or European pay scales to emerging nations could mean shutting down local factories—hurting people, not helping them.

There are major sovereignty issues as well. Anti-globalization groups speak in the name of Third World countries, but democratically elected governments in countries such as Mexico and India often disagree with them. They want more corporate investment, not less; freer trade, not more restricted markets; and the enforcement of local labor laws, not the imposition of foreign ones. Moreover, Mexico, India, and other nations insist on speaking for themselves.

Culture can be a serious problem. Child labor in factories is opposed by anti-globalization forces, but in many countries it is a major source of income, keeping families together and girls out of prostitution. Besides, it is commonly accepted on American farms today and was legal during the long period when the U.S. itself was a developing country. The environment poses a similar conundrum. Opposition to the Three Gorges dam in China is intense because it will displace many farmers. But dam-building was crucial in controlling water and generating electricity in the U.S. Without dams, California and much of the West could not have been settled. Imposing high 21st century labor and environmental standards on developing countries runs the risk of appearing hypocritical and undermining growth.

Despite these difficulties, smart CEOs should proceed in opening a dialogue with the reformers. Many have already successfully negotiated with some of the groups. Gap Inc., Nike Inc., and others have adopted codes of conduct for their overseas plants, hiring monitors to oversee compliance. Levi Strauss Co. has ethical manufacturing standards for its overseas operations. Home Depot Inc. has adopted an eco-friendly lumber supply program with the Rainforest Action Network. Starbucks Corp. is working with Conservation International to buy coffee from farmers preserving forests.

The truth is that many of the demands of the anti-globalization groups reflect the values of middle-class consumers in the U.S. and Europe, especially the young. It may be hard, but by working with reasonable reformers of the global system, corporations can not only help others, they just might help themselves. ●

Poverty and Environmental Degradation

Akin L. Mabogunje
Environment, Jan/Feb. 2002, Vol. 44, Issue 1

Globalization, Poverty and the Environment

Perhaps the single most important development in the world today is what is generally referred to as "globalization." Globalization is partly a result of the tremendous advances in information technology that have, in effect, shrunk the world and linked distant parts of the Earth, creating global relationships. Globalization is also a result of the expanding reach of the capitalist mode of production. Changes in technology and manufacturing organization have fostered the emergence of transnational corporations that have been able to amass wealth within and beyond individual nation-states such that their roles in the economy of their countries and of other countries rival or exceed those of nation-states. Communication technologies have enabled enormous financial resources to be moved from one end of the world to another in a matter of minutes. The instantaneous transfer of vast economic resources has the potential to make or break the economic fortunes of countries and affect the lives and employment opportunities of large numbers of people. Therefore, nation-states are forced to vigorously compete for foreign investment to enhance the rate of growth of their economies. To attract these investments, nation-states must achieve minimum levels of infrastructure development and, more importantly, maintain a certain degree of economic, social, and political stability.

Manufacturing operations have evolved from the classic model (epitomized by the vehicle production operations of Henry Ford in the early twentieth century), in which a huge factory produces all the components as well as the end-product, to an increasingly flexible method of production whereby components are produced in different countries and then assembled at another location close to the market site.

Therefore, although globalization exacerbates poverty in some places and among some groups, it also has a democratizing potential that may be essential to breaking out of poverty. Developing economies cannot get out of poverty without attracting transnational corporations, but at the same time, they cannot attract these corporations unless they have achieved a certain level of development. Because many developing-country economies are in the early stage of the transformation to a free-market, capitalist mode, the conditions necessary to attract international investment are difficult to fulfill, particularly for South Asia and sub-Saharan Africa.

Poverty and Environmental Degradation

Despite the constraints globalization places on economic growth and the insecurity that arises from regional armed conflicts, advances in health sciences—especially in epidemiology—have led to a human population explosion. Between 1960 and 2000, the world's population grew from less than 3 billion to some 6 billion. World population reached 6.1 billion in mid-2000 and is currently growing at an annual rate of 1.2 percent (about 77 million people). The United Nations estimates that by 2050, world population will reach between 7.9 billion and 10.9 billion people.

Population in developed countries is expected to change little during the next 50 years and is even expected to decrease in some countries. However, in the developing world, population is expected to increase by 3.3 million between 2000 and 2050.

A remarkable shift of global population from rural to urban areas has occurred in developed and developing regions of the world. In fact, by 2030, the urban population is expected to be twice the size of the rural population globally. The shift in population distribution from rural to urban areas has been accompanied by a shift in the concentration of the poor. Poverty in urban centers has been increasing more rapidly than in rural areas. According to a United Nations estimate, 600 million people in urban areas in developing countries (almost 28 percent of the developing world's urban population) cannot meet their basic needs for shelter, water, and health. In fact, about half the urban population in poor countries is living below official poverty levels. This number is expected to rise phenomenally over the next few decades. Rapid population growth and urbanization, coupled with the need to produce for export, has negatively affected the environment in at least seven ways:

Deforestation. The agricultural practices in developing countries are still relatively primitive, depending largely on bush-fallow cultivation, with the repeated clearing and burning of shrub and forest to make room for food crops. Equally significant is the deforestation arising from the need for firewood. For instance, it is estimated, that firewood and brush provide about 52 percent of the domestic energy supply in sub-Saharan Africa; charcoal, another forest product, is also [a] major source of domestic energy.

Desertification. Overcultivation and overgrazing on marginal lands are the major causes of desertification. Although desertification results from many factors and occurs in a variety of environments, rangelands are particularly at risk because they are often found in arid and semiarid regions. In the tropical grassland regions that often border deserts, overgrazing is a potent cause of desertification because feeding the livestock population (which is rapidly expanding to meet increased demand) requires frontier expansion. Desertification also arises from the removal of wood for fuel and the salinization of croplands caused by poorly managed irrigation.

Biodiversity loss. The wide range of ecosystems on which the poor eke out a living has been degraded, and the ecosystems' diverse communities of plants and animals have been put at risk in the process. According to the World Resources Institute, most scientists agree that between 5 and 10 percent of closed tropical forest species will become extinct each decade at current rates of forest loss and disturbance. This loss amounts to about 100 species a day. Indeed, about one-third of the forests that existed in 1950 have been cleared, primarily for agriculture, grazing, or firewood collection. The U.S. National Academy of Sciences estimates that more than 50 percent of all the Earth's species live in tropical rainforests: A typical four-square-mile patch of rainforest contains as many as 1,500 species of flowering plants, 750 tree species, 125 mammal species, 400 bird species, 100 reptile species, 60 amphibian species, and 150 butterfly species.

Erosion. Population pressure has led to a reduction in the fallow period and to overcultivation of cropland, particularly in developing countries, where poverty ensures that bush-fallow farming predominates. As a result of overcultivation and forest clearing, soil erosion has become widespread. For instance, in Ethiopia, annual topsoil losses of up to 296 metric tons per hectare have been recorded on relatively steep slopes. Even in countries with somewhat moderate slopes, erosion can proceed rapidly where such areas are unprotected by vegetation. In West Africa, losses of 30 to 55 metric tons per hectare have been noted on slopes of only 1 to 2 percent. In regions with unstable sedimentary rock formations, such as in southeastern Nigeria, gully erosion devastates a considerable area of land. Wind erosion is also significant in drier, marginal lands close to the deserts.

Urban pollution. Urban pollution represents an increasing feature of cities and metropolitan areas in developing countries. It begins with the difficult shelter conditions of squatter settlements, which consist of makeshift huts on land to which the poor have no ownership rights and which usually lack adequate water supply and sanitation facilities. Air pollution becomes a serious concern in such areas. The dependence of the poor on biomass fuels for cooking and other domestic uses increases the concentration of suspended particulates, which often reach levels that exceed World Health Organization (WHO) standards in areas where the poor are concentrated. The need of the poor for cheap means of transport within urban areas has encouraged the proliferation of highly polluting transportation modes such as single-stroke engine motorcycles. Poorly maintained secondhand vehicles heighten the level of air pollution in most cities of developing countries.

Water pollution. Contaminated drinking water transmits diseases such as diarrhea, typhoid, and cholera. In developing countries, diarrheal diseases are believed to have killed about 3 million children annually in the early 1990s and 1 million adults and children older than 5 years annually in the mid-1980s. The lack of solid waste management in squatter settlements is also visibly disturbing. These areas generally receive minimal garbage collection service or none at all. For example, in 1993, in Dhaka, Bangladesh, 90 percent of the slum areas did not have regular garbage collection services. The problems resulting from such conditions are obvious—odors, disease vectors, pests that are attracted to garbage (including rats, mosquitoes, and flies), and the overflowing drainage channels clogged with garbage. Leachate from decomposing and putrefying garbage contaminates water sources. Because the poorest areas of cities are generally those that receive the fewest sanitation services, the uncollected solid wastes usually include a significant proportion of fecal matter.

Water pollution is also a serious problem in areas where farmers have been given fertilizers and pesticides to increase agricultural productivity. In India, pollution caused by the leaching of nitrogen fertilizers has been detected in the ground water in many areas. In parts of India's Haryana State, for example, well water with nitrate concentrations ranging from 114 milligrams per liter (mg/L) to 1,800 mg/L (far above the 45 mg/L national standard) have been reported. Pesticides that governments have supplied to peasant farmers contaminate sources of ground water, endanger local water supplies, and pollute aquatic systems. Indeed, according to a 1990 estimate published by WHO, occupational pesticide poisoning may affect as many as 25 million people, or 3 percent of the agricultural workforce each year in developing countries. In Africa alone, where some 80 percent of the populace is involved in agriculture, as many as 11 million cases of acute pesticide exposures occur each year.

Climate change. The melting snows of Kilimanjaro provide dramatic evidence that climate change is already affecting the Earth. The Third Assessment Report of the Intergovernmental Panel on Climate Change projects that African countries are especially vulnerable to climate change because much of its agriculture is rain-fed, and it experiences a high frequency of droughts and floods. In particular, grain yields are projected to decline. Coastal settlements in such regions as Egypt, southeastern Africa, the Gulf of Guinea, Senegal, and Gambia will be affected by rising sea levels and coastal erosion. All over the world, the range of infectious disease will likely increase, and significant extinctions of plant and animal species are projected. Desertification is expected to worsen, and most importantly, the numbers and impact of extreme droughts and floods are expected to grow. All of these projections are made worse by the limited ability of the poor to adapt to climate change. ●

Questions for Writing About Globalization

1. What is globalization? Define the main elements or aspects of globalization and, using information from the articles and your experience, give examples of each.

2. What are the positive and negative aspects of globalization? Use evidence from the articles and your experience to support your ideas.

3. Using evidence from at least three articles, discuss whether being part of the international trade system helps individuals and small communities in the developing world.

4. How does globalization affect cultural traditions? Use evidence from the articles and your experience to support your ideas.

5. How does globalization affect the environment? Use evidence from the articles and your experience to support your ideas.

6. Should developing countries be forced to protect the environment even though the countries that are already wealthy, the United States and Europe, didn't protect the environment as they developed? Use evidence from the articles and your experience to support your ideas.

7. Should workers in developing countries be paid the same wages as those in developed countries? Use evidence from the articles and your experience to support your ideas.

8. What responsibilities do transnational corporations have toward the people, culture, and environment in the countries where they establish connections? Use evidence from the articles and your experience to support your ideas.

More Questions for Writing About Globalization

This theme can be expanded by considering some of the questions below. You can use the Additional Resources on Globalization on the *Sourcework* website and other sources of your own.

- What is fair trade and is it a realistic option?
- How can cultural diversity be preserved in the face of a spreading global monoculture?
- What is sustainable development and how does it protect local cultures and environments?
- How can micro-credit lending systems and cooperatives help small businesses in developing countries?
- What effect has globalization had on women's rights and opportunities in both developing and developed countries?

NOTE: To practice in-class writing on the Globalization theme, see the *Sourcework* website at http://esl.college.hmco.com/students.

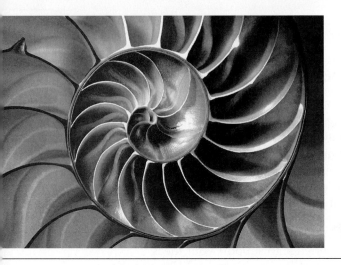

Nonviolent Social Change:

Working for a Better World

You must become the change you want to see. —*Mahatma Gandhi*

You must do the thing you think you cannot do. —*Eleanor Roosevelt*

Only a small group of dedicated citizens can change the world; indeed, it's the only thing that ever has. —*Margaret Mead*

How wonderful it is that nobody need wait a single moment before starting to improve the world. —*Anne Frank*

We must find an alternative to violence. The eye for an eye philosophy leaves everyone blind. —*Martin Luther King Jr.*

Getting Started

The quotations above are comments made by individuals who have written about and worked toward changes in society. To begin thinking about the topic of social change, choose one of the quotations, find out something about the person who said it, and explain to the class what you think it means.

Introduction to the Theme

Most of us want a better world. However, we may differ on just what "better" means and on how to achieve the kind of world we want. Therefore, many attempts to create a better world involve violent conflict, in which one group forces change on another in the form of war or conquest. Yet history also includes a record of nonviolent changes which have, in fact, been more effective and more lasting, and have meant the sacrifice of fewer people.

This unit looks at the place of nonviolent social change in human affairs. The first article, "Are Humans Hard-Wired to Behave Aggressively?" suggests that humans may have a biological tendency toward aggressive behavior. "Primates—A Natural Heritage of Conflict Resolution" argues that peacemaking and aggression work together in both animal and human society. The third selection, "An Experiment in Love," describes the principles behind the philosophy of nonviolence. The fourth article, "Liberation Without War," discusses the conditions that are necessary before nonviolent resistance will work. The last article, "Healing Lessons From Another War-Torn Society—Mozambique," describes how villagers in Mozambique, an African country that has endured years of war, recreate a sense of community, bringing those who have fought against each other back together after the conflict ends. Finally, the video "A Force More Powerful: A Century of Nonviolent Conflict" offers visual accounts of six situations in which change was brought about by nonviolent means.

> **NOTE:** For discussion questions on each article, go to the *Sourcework* website at http://esl.college.hmco.com/students.

Are Humans Hard-Wired to Behave Aggressively?

Margie Wylie
Toronto Star (Canada), March 21, 2003

The Y chromosome could be the culprit in war. But we are in process of getting domesticated.

When technology has made the world smaller than ever, why does mankind still resort to settling international differences with the blunt instrument of war?

The clues may be in our genes. An emerging and controversial branch of science suggests that humans are, at least in part, hard-wired for aggression and other troublesome behaviours.

Many modern problems are caused "simply by doing well what we have evolved to do: garner, consume, be fertile, give to our children, and not look too far ahead," University of Michigan evolutionary ecologist Bobbi S. Low wrote in her book *Why Sex Matters: A Darwinian Look At Human Behavior.*

Harvard anthropologist Richard Wrangham fingers the Y chromosome as the culprit in war.

In his book *Demonic Males: Apes And The Origins Of Human Violence,* Wrangham argues that more aggressive men were the most successful breeders back in our dim evolutionary past.

While females have evolved around the priority of protecting their young, and thus are more risk-averse, "sexual selection has favoured male temperaments that are attracted to high-risk, high-gain ventures," Wrangham said. "That leads to . . . wildness that hikes insurance rates for young men and a greater willingness to risk their lives and the lives of others."

Wrangham bases his work in part on observations of chimpanzees, one of humanity's closest evolutionary cousins. Male chimps fight one another directly for access to females, he says. But they also make group raids into neighbouring clans, killing out-of-group males without provocation or apparent immediate gain. In other words, they wage war.

Of course, the reproductive advantage that conferred on human males thousands of years ago has disappeared in modern society. Why, then, does the behaviour persist?

Low explains that the behaviours evolution favoured tended to offer "secondary rewards"—that is, they felt good, and still do. This unties the impulse from its survival purpose: young men don't drive recklessly because it ensures more offspring; they do it because it feels good.

Geneticists have just begun to link DNA sequences to certain behaviours. So far, it's been slow going.

"Behaviours are at least 50 per cent or so non-genetic, and of the genetic contribution, it's probably spread between many, many different genes," Dean H. Hamer, a behavioural geneticist told the recent Future of Life Conference.

Critics, meanwhile, say these scientists vastly overestimate the pull of genes on behaviour.

"The whole idea that aggression is somehow ingrained in our genes is pure hogwash," said Stanford biologist Paul R. Ehrlich, who wrote *Human Natures: Genes, Cultures and the Human Prospect* as a counterpoint to the growing chorus of voices supporting genetic theories.

"There's absolutely no data to indicate that more aggressive people have more offspring than others," he said. In primates, in fact, "sneaky males" who skirt confrontations to mate surreptitiously "do just as good or better than the aggressive ones."

Ehrlich favours an environmental explanation of behaviour.

Others worry that genetic theories offer a convenient excuse to give in to badness. Why try to find answers to war or even crime if our genes make us do it?

The scientists respond that humans are more than automatons.

Harvard economist Terry Burnham, co-author of *Mean Genes: From Sex To Money To Food, Taming Our Primal Instincts,* argues that the influence of those genes is strong enough that we can't hope to overcome it by willpower alone. The answer is to create structures that channel our tendencies in ways that benefit us.

"Humans are built to kill each other in certain settings," Burnham said. "If you want to prevent killing, as I do, then you need to engineer a world that doesn't lead people to murder and war."

Wrangham agreed.

In Bonbono monkeys, he said, females keep male aggression in check by travelling in packs and defending one another. While he doesn't suggest women do the same, he thinks they could use the ballot box to shift foreign policy.

But waiting for evolution to breed out our bad traits can take a long time.

Bonbono monkeys, famous for their loving societies, split off from chimpanzees some 2.5 million years ago, Wrangham said; biologists guess they evolved their peaceful leanings only about 10,000 years ago.

So, if evolution is dealing its hand too slowly, why not speed things up by engineering out warlike tendencies?

Not likely, said Hamer. For one thing, "gene therapy has not yet worked in the simplest case of replacing a gene in an adult individual," he remarked at the conference. Even if we had the technology, genes that affect behaviour tend to affect multiple behaviours at once. For example, he said, "the same gene that causes some people to be anxious and depressed and moody is also a gene that, if you take it away, makes people much less interested in sex."

But there is some hope. Wrangham argues in an upcoming book that humans have made evolutionary strides toward being less aggressive, at least inside groups.

Domesticated animals, bred for docility, have as much as a quarter less brain mass than their wild cousins, he said. And the peaceful Bonbonos have brains about 10 percent smaller than their fierce chimpanzee cousins.

Not coincidentally, Wrangham said, modern humans have lost about 10 per cent of their brain mass in the last 30,000 years. While most biologists explain the difference by body size—ancient humans had larger bodies and thus larger brains—Wrangham thinks we're simply in the process of domesticating ourselves.

"We couldn't possibly live in big cities if we were chimps. We'd attack each other all the time," he said. "We are species that are learning to control our violent behaviour, at least inside groups." ●

Primates—A Natural Heritage of Conflict Resolution

Frans B.M. de Waal
Science, April 28, 2000 Vol. 289 Issue 5479

The traditional notion of aggression as an antisocial instinct is being replaced by a framework that considers it a tool of competition and negotiation. When survival depends on mutual assistance, the expression of aggression is constrained by the need to maintain beneficial relationships. Moreover, evolution has produced ways of countering its disruptive consequences. For example, chimpanzees kiss and embrace after fights, and other nonhuman primates engage in similar "reconciliations." Theoretical developments in this field carry implications for human aggression research. From families to high schools, aggressive conflict is subject to the same constraints known of cooperative animal societies. It is only when social relationships are valued that one can expect the full complement of natural checks and balances.

Implications for Human Behavior

Ironically, research on how animals spontaneously make up after fights was for a long time ahead of how humans accomplish the same goals. This situation is rapidly changing, though, now that basic human research in this area is gathering steam, with some research shifting focus from aggression to conflict, negotiation, and compromise. For example, projects are under way in several countries to measure the development of conciliatory behavior in children.

The same ethological observation techniques developed for animals are applicable to children in the schoolyard or other settings of unstructured activity. Among preschoolers, two forms of conflict resolution have been noticed: peaceful associative outcomes, in which both opponents stay together and work things out on the spot, and friendly reunions between former opponents after temporary distancing. These two complementary forms of child reconciliation, expressed in play invitations, body contacts, verbal apologies, object offers, self-ridicule, and the like, have been found to reduce aggression, decrease stress-related agitation (such as jumping up and down), and increase tolerance. The striking similarity of these findings to those on nonhuman primates suggests causal, as well as functional, parallels. One of the single best predictors of peacemaking is positive contact between children before eruption of the conflict, suggesting a concern with the continuity and integrity of interactions with peers.

Preference for integrative versus confrontational solutions to conflict is different for children from different cultural backgrounds. For example, Kalmyk and Russian children hold hands after fights while reciting mirilka, or peacemaking rhymes such as, "Make peace, make peace, don't fight; if you fight, I'll bite, and we can't bite since we're friends." Recent reviews of the literature on child conflict resolution stress the same themes as the primate literature, such as how friendship increases conciliatory tendency and how peacemaking skills are acquired through interaction with peers and siblings. An impoverished social environment (as in the homeless) deprives children of this essential aspect of socialization, causing deficits in conflict management and moral development. With the recent interest in conflict resolution at schools, there is a great need for basic information about how children behave among peers. Conflict resolution programs will need to be evaluated against behavioral change. This will require observational techniques not unlike those applied in the above primate studies complemented with attention to the unique role of language.

In human adults, the topic of peacemaking is less well studied. The little systematic research that exists confirms that, rather than the rate and intensity of open conflict, it is the way conflict is being handled and resolved that matters most, for example, for marriage stability. There also exist cross-cultural comparisons that indicate how in human society reconciliation has been institutionalized, elaborated on, ritualized, and surrounded with a great many societal influences, such as the role of elders, conciliatory feasts, and compensatory payments. Peacemaking is a universal human preoccupation: some societies, such as the Malayan Semai, say that they fear a dispute more than they fear a tiger. No wonder that the Semai's becharaa'—an assembly of the disputants, their relatives, and the rest of the community—is opened by lengthy monologues in which the elders emphasize the mutual dependency within the community and the need to maintain harmony.

People everywhere seem to follow the relational model by taking overlapping interests into account when facing conflict, even at the international level. The European Community was founded on the premise that the best way to bring the parties together after World War II, and to ensure a peaceful future, was to promote economic ties, hence to raise the cost of damage to these relationships.

The conclusion from this growing area of research is that human aggressive conflict is best understood as an integral part of the social network. It operates within a set of constraints as old as the evolution of cooperation in the animal kingdom. Certain forms of aggression, such as warfare and random shootings, fall outside this framework, but the majority of aggression arises within the face-to-face group or family. It is this context that shaped human social psychology for millions of years, including both discordant and integrative social tendencies. And so, in a time when Lorenz's message about the dark side of human nature still finds an echo in popular writings about nonhuman primates, other research is increasingly taking a perspective that includes the social impact of conflict, and how that impact is being buffered. Without denying the human heritage of aggression and violence, this research demonstrates an equally old heritage of countermeasures that protect cooperative arrangements against the undermining effects of competition. ●

Living Links, Center for the Advanced Study of Human and Ape Evolution, Yerkes Regional Primate Research Center, and Psychology Department, Emory University, Atlanta, GA 30322, USA. E-mail: dewaal@emory.edu

An Experiment in Love

Martin Luther King, Jr.
A Testament of Hope: The Essential Writings of Martin Luther King, Jr. (*edited by James Melvin Washington. 1986, San Francisco: Harper & Row Publishers*)

King relied heavily on the systematic analysis of the Christian concept of "love" in the work of Anders Nygren, a noted Swedish theologian. In his important study titled Agape and Eros *(1953), Nygren argued that the New Testament concept of love, transliterated from the Greek as "agape," is the most powerful creative force in the universe. It is God's love for humanity. According to Nygren, "Agape does not recognize value, but creates it. Agape loves and imparts value by loving. The man who is loved by God has not value in himself, what gives him value is precisely the fact that God loves him." Paul Tillich, on the other hand, argued quite correctly that the New Testament defines love in terms of eros as well as agape. King, a Tillichian scholar, overlooks critical discussions of Nygren's interpretation, and actually misinterprets Nygren's view at a number of points. But, as Harold Bloom is fond of saying, every translation and interpretation involves some degree of "misprison." That is, it involves some creative form of often unintentional misinterpretation. Fortunately, King's interpretation both of the New Testament concept of love and Nygren's analysis of it introduced a fresh application of the concept from the standpoint of Christian social ethics when he argues in this article that "Agape is a willingness to go to any length to restore community."*

From the beginning a basic philosophy guided the movement. This guiding principle has since been referred to variously as nonviolent resistance, noncooperation, and passive resistance. But in the first days of the protest none of these expressions was mentioned: the phrase most often heard was "Christian love." It was the Sermon on the Mount, rather than a doctrine of passive resistance, that initially inspired the Negroes of Montgomery to dignified social action. It was Jesus of Nazareth that stirred the Negroes to protest with the creative weapon of love.

As the days unfolded, however, the inspiration of Mahatma Gandhi began to exert its influence. I had come to see early that the Christian doctrine of love operating through the Gandhian method of nonviolence was one of the most potent weapons available to the Negro in his struggle for freedom. About a week after the protest started, a white woman who understood and sympathized with the Negroes' efforts wrote a letter to the editor of the *Montgomery Advertiser* comparing the bus protest with the Gandhian movement in India. Miss Juliette Morgan, sensitive and frail, did not long survive the rejection and condemnation of the white community, but long after she died in the summer of 1957 the name of Mahatma Gandhi was well known in Montgomery. People who had never heard of the little brown saint of India were now saying his name with an air of familiarity. Nonviolent resistance had emerged as the technique of the movement, while love stood as the regulating ideal. In other words, Christ furnished the spirit and motivation, while Gandhi furnished the method.

One of the glories of the Montgomery movement was that Baptists, Methodists, Lutherans, Presbyterians, Episcopalians, and others all came together with a willingness to transcend denominational lines. Although no Catholic priests were actively involved in the protest, many of their parishioners took part. All joined hands in the bond of Christian love. Thus the mass meetings accomplished on Monday and Thursday nights what the Christian Church had failed to accomplish on Sunday mornings.

In my weekly remarks as president of the resistance committee, I stressed that the use of violence in our struggle would be both impractical and immoral. To meet hate with retaliatory hate would do nothing but intensify the existence of evil in the universe. Hate begets hate; violence begets violence; toughness begets a greater toughness. We must meet the forces of hate with the power of love; we must meet physical force with soul free. Our aim must never be to defeat or humiliate the white man, but to win his friendship and understanding.

In a real sense, Montgomery's Negroes showed themselves willing to grapple with a new approach to the crisis in race relations. It is probably true that most of them did not believe in nonviolence as a philosophy of life, but because of their confidence in their leaders and because nonviolence was presented to them as a simple expression of Christianity in action, they were willing to use it as a technique. Admittedly, nonviolence in the truest sense is not a strategy that one uses simply because it is expedient at the moment; nonviolence is ultimately a way of life that men live by because of the sheer morality of its claim. But even granting this, the willingness to use nonviolence as a technique is a step forward. For he who goes this far is more likely to adopt nonviolence later as a way of life.

It must be emphasized that nonviolent resistance is not a method for cowards; it does resist. If one uses this method because he is afraid or merely because he lacks the instruments of violence, he is not truly nonviolent. This is why Gandhi often said that if cowardice is the only alternative to violence, it is better to fight. He made this statement conscious of the fact that there is always another alternative: no individual or people need submit to any wrong, nor need they use violence to right that wrong; there is the way of nonviolent resistance. This is ultimately the way of the strong man. It is not a method of stagnant passivity. The phrase "passive resistance" often gives the false impression that this is a sort of "do-nothing method" in which the resister quietly and passively accepts evil. But nothing is further from the truth. For while the nonviolent resister is passive in the sense that he is not physically aggressive toward his opponent, his mind and emotions are always active, constantly seeking to persuade his opponent that he is wrong. The method is passive physically but strongly active spiritually. It is not passive non-resistance to evil, it is active nonviolent resistance to evil.

A second basic fact that characterizes nonviolence is that it does not seek to defeat or humiliate the opponent, but to win his friendship and understanding. The nonviolent resister must often express his protest through noncooperation or boycotts, but he realizes that these are not ends themselves; they are merely means to awaken a sense of moral shame in the opponent. The end is redemption and reconciliation. The aftermath of nonviolence is the creation of the beloved community, while the aftermath of violence is tragic bitterness.

A third characteristic of this method is that the attack is directed against forces of evil rather than against persons who happen to be doing the evil. It is evil that the nonviolent resister seeks to defeat, not the persons victimized by evil. If he is opposing racial injustice, the nonviolent resister has the vision to see that the basic tension is not between races. As I like to say to the people in Montgomery: "The tension in this city is not between white people and Negro people. The tension is, at bottom, between justice and injustice, between the forces of light and the forces of darkness. And if there is a victory, it will be a victory not merely for fifty thousand Negroes, but a victory for justice and the forces of light. We are out to defeat injustice and not white persons who may be unjust."

A fourth point that characterizes nonviolent resistance is a willingness to accept suffering without retaliation, to accept blows from the opponent without striking back. "Rivers of blood may have to flow before we gain our freedom, but it must be our blood," Gandhi said to his countrymen. The nonviolent resister is willing to accept violence if necessary, but never to inflict it. He does not seek to dodge jail. If going to jail is necessary, he enters it "as a bridegroom enters the bride's chamber."

One may well ask: "What is the nonviolent resister's justification for this ordeal to which he invites men, for this mass political application of the ancient doctrine of turning the other cheek?" The answer is found in the realization that unearned suffering is redemptive. Suffering, the nonviolent resister realizes, has tremendous educational and transforming possibilities. "Things of fundamental importance to people are not secured by reason alone, but have to be purchased with their suffering," said Gandhi. He continues: "Suffering is infinitely more powerful than the law of the jungle for converting the opponent and opening his ears which are otherwise shut to the voice of reason."

A fifth point concerning nonviolent resistance is that it avoids not only external physical violence but also internal violence of spirit. The nonviolent resister not only refuses to shoot his opponent but he also refuses to hate him. At the center of nonviolence stands the principle of love. The nonviolent resister would contend that in the struggle for human dignity, the oppressed people of the world must not succumb to the temptation of becoming bitter or indulging in hate campaigns. To retaliate in kind would do nothing but intensify the existence of hate in the universe. Along the way of life, someone must have sense enough and morality enough to cut off the chain of hate. This can only be done by projecting the ethic of love to the center of our lives.

In speaking of love at this point, we are not referring to some sentimental or affectionate emotion. It would be nonsense to urge men to love their oppressors in an affectionate sense. Love in this connection means understanding, redemptive good will. When we speak of loving those who oppose us, we refer to neither *eros* nor *philia;* we speak of a love which is expressed in the Greek word *agape. Agape* means understanding, redeeming good will for all men. It is an overflowing love which is purely spontaneous, unmotivated, groundless, and creative. It is not set in motion by any quality or function of its object. It is the love of God operating in the human heart.

Agape is disinterested love. It is a love in which the individual seeks not his own good, but the good of his neighbor (I Cor. 10:24). *Agape* does not begin by discriminating between worthy and unworthy people, or any qualities people possess. It begins by loving others *for their sakes.* It is an entirely "neighbor-regarding concern for others," which discovers the neighbor in every man it meets. Therefore, *agape* makes no distinction between friends and enemy; it is directed toward both. If one loves an individual merely on account of his friendliness, he loves him for the sake of the benefits to be gained from the friendship, rather than for the friend's own sake. Consequently, the best way to assure oneself that love is disinterested is to have love for the enemy-neighbor from whom you can expect no good in return, but only hostility and persecution.

Another basic point about *agape* is that it springs from the *need* of the other person—his need for belonging to the best in the human family. The Samaritan who helped the Jew on the Jericho Road was "good" because he responded to the human need that he was presented with. God's love is eternal and fails not because man needs his love. Saint Paul assures us that the loving act of redemption was done "while we were yet sinners"—that is, at the point of our greatest need for love. Since the white man's personality is greatly distorted by segregation, and his soul is greatly scarred, he needs the love of the Negro. The Negro must love the white man, because the white man needs his love to remove his tensions, insecurities, and fears.

Agape is not a weak, passive love. It is love in action. *Agape* is love seeking to preserve and create community. It is insistence on community even when one seeks to break it. *Agape* is a willingness to go to any length to restore community. It doesn't stop at the first mile, but it goes the second mile to restore community. It is a willingness to forgive, not seven times, but seventy times seven to restore community. The cross is the eternal expression of the length to which God will go in order to restore broken community. The resurrection is a symbol of God's triumph over all the forces that seek to block community. The Holy Spirit is the continuing community creating reality that moves through history. He who works against community is working against the whole of creation. Therefore, if I respond to hate with a reciprocal hate I do nothing but intensify the cleavage in broken community. I can only close the gap in broken community by meeting hate with love. If I meet hate with hate, I become depersonalized, because creation is so designed that my personality can only be fulfilled in the context of community. Booker T. Washington was right: "Let no man pull you so low as to make you hate him." When he pulls you that low he brings you to the point of defying creation, and thereby becoming depersonalized.

In the final analysis, *agape* means a recognition of the fact that all life is interrelated. All humanity is involved in a single process, and all men are brothers. To the degree that I harm my brother, no matter what he is doing to me, to that extent I am harming myself. For example, white men often refuse federal aid to education in order to avoid giving the Negro his rights; but because all men are brothers they cannot deny Negro children without harming their own. They end, all efforts to the contrary, by hurting themselves. Why is this? Because men are brothers. If you harm me, you harm yourself.

A sixth basic fact about nonviolent resistance is that it is based on the conviction that the universe is on the side of justice. Consequently, the believer in nonviolence has deep faith in the future. This faith is another reason why the nonviolent resister can accept suffering without retaliation. For he knows that in his struggle for justice he has cosmic companionship. It is true that there are devout believers in nonviolence who find it difficult to believe in a personal God. But even these persons believe in the existence of some creative force that works for universal wholeness. Whether we call it an unconscious process, an impersonal Brahman, or a Personal Being of matchless power and infinite love, there is a creative force in this universe that works to bring the disconnected aspects of reality into a harmonious whole. ●

Liberation Without War

Jack DuVall
Sojourners Magazine, February 2004, Volume 33 Number 2

When the Romans imprisoned the apostle Paul and he was taken to be whipped, Paul asked his captors, "Is it lawful for you to whip a Roman citizen?" So a captain asked him: "Are you a Roman?" Paul answered, "Yes." The captain replied, "It took me a great deal of money to buy my freedom," showing skepticism that Paul—who probably looked like a penniless slave—was a Roman, and therefore free. Paul declared: "I was free born."

Represented in that exchange was a fundamental division in human thinking: between those who believe that only an external agency—money, personal influence, violence—can deliver people from oppression, and those who understand that each individual has the innate right to be free *and* the ability to become free.

Che Guevara, the violent revolutionary, once said: "I am not a liberator. Liberators do not exist. The people liberate themselves." Unfortunately, what the people can do to liberate themselves from tyranny or injustice has received far less attention than what terrorists, conquerors, or charismatic leaders have tried to do.

In many historical cases—such as the emancipation of American slaves during the Civil War, defeating Nazism in World War II, the Cold War with the Soviet Union— leaders saw no alternative to using or threatening military force against armed adversaries. When hostilities ended, relative freedom and peace ensued. And so armed might has been seen as the means of liberation.

When it became apparent in summer 2003 that stability in Iraq had not followed the military ouster of Saddam Hussein, some claimed that civil disorder always accompanied changes to democracy, citing the fall of Eastern European regimes in 1989. But no museums of antiquities were looted in Warsaw or Berlin when civilian-based movements brought down authoritarian governments, nor did chaos reign in Manila when Filipinos chased out a dictator three years before

When nonviolent movements mobilize people to use strikes, boycotts, civil disobedience, and other disruptive tactics—through a strategy to subvert an unjust regime's power—democracy ensues more often than when violence is used. If we disregard the costs of regime change through terror of war, by not comparing them to the risks and opportunities of nonviolent conflict, then we are issuing a blank check to the belief that liberation is always violent.

Terrorists believe that power comes from killing—they are attached to that belief as strongly as many are to their religious beliefs. But even though many people believe that weapons have power, most people who want to fight for their rights or justice are more interested in winning than in being killed—and they will listen to proof that violence is less effective than other methods of struggle.

The logic is this: Those who threaten violence want something from those being threatened. That's a transaction, and each party to a transaction has leverage. If you refuse to give me what I want, even if I threaten you with violence, I cannot succeed unless I can pay the cost of ending your resistance. A civilian-based nonviolent movement succeeds when it drives up the cost of suppressing the people to the point that a regime's defenders are unwilling or unable to pay it.

This process is deliberate and systematic. First, a movement's members must set aside their partisan, ethnic, or ideological differences and unify behind the goal of liberating the country from its oppressors. Then the movement has to reduce civilians' fear of participating by first using nonviolent tactics entailing less physical risk, such as not paying taxes, work stay-aways, and commercial boycotts. This broadens a movement's base, as it recruits people who won't be violent but still want to act. Distributing the scope of resistance beyond the capital also strains the regime's outermost, least reliable agents.

The movement also has to challenge the regime's legitimacy. Tactics that tempt repression can force rulers to discredit themselves in the world's eyes. That takes nonviolent discipline, to crystallize the meaning of the choice between the regime and the opposition.

Then more disruptive actions, such as a general strike or larger demonstrations, can be sequenced to make it hard for an oppressor to maintain the semblance of control. When it's clear that nothing will be normal until the regime changes, even the military will begin to doubt the intelligence of endless obedience.

Finally, the movement has to anticipate repression and perhaps be ready to settle for intermediate goals, until its own strength is sufficient—it has to know when to buy time and when to reach for victory.

We are talking, of course, about staging a revolution. Thomas Jefferson believed that when a bad government could not be reformed, the people had a "right of revolution." He lived when nonviolent action was almost unknown as a political strategy, but he believed so strongly in the people's prerogatives that he countenanced the idea of violent revolt. Having no attachment to violence, Jefferson, if he lived today, would embrace this right of bloodless resistance. And he would see its relationship to producing government genuinely based on the people's consent.

Mohandas Gandhi often invoked the biblical maxim that "as you sow, so shall you reap,"—that your achievement will reflect your methods. The history that Gandhi helped launch has confirmed that truth:

- In the 1960s, African-Americans used sit-ins and marches to pull apart racial segregation—yielding more tolerance and justice, imperfect as it is, than seemed possible beforehand.
- In Poland in 1980, workers used strikes to win the right to organize a free trade union, galvanizing the people to insist on fuller rights. When Solidarity took power, no one died.
- In South Africa in the 1980s, blacks in townships and factories used boycotts and strikes until apartheid lost the support of business and outside interests, compelling a new president to negotiate.
- In Serbia in 2000, a dictator was unseated after a nonviolent campaign liquefied the loyalty of the military—who refused his orders. Then a new, democratically chosen president took power.

"Nonviolence" may be a preferable form of behavior, but nonviolent action isn't effective unless it is driven by a strategy to take power. Gandhi did not want to make peace with the British. He incited a conflict in order to force them out of India.

Some think the Indians prevailed because the British were gentlemen (as if the Amritsar massacre hadn't happened). But that mistaken view reinforces another misconception: that violent oppressors can only be defeated with more violence. Yet there is no historical correlation between the degree of a regime's brutality and its hold on power. Everyone believed that Saddam Hussein was impregnable because he'd kill anyone who dissented. So most Iraqis were afraid to act. However, the fear of action does not mean that action, once taken, will fail.

In 2002, an Iraqi opponent of Saddam said he liked nonviolent resistance, but that Saddam was like Stalin—therefore it wasn't possible. He was asked what would happen if 5,000 people demonstrated in Baghdad. He said they'd all be shot. What if 20,000 should demonstrate? Same result, though much bloodier, he said. But what if 100,000 Iraqis should protest, demanding that Saddam go? He hesitated. Well, if that happened, he said, then things might go differently. Why? Because if that many Iraqis were determined to resist, the dictator's defenders would realize that fear as an instrument of power no longer worked—that Saddam had lost control of the country. Suddenly an impervious regime had been reduced in this Iraqi's mind to a strategic problem.

Fortunately, there is a proven way to capsize murderous regimes: strategic, civilian-based resistance. But we can no longer afford to wait for indigenous movements to engage in the trial-and-error process of locally reinventing nonviolent struggle and overcoming their oppressors. We have to help them succeed.

They don't need enormous subsidies, and they don't need Americans parachuting in to tell them what to do. Only indigenous movements have the legitimacy necessary to rally popular support. But to outmaneuver tyrants, many need training in the strategies of nonviolent action as well as better information technology. A nongovernmental, international body—not serving any nation's interests, but pooling resources from many—should provide this help.

In the meantime, governments must ratchet up pressure on such regimes. For example, Burma's military junta, which imprisoned the Nobel Prize-winning leader of its nonviolent opposition, still gets help from India, China, other Asian nations, and Western corporations doing business with Burma. Other dictatorships are also fortified by our detachment and our trade. Political oppression anywhere is now everyone's business, because the violence it breeds can appear anywhere.

Just as St. Paul understood that his freedom was God-given, a natural right, the world is coming to acknowledge that rights are not conferred by states—they must be honored by states because they belong to individuals. Eventually it will be accepted everywhere that each person's rights come before any ruler's will and that no government is legitimate unless it is based on the people's consent.

The day when that becomes a universal fact will not arrive until the world realizes that rights are won more surely by the people than by terrorists or armies. To make nonviolent struggle the global boulevard to political liberation, we must relentlessly propagate the ideas and strategies that pave its way to victory. Former president Jimmy Carter has said that "nonviolent valor can end oppression." But not until we all enlist to help the valiant. ●

Healing Lessons From Another War-Torn Society—Mozambique

Helena Cobban
Christian Science Monitor May 8, 2003

After the guns of war fall silent, what happens to the people whose main role during the war was to be professional fighters? This is an important challenge for US communities as they welcome back soldiers previously deployed in Iraq.

I came to this small town in southern Mozambique to discuss this with a group of men brought together by an organization of people who had fought—on both sides—in the civil war that ravaged this sprawling, ocean-side country from 1976 through 1992.

We perched on a circle of chairs set outside the local office of a human rights group. Participants included two rights activists, four men who had fought in the civil war, and a traditional healer. They all stressed that communities need to take special steps to reintegrate community members who return home after participation in, or close exposure to, a war.

Jorge Moine, the healer, explained that when a community member returns from war, his or her parents would traditionally sit by a holy tree, and ask the family's ancestors for guidance on reintegrating the returning one. Then there would be special ceremonies to "cleanse" the former fighter of the taint of war before he would be allowed back into the home.

"Some people might do traditional ceremonies. Others might go to a church and say a special mass for this purpose," he said. But one way or another, the transition from wartime behavior to peacetime behavior should be meaningfully marked.

During Mozambique's war, around a million of this impoverished country's 16 million citizens were killed, 5 million were displaced, and numerous shocking atrocities were committed. Despite that violence and upheaval, once the government and the insurgent Mozambique National Resistance (RENAMO) concluded a peace agreement in October 1992, the country rapidly returned to peace. And the peace has proven robust ever since.

How did Mozambique achieve this? Even throughout the civil war, it retained many strong cultural resources for peacemaking and conflict resolution. The ancient traditions of the 16 or so different language groups were one such resource—as were many of its Christian churches.

Churches played an important role throughout the process of making and then consolidating the peace. The first contacts between the government and RENAMO leaders were brokered by local Christian leaders, and the 17 months of negotiations were hosted—in Rome—by a Catholic lay organization, Sant'Egidio. During negotiations, numerous members of the clergy and traditional healers worked in their different ways to prepare the population for the transition to peace.

How did these community leaders help individual Mozambicans deal with the sense of hurt that arose from the atrocities committed during the war? In other countries, such acts would likely have led to calls for revenge—or at least for post-war punishment. In Mozambique, most community leaders met the desire for retribution by explaining that the heinous acts had been committed in the extraordinary circumstances of war, but that with peace, the rules that govern "normal," peaceful life would come back into operation. Wartime atrocities were thus attributed much more to the social breakdown of war itself, rather than to intentional acts undertaken by specific individuals.

I asked the group here if they thought people who'd committed bad acts during the war should be punished.

"If you did that, the whole of Mozambique should have been punished!" one combat veteran replied.

"War is war," another explained. "Everything that happens in war is violent. You can't pick out certain parts of it as worse than the rest."

I found such views expressed by nearly all the people I talked to during two weeks of intensive discussions of this issue. Only one or two of the 30 or so Mozambicans I heard from expressed any concern that the general amnesty, for war-era atrocities included in the 1992 peace agreement may have fostered a climate of "impunity" for former perpetrators.

Many Western rights activists believe that when wars end, all atrocities committed during them should be prosecuted in war-crimes courts. But these activists should pay attention to the fact that in Mozambique in 1992—as in South Africa—it was only an offer of amnesty for former atrocities that allowed a period of conflict and gross rights-abuse to end.

Another lesson Westerners might take from Mozambique is the care people here take to reintegrate former combatants into normal society once the war has ended. The US "discovered" posttraumatic stress disorder in the 1970s. But Mozambique's indigenous leaders have been paying special attention for centuries to the sensitive transition individuals have to make when they exit the war zone and return to peaceful society.

That transition, Mozambicans believe, requires not only the rituals that mark it clearly, but also solid help in connecting former soldiers to productive work and normal family life.

The programs designed to help this happen were far from perfect. But still, 92,000 former combatants from both sides were demobilized—and the peace agreement has sunk remarkably strong roots in the past 10 years.

People who want to see how societies can escape endless cycles of violence can learn a lot by studying Mozambique: an African country that has done just that. ●

A Force More Powerful:
A Century of Nonviolent Conflict (Video)

Steven York (writer and producer)
Produced by York Zimmerman, Inc. 1999

About the video

This video shows six examples of nonviolent social changes:

- Civil Rights Movement in the United States, 1958–1968
- Indian Independence Movement, 1933–1948
- Movement to End Apartheid in South Africa, 1985–1994
- Resistance to German occupation in Denmark, 1940
- Polish Labor Movement, 1980
- The struggle against Pinochet in Chile, 1983. ●

Questions for Writing About Nonviolent Social Change

1. Choose one section of the video and write a review of it, in which you describe what happens and tell whether you think it presents an effective argument for using nonviolence.
2. Which has been more important in human evolution—the tendency to resolve conflicts with violence or with peaceful reconciliation? Use evidence from the articles along with your view of human nature to support your opinion.
3. Martin Luther King, Jr. describes six characteristics of nonviolent resistance. Analyze a historical conflict that was resolved peacefully and discuss how each of the characteristics was revealed in that situation. You can choose one of the events in the video or any other event you know about from any part of the world.
4. When is nonviolence an effective strategy? Use evidence from the articles along with your view of human nature to support your ideas.
5. Choose a conflict that you know something about that is now happening somewhere in the world. Do you see a way that nonviolence could be used in that conflict? Why or why not? Use evidence from the articles and other sources to support your ideas.
6. Choose a personal conflict you have witnessed or been involved in. Do you see a way that nonviolence could be used to resolve that conflict? Use evidence from the articles along with your view of human nature to support your opinion.
7. Is war inevitable? Use evidence from the articles along with your view of human nature to support your ideas.

More Questions for Writing About Nonviolent Social Change

This theme can be expanded by writing about any of the questions that follow or by exploring Additional Resources on Nonviolent Social Change on the *Sourcework* website. In some cases, you may need to find additional sources of your own.

* Choose a conflict in history that was resolved without violence and trace the causes and the resolution of the problem. Why did nonviolence succeed in that case?
* What do veterans, those who have actually fought in wars, think about the effectiveness of violence versus nonviolence? Interview as many veterans from a variety of wars as possible and describe their views. Use published sources to strengthen your conclusions.
* Are some cultures more violent than others? Compare the beliefs about and practice of violence in two cultures you are familiar with.
* Both terrorists and nonviolent resisters are revolutionaries who use extreme tactics to try to force social change. What similarities and differences do you see between these two groups who want to change society?

NOTE: To practice in-class writing on the Nonviolent Social Change theme, see the *Sourcework* website at http://esl.college.hmco.com/students.

Bioethics:

When Science and Values Collide

"Science is often perceived to be an objective, analytical, and rational endeavor unaffected by morals and value. However, far from occurring in a social vacuum, I believe that science and especially medical science, is a human endeavor, the practice of which is influenced by our political, cultural, religious, and ethical values." —*Vaille Dawson, 1996 (Capra, 1983; Charlesworth, Farral, Stokes and Turnbull, 1989)*

Getting Started

Below are two examples of the kinds of issues that arise when the pursuit of science and application of technology come into conflict with human life in day to day situations. Read each situation and consider your opinion about them.

Huntington's disease dilemma

Mr. F, a 42-year-old man, and George, his 21-year-old son, come to a genetic testing center for advice. George wants to be tested for the gene associated with Huntington's disease, a progressive, fatal, inherited brain disorder that usually strikes its victims in middle age. There is a 50 percent chance that Mr. F has inherited the gene for Huntington's disease and, if so, a 50 percent chance he has passed it along to his son George. Mr. F doesn't yet show symptoms of the disease and he doesn't want to be tested. He prefers to live his life and make decisions without knowing whether or not he has the gene. George, on the other hand, wants to know if he has inherited the gene so he can plan his life accordingly.

If George gets tested and is found to carry the gene for Huntington's disease, his father, Mr. F, must also carry the gene. The two men agree that, given their close relationship, it would be impossible for George to keep his secret from his father.

Does George have a right to know whether or not he carries a disease gene even if it interferes with his father's wish not to know his genetic status?

Buying and Selling Organs

Jessica B, a 10-year-old girl from a wealthy American family, is suffering from liver disease. Her condition would be greatly improved with a liver transplant. Without one, she will die. She has been on a waiting list for a liver donation for a year, but her condition is deteriorating. It is likely that she will die before she reaches the top of the waiting list. In the United States, organ transplantation is gift-based. That is, organs can not be sold legally. All organ donation is done voluntarily. Jessica's parents have discovered an attorney who would locate and contact a person who is willing to give up part of his liver for a payment. The attorney would also be able to make arrangements with a hospital that would accept the organ as a voluntary gift with Jessica designated as the recipient.

1. Do you think Jessica's parents should be allowed to pay to obtain a liver for their daughter?
2. Are there some situations in which you think buying and selling organs would be okay and other situations in which it wouldn't?

Introduction to the Theme

Our decisions about how we use scientific knowledge are influenced by our values and what we believe is ethical. Thus, for example, the ability to transplant an organ from one human to another is scientifically possible, but decisions about how this process is carried out are based on our beliefs about what is right or wrong. It is our values that lead us to decide who will donate organs, how they will be donated, and who will receive them.

In the past 30 years, a field of study called *bioethics* has emerged in an effort to address some of the ethical issues that arise when applying scientific knowledge. Bioethicists, those who work in bioethics, have attempted to develop common guidelines to use when making decisions about the ethical use of scientific knowledge.

Bioethics is an effort to bridge the gap between available scientific information and our use of that knowledge in our daily lives. The first three articles in this unit, "Controversial Transplant a Success," "It's Aids, *not* Tuskegee: Inflammatory Comparisons Won't Save Lives in Africa" and "Bioethics for Clinicians: 20. Chinese Bioethics," offer case studies of current bioethical issues.

The fourth article, "Birth to Death: Science and Bioethics," discusses the gap between science and values and presents the need for a bioethical framework for making ethical decisions. The final article, "Taking Sides: Clashing Views on Bioethical Issues," presents a set of principles for making bioethical decisions. These principles, developed in the late 1970s, provide guidelines for conducting ethical research involving human subjects. Their use has spread to many other areas including the practice of medicine, genetic engineering, the environment, and sociopolitical issues.

A brief summary of each principle follows because these principles are central to the ideas and language that are used in bioethical discussions.

Autonomy The principle of autonomy concerns people's ability to make decisions for themselves based on their own thoughts. This principle suggests that people ought to be able to determine for themselves what is best for them as long as their decision does not harm others.

Beneficence Beneficence means to act in a way that benefits others. It concerns a moral obligation to behave in a way that results in the most good and least harm.

Justice This is the moral obligation to fairness. It implies that people in like circumstances should be treated equally. In other words, our treatment of people or situations, or our decisions about how we will act in a situation must be consistent.

Often, issues of how to use scientific knowledge become controversial because these three principles conflict with each other. Doctors must often decide between respecting their patients' decision (autonomy) and providing the care they believe is most benevolent. In considering the three case studies presented at the beginning of this unit, you may discover that differing opinions about the outcome of each case were a result of the bioethical principles in conflict.

NOTE: For discussion questions on each article, go to the *Sourcework* website at http://esl.college.hmco.com/students.

Case Studies in Bioethics

Case Study 1

Controversial Transplant a Success

Steve Karnowski
Associated Press Online, Oct. 18, 2000

Doctors declared success Wednesday in the groundbreaking case of an ailing 6-year-old girl who received a transplant of umbilical cord blood from her made-to-order baby brother.

Molly Nash of Englewood, Colo., received the blood three weeks ago in hopes it would save her life. The girl suffers from Fanconi anemia, a rare genetic disorder that prevented her body from making bone marrow. Without the transplant, the disease almost certainly would have killed the Englewood, Colorado, girl by age 35, perhaps decades earlier.

Three weeks after the transplant, tests show it is working, and Molly is nearly ready to leave the hospital, said Dr. John Wagner of the University of Minnesota. The infused cells are taking over the functions of Molly's bone marrow, making platelets and disease-fighting white blood cells, Wagner said.

"The bone marrow graft is recovering extremely well," he said. "So we have a success."

The cord blood came from Molly's brother, Adam, a test-tube baby who was born Aug. 29 after his parents genetically screened and selected an embryo to make sure he would be free of Molly's disease and would be a compatible tissue donor.

It was the first known case in which parents created a baby genetically selected to help save a sibling's life.

Molly's quick recovery has elated her parents. Lisa Nash said her daughter loves to dance but hadn't felt like it for around six months, until now.

"The other night she and I were playing in her room, and a song came on and she got on the floor and started dancing," she said. "And that was when we knew that this was the right thing to have done."

Wagner said he expects Molly to be released from the hospital within a week, and doctors will closely follow her over the next two months. While she is not out of the woods, she now has a good chance at a normal life, the doctor said.

Wagner said he hopes Molly's success influences the debate over research using human embryos and helps free up more funding.

"Embryo research could have real benefits to people," Wagner said. "This is just one example of it."

The topic is controversial because fertilized embryos that aren't implanted in a woman's uterus are kept frozen or allowed to die. Pope John Paul II is among those who have attacked the practice of discarding unused embryos.

Jeffrey Kahn, director of the University of Minnesota's Center for Bioethics, acknowledged that genetic screening might be misused but said the Nash case shows how it can be positive.

"A healthy child can also save the life of a sick sibling," he said. "And that's all to the good."

In the Nash case, doctors fertilized 12 of Lisa Nash's eggs, tested 10 of the embryos, selected the one that became Adam, and froze the rest except for one embryo that tested positive for Fanconi anemia, Lisa Nash said.

The Nashes said they believe they did the right thing for their family and for other children with genetic diseases who might benefit from similar procedures, such as patients with sickle-cell anemia.

If Molly is still doing well a year from now, the mother said, the Nashes will use the remaining embryos to try to have more children. ●

Case Study 2

It's AIDS, not *Tuskegee: Inflammatory Comparisons Won't Save Lives in Africa*

David Ho
Time, Sept. 29, 1997

In the current issue of the New England Journal of Medicine, Peter Lurie and Dr. Sidney Wolfe of the advocacy group Public Citizen charge that some U.S.-sponsored *AIDS*-research projects in Africa are unethical. The Journal's editor, Dr. Marcia Angell, goes even further, comparing these studies to the infamous *Tuskegee* experiment in which black men in the South were deliberately deceived and denied effective treatment in order to determine the natural course of syphilis infection. This comparison is *inflammatory* and unfair, and could make a desperate situation even worse.

Doctors in the U.S. have known since 1994 that the drug AZT can substantially reduce the chance of transmission of the *AIDS* virus from an infected woman to her newborn child. Unfortunately, administering AZT to pregnant women is complicated and quite expensive—about $1,000 per mother. That's far beyond the means of most developing countries, where 1,000 newborns are infected each day.

Hoping to find an AZT regimen they could afford, African researchers sought sponsorship from U.S. health agencies and launched a number of scientific studies in which some mothers were given short treatments with AZT and some, for the purpose of comparison, received a placebo. It is the inclusion of these placebo groups that the critics find objectionable. Giving a sugar pill to an *AIDS* patient is considered ethically unacceptable in the U.S. To give one to a pregnant African, Dr. Angell writes, shows a "callous disregard of [a patient's] welfare for the sake of research goals."

These clinical trials, however, were created for Africans, by Africans, with the good of their people in mind and with their informed consent. The studies were designed to be responsive to local needs and to the constraints of each study site. African scientists have argued that it is not in their best interest to include a complicated and costly AZT regimen for the sake of comparison when such a regimen is not only unaffordable but logistically infeasible. They have, instead, opted for a study design that is achievable in practice and is likely to provide lifesaving answers expeditiously, even though it includes a group of women receiving a placebo. While the inclusion of this placebo group would not be acceptable in the U.S., the sad truth is that giving nothing is the current standard of care in Africa.

The ethical debate here is obviously a complex one, without a clear distinction between right and wrong. *Comparisons* to *Tuskegee* don't help; neither does the imposition of Western views, or what Dr. Edward Mbidde of Uganda calls "ethical imperialism." Calm and careful deliberations are in order. Insisting on the infeasible in the name of ethical purity is counterproductive in the struggle to stop this deadly virus. ●

Case Study 3

Bioethics *for Clinicians: 20. Chinese* Bioethics

Kerry W. Bowman and Edwin C. Hui
Canadian Medical Association Journal, Nov. 28, 2000

Mr. *Y* is a 75-year-old Chinese Canadian who has been admitted to an intensive care unit because of respiratory failure. He has a long history of respiratory problems. Mechanical ventilation is started. Mr. *Y* is oriented to time, person and place. He spends much of his time reading and enjoys his family's visits. Attempts to wean him from the ventilator have failed; consequently, he is facing a situation of permanent dependence on the breathing machine. It is unclear as to what Mr. *Y*'s wishes related to this would be. The physician in charge wishes to inform Mr. *Y* that he is unable to get him to a point where he can be taken off the ventilator and wants to introduce the option of gradually weaning him off the ventilator and keeping him comfortable so that nature may take its course and he may die in peace. The patient's eldest son is described to the health care team as "the decision-maker." He approaches the physician and asks emphatically that his father not be told that he is permanently dependent on the ventilator as it would take away his hope, terrify him and, in turn, make him sicker. The son feels that telling his father would be cruel and is therefore unjustifiable.

In the Confucian social hierarchy, the elderly sick person can expect to be cared for by his or her family. The patient is relieved of a large share of personal responsibility, including decision-making, even though he or she may be rational and competent. Furthermore, from a Confucian point of view, which is governed by the rule of filial piety and protection, a parent should not be given the news of a terminal illness; it is considered morally inexcusable to disclose any news that may cause further harm to one's parent.

In the face of serious illness, Mr. *Y*'s family, much like many people of non-Western cultures, believe that focusing on the negative may be a way of creating negative outcomes. His family has made it clear that hope was central to their concern for their father. All societies seem to recognize "the need for hope," yet each differs in understanding the conditions for hope. In contemporary North American health care, the doctor is often perceived to be someone who works in partnership with the terminally ill patient to maintain the patient's dignity, quality of life, personal choice over treatments, and hope. In Western terms, therefore, hope appears to be upheld through autonomy and active treatment choices and regimens.

However, Mr. *Y*'s family believes that hope is best maintained through the family's absorption of the impact of the illness and diagnosis, and through the family's control of medical information transmitted to Mr. *Y*. Their wishes reflect a belief in the shared responsibility of the illness with other family members, and an awareness of the potential physical or emotional harm that truth-telling might bring. The negotiated approach results in asking Mr. *Y* if he would like to receive medical information and be involved in his treatment planning or, as his son has requested, use the son as decision-maker. Mr. *Y* indicates the latter preference. A consultation between the physician and the family takes place. The negotiated treatment plan consists of 2 further days of ventilation and then a gradual withdrawal of ventilation, with supportive care and comfort measures given the highest priority. ●

Bioethics and Bioethical Principles

Birth to Death: Science and Bioethics

David C. Thomasma and Thomasine Kushner (editors)
Cambridge University Press, 1996

Bioethics is not something necessarily esoteric. When you and your loved ones encounter modern medicine and modern care facilities you meet directly what C. P. Snow articulated as the "Clash of two cultures." Scientific culture and human values culture compete for our loyalties daily, but never more so than when we or someone we care for becomes seriously ill or is dying, and needs the assistance of the health care system.

In the personages of physicians, nurses, social workers, therapists, admitting clerks, nursing home administrators, case managers, and all the others we encounter individuals who not only aim for the best interests of the sick, but also represent the scientific culture of modern medicine. Due to the rapid rise of scientific and technological advancement everywhere, and especially in medicine, enormous changes must take place, willy-nilly, in our human values culture, as we call it, whether we like those changes or not. Furthermore, science and technology require rethinking cherished values about the moral status of animals, children, the dying, the mentally compromised, and even those who are healthy and must support the medical care system. Rethinking these cherished values is important because they lead us to examine even more profound assumptions about ourselves. These profound assumptions we can call "second-order" considerations, questions such as what counts as a person either when we have frozen embryos in storage or in parents with advanced Alzheimer's disease, what is personal identity, can animals actually have rights, is there a moral difference at all between animals and humans, what will happen to social values if we try to alter the gene pool, how should we treat "marginal" people, are there duties that cut across generations, and what about the environment in all this?

When we begin to root around in these questions, we enter the realm of what we call "third-order" considerations as well. These lead us to question what sort of ethical system we ought to employ: can we use the virtues we were taught, is a rights-based or principle-based ethics best, are there inalienable rights that must never be violated, do ends justify the means, should utilitarianism be used to resolve conflicts, is there some other ethical theory that might be better, are we to hold conflicting theories together like a collage, using whichever works at the moment (this is called Post-modernism)?

We do not need a degree in medicine, philosophy, or theology to grapple with these issues. After all, what Plato or Aristotle might have to say on any of these topics is interesting, but does not determine to any great extent what behaviors we exhibit as our grandmother slowly loses her edge, or as a child is born prematurely and must be placed in an intensive care unit, or as we invest in the stock of a private nursing home corporation, or as we survey dogs in a pound that, if not chosen by a family, may wind up being used in cardiology research.

In other words, when we confront the medical culture in our daily lives, we are involved in bioethics. We participate in the decisions that mesh our values with those of scientific culture. It is these decisions that are more important than theoretical reflection, since they shape our understanding of other values, and, by doing so, shape us as well. ●

Taking Sides: Clashing Views on Bioethical Issues

Carol Levine (editor)
Guilford, Connecticut: Dushkin/McGraw-Hill: (1999, 8th edition)

Ethical dilemmas in medicine are, of course, nothing new. They have been recognized and discussed in Western medicine since a small group of physicians—led by Hippocrates—on the Isle of Cos in Greece, around the fourth century B.C., subscribed to a code of practice that newly graduated physicians still swear to uphold today. But unlike earlier times, when physicians and scientists had only limited abilities to change the course of disease, today they can intervene in profound ways in the most fundamental processes of life and death. Moreover, ethical dilemmas in medicine are no longer considered the sole province of professionals. Professional codes of ethics, to be sure, offer some guidance, but they are usually unclear and ambiguous about what to do in specific situations. More important, these codes assume that whatever decision is to be made is up to the professional, not the patient. Today, to an ever-greater degree, laypeople—patients, families, lawyers, clergy, and others—want to and have become involved in ethical decision making not only in individual cases but also in large societal decisions, such as how to allocate scarce medical resources, including high-technology machinery, newborn intensive care units, and the expertise of physicians. While questions about the physician-patient relationship and individual cases are still prominent in bioethics, today the field covers a broad range of other decisions as well, such as the use of reproductive technology, the harvesting and transplantation of organs, equity in access to health care, and the future of animal experimentation.

Bioethics began in the 1950s as an intellectual movement among a small group of physicians and theologians who started to examine the questions raised by the new medical technologies that were starting to emerge as the result of the heavy expenditure of public funds in medical research after World War II. They were soon joined by a number of philosophers who had become disillusioned with what they saw as the arid abstractions of much analytic philosophy at the time and by lawyers who sought to find principles in the law that would guide ethical decision making or, if such principles were not there, to develop them by case law and legislation or regulation. Although these four disciplines—medicine, theology, philosophy, and law—still dominate the field, today bioethics is an interdisciplinary effort, with political scientists, economists, sociologists, anthropologists, nurses, allied health professionals, policymakers, psychologists, and others contributing their special perspectives to the ongoing debates.

Ethical Principles

In its four years of deliberation, the National Commission for the Protection of Human Subjects of Biomedical and Behavioral Research grappled with some of the most difficult issues facing researchers and society: When, if ever, is it ethical to do research on fetuses, on children, or on people in mental institutions? This commission—which was composed of people from various religious backgrounds, professions, and social strata—was finally able to agree on specific recommendations on these questions, but only after they had finished their work did the commissioners try to determine what ethical principles they had used in reaching a consensus. In their Belmont Report (1978), named after the conference center where they met to discuss this question, the commissioners outlined what they considered to be the three most important ethical principles (respect for persons, beneficence, and justice) that should govern the conduct of research with human beings. These three principles, they believed, are generally accepted in our cultural tradition and can serve as basic justifications for the many particular ethical prescriptions and evaluations of human action.

Because of the principles' general acceptance and widespread applicability, they are at the basis of most bioethical discussion. Although philosophers argue about whether other principles—preventing harm to others or loyalty, for example—ought to be accorded equal weight with these three or should be included under another umbrella, they agree that these principles are fundamental.

Respect for Persons

Respect for persons incorporates at least two basic ethical convictions, according to the Belmont Report. Individuals should be treated as autonomous agents, and persons with diminished autonomy are entitled to protection. The derivation from Kant is clear. Because human beings have the capacity for rational action and moral choice, they have a value independent of anything that they can do or provide to others. Therefore, they should be treated in a way that respects their independent choices and judgments. Respecting autonomy means giving weight to autonomous persons' considered opinions and choices, and refraining from interfering with their choices unless those choices are clearly detrimental to others. However, since the capacity for autonomy varies with age, mental disability, or other circumstances, those people whose autonomy is diminished must be protected—but only in ways that serve their interests and do not interfere with the level of autonomy that they do possess.

Two important moral rules are derived from the ethical principle of respect for persons: informed consent and truth telling. Persons can exercise autonomy only when they have been fully informed about the range of options open to them, and the process of informed consent is generally considered to include the elements of information, comprehension, and voluntariness. Thus, a person can give informed consent to some medical procedure only if he or she has full information about the risks and benefits, understands them, and agrees voluntarily—that is, without being coerced or pressured into agreement. Although the principle of informed consent has become an accepted moral rule (and a legal one as well), it is difficult—some say impossible—to achieve in a real-world setting. It can easily be turned into a legalistic parody or avoided altogether. But as a moral ideal it serves to balance the unequal power of the physician and patient.

Another important moral ideal derived from the principle of respect for persons is truth telling. It held a high place in Kant's theory. In his essay "The Supposed Right to Tell Lies from Benevolent Motives," he wrote: "If, then, we define a lie merely as an intentionally false declaration towards another man, we need not add that it must injure another . . . ; for it always injures another; if not another individual, yet mankind generally. . . . To be truthful in all declarations is therefore a sacred and conditional command of reasons, and not to be limited by any other expediency."

Other important moral rules that are derived from the principle of respect for persons are confidentiality and privacy.

Beneficence

Most physicians would probably consider beneficence (from the Latin *bene,* or good) the most basic ethical principle. In the Hippocratic Oath it is used this way: "I will apply dietetic measures for the benefit of the sick according to my ability and judgment; I will keep them from harm and injustice." And further on, "Whatever houses I may visit, I will comfort and benefit the sick, remaining free of all intentional injustice." The phrase *Primum non nocere* (First, do no harm) is another well-known version of this idea, but it appears to be a much later, Latinized version—not from the Hippocratic period.

Philosopher William Frankena has outlined four elements included in the principle of beneficence: (1) One ought not to inflict evil or harm; (2) one ought to prevent evil or harm; (3) one ought to remove evil or harm; and (4) one ought to do or promote good. Frankena arranged these elements in hierarchical order, so that the first takes precedence over the second, and so on. In this scheme, it is more important to avoid doing evil or harm than to do good. But in the Belmont Report, beneficence is understood as an obligation— first, to do no harm, and second, to maximize possible benefits and minimize possible harms.

Justice

The third ethical principle that is generally accepted is justice, which means "what is fair" or "what is deserved." An injustice occurs when some benefit to which a person is entitled is denied without good reason or when some burden is imposed unduly, according to the Belmont Report. Another way of interpreting the principle is to say that equals should be treated equally. However, some distinctions—such as age, experience, competence, physical condition, and the like—can justify unequal treatment. Those who appeal to the principle of justice are most concerned about which distinctions can be made legitimately and which ones cannot (see the issue on insurance and genetic testing).

One important derivative of the principle of justice is the recent emphasis on "rights" in bioethics. Given the successes in the 1960s and 1970s of civil rights movements in the courts and political arena, it is easy to understand the appeal of "rights talk." An emphasis on individual rights is part of the American tradition, in a way that emphasis on the "common good" is not. The language of rights has been prominent in the abortion debate, for instance, where the "right to life" has been pitted against the "right to privacy" or the "right to control one's body." The "right to health care" is a potent rallying cry, though it is one that is difficult to enforce legally. Although claims to rights may be effective in marshaling political support and in emphasizing moral ideals, those rights may not be the most effective way to solve ethical dilemmas. Our society, as philosopher Ruth Macklin has pointed out, has not yet agreed on a theory of justice in health care that will determine who has what kinds of rights and—the other side of the coin—who has the obligation to fulfill them. ●

Questions for Writing About Bioethics

1. What is bioethics? Use one or more of the case studies to help explain the meaning of bioethics.
2. In each of the case studies, there is an ethical dilemma. Choose one of the case studies and analyze how the principles of bioethics apply to that situation.
3. Discuss how you would apply the rule of *autonomy,* including informed consent and truth telling, to the case of Mr. Y, the Chinese Canadian who wanted his sons to make decisions for him.
4. Did the researchers using AZT in Africa follow the principle of beneficence when they withheld the drug from some patients, thus endangering their babies' lives? Why or why not? How does the conflict between individual rights and the common good enter into this discussion?
5. Do you see any conflict with the principle of respect for persons in the case of Adam Nash, the baby who was conceived to save his sister's life? Discuss reasons for your position.
6. Do you feel that the three bioethical principles of *autonomy, benevolence* and *justice* reflect the values of your family's culture and your personal values? Use several of the articles from this unit or from the *Sourcework* website bibliography to support your ideas.

More Questions for Writing on Bioethics

Below are additional ideas for writing about bioethics that can be developed into research papers. On the *Sourcework* website you will find a list of sources that may help you with these topics. You will also need to find some of your own sources.

1. How can the bioethical principles of *autonomy, benevolence* and *justice* be used to help explain controversies such as genetic engineering, research ethics or assisted suicide? Select one of these topics, identify and discuss the arguments made in support and opposition. Then consider how these arguments reflect the three bioethical principles.
2. Controversies in medicine and science in general are often a result of bioethical principles coming into conflict with one another. Explore one issue and discuss how and why specific principles conflict with each other. Below are several examples of possible issues.

   - Use of animals in research
   - Use of genetic engineering in plants
   - Birth control and human population growth
   - Organ transplantation
   - Buying and selling organs

3. Identify a key person in the field of bioethics. How has this person influenced bioethical thought?
4. How and why did the field of bioethics begin?

NOTE: To practice in-class writing on the bioethics theme, see the *Sourcework* website at http://esl.college.hmco.com/students.

Introduction

Students wrote the three essays in this appendix using the writing process presented in Part One of *Sourcework*. The students who wrote the first two essays, "Risky Business" and "Changing Expectations of Marriage," read articles, and discussed the theme with their classmates before writing their own essays. For both students, this was the first time they had written a paper using sources. Notice that the papers are short, 3–5 pages, and refer only to a small number of sources.

The third paper "Vegetarianism?" was written by a student who had already written several guided-research papers. In this paper, the student chose her own topic and found her own sources. Notice that the paper is longer and refers to more sources.

All three students worked closely with their classmates throughout the process of writing their papers. This collaboration helped them in each step of the writing process.

Example Essay 1

Research Question: Why do people take risks?

Risky Business

What would you do if your friend asked you to try white-water rafting with her? As soon as my friend asked me last month, I answered, "It sounds good. I'll try it!" By comparison, when I told another friend that I would go rafting, she said to me, "How scary! Why do you want to do such a risky thing?" There is a difference between her opinion about thrills and mine. "Risk" has both positive and negative aspects. The positive aspect of risk, that it might give us success in something challenging, makes me try rafting, while the negative aspect, that it might take something important from us such as life or money, makes my friend scared. The uncertain result of risks is sometimes an advantage and sometimes a disadvantage for us. Why do people take risks even though there is a possibility that they may lose something? Biological need, social environment, and psychological satisfaction are three reasons why people take risks.

The first reason why people take risks is to meet a biological need inherited from their ancestors. Some people think the tendency to take risks is just personal taste, but it is not. People are attracted to risk taking, in part, because they have certain genes that stimulate their behavior. The article "For Our Ancestors, Taking Risks Was a Good Bet" (1999) discusses research by Israeli scientists that suggests that people who have a strong interest in taking risks may have inherited what has been called the "thrill-seeking" gene. This gene helps the chemical dopamine enter into nerve cells more easily. Dopamine controls feelings of pleasure and emotion. In addition to this thrill-seeking gene, the study found that risk takers have another gene that influences levels of serotonin, a mood chemical that is linked to feelings of satisfaction. In other words, risky situations stimulate the release of these chemicals and people with these thrill-seeking genes feel a greater sense of pleasure and satisfaction.

These thrill-seeking genes have been inherited from ancestors who lived in a dangerous environment and had to be able to successfully face risk in order to survive. For instance, they had to risk their lives when they had to kill fierce animals for food or find a way to survive during a drought. John Tooby, who runs the Center for Evolutionary Psychology at the University of California at Santa Barbara, writes that the people who survived and passed their genes on, were the ones who did well in risky situations (cited in Taro-Greenfield, 1999). Although now people no longer have to make use of this survival characteristic, they are still very much attracted to risk-taking activities because of these genetic influences.

People may have the thrill-seeking genes, but daily life is now so controlled and follows such a safe routine that it is hard to find something exciting and challenging enough to stimulate them. Michael Apter, the author of "The Dangerous Edge: The Psychology of Excitement," points out that our society has become an increasingly safe place to be; however, risk taking is necessary for humans (cited in Bowers, 1995). It is clear that the safety results in boredom and people seek risks in order to escape that boredom. In, "Taking the Bungee Plunge," Ginia Bellafonte (1992, p. 61) writes, "Bungee jumping, the non-art of flinging yourself into midair with an ankle strapped to elastic, can be an exhilarating thrill in an otherwise dreary nine-to-five existence." Through facing the challenge of risky activities, people are seeking some positive thrills, which are missing from their monotonous lives.

In addition to trying to escape the boredom that results from a safe society, people take risks to satisfy psychological needs. The contradiction between human nature that stimulates people to look for thrills and our safe society which lacks thrills causes people to seek psychological satisfaction through risk taking. There are two kinds of psychological needs that are met through risk taking: a feeling of excitement and a sense of accomplishment. First, people escape from everyday life and try risky activities to get excitement (Bellafonte, 1992; Bowers, 1995). For instance, gamblers and investors seek not only money but also the excitement that arises from the risk of losing money. There are also people who find this excitement through extreme sports. Kate Douglas, an extreme sports player, feels that her emotions and awareness are stimulated by bungee jumping (cited in Bowers, 1995).

Moreover, the successful conquest of a risk provides people with a sense of self-accomplishment, the second psychological need. Bowers (1995) writes that meeting the challenge of a risky situation is a way to make life feel more meaningful. For example, I wanted to take the entrance exam for a highly rated high school even though the possibility that I would pass was only fifty percent. My family opposed my effort, telling me it was too risky to focus on entering this high school. Fortunately, I took and passed the exam. If I had taken and passed the exam for a less challenging school, I would not have gained as great a feeling of accomplishment. However, because I pushed my limit and took a risk, my feeling of success was greater. Cathy Hanesworth, an extreme sports enthusiast, wrote, "If you can prove to yourself that you can do something that is very scary, you can carry that confidence with you into any situation because you have pushed your physical and mental limits farther than your comfort zone" (cited in Bellafonte, 1992, p. 61). In short, it is self-satisfaction that attracts us to risk taking.

In conclusion, it is difficult to find risk-taking experiences because modern society has become much too safe and mundane. The challenges presented by taking risks provide us incredible payoffs. We acquire a great deal of self-assurance and self-fulfillment. These social and psychological needs also originate from the genetic traits of our ancestors. When these three factors are combined, it compels someone like me to say yes to an offer of white-water rafting. It may be scary and the outcome may be uncertain, but it is also a way to help make my life feel more valuable.

References

Bellafonte, G. (1992, May/June). Taking the bungee plunge. *Utne Reader,* 61.

Bowers, J. (1995, October). Going over the top. *Women's Sports and Fitness, 283,* 29.

Taro-Greenfield, K. (1998, September 8). For our ancestors, taking risks was a good bet.

　　Time, 154, 12.

Example Essay 2

Research Question: How does culture influence people's concept of marriage?

Changing Expectations of Marriage in Asia

A young woman in Korea might date fifteen different men before choosing one to be her husband. Her grandmother might be shocked by this. Her mother would probably shake her head in disbelief. Forty years ago, marriages were arranged by the family and a young woman had no voice in who her future husband would be. Once married, she simply accepted her role as a caretaker for her husband and children and did not expect that her own personal interests would be recognized. This attitude toward marriage is changing in Asia as women look for ways to pursue their own dreams. There are three main reasons why women's expectation of marriage is higher than it was 40 years ago in Asian countries: a desire for personal fulfillment, a desire for financial self-reliance, and a simple desire to be able to choose one's husband.

The first thing that contributes to women's high expectation of marriage is that their desire to pursue personal goals has become more important in Asia. This means that they don't want to give up their own lives any more after marriage. Actually, until recently many women in Asian countries haven't been allowed to have careers. They had to give up their personal lives for their family. In "What Does Life Tell Us About Love?" Kavita Daswani (cited in Wark, 2003, p. 42) writes, "There is an element of sacrifice and obligation: we are expected to make many things secondary once the husband comes along, to devote our energies to him, and his house and the building of another family unit." In other words, married women's first priority is traditionally to spend their time taking care of their husband and children, their house, and the progression of their family. They haven't had enough time to look after themselves and achieve their own career goals in traditional

Asian countries like India. The point here, however, is that many women in Asian countries also want their own lives, and don't just want to live for their husband and children. They hope to find a career that enables them to develop as well as earns them money. As a result, they either postpone getting married or look for a more open-minded husband. In "I Take Thee, for Weekends Only," Kay Itoi (1999) discusses how Japanese women's opinion about marriage is changing. "Tired of following in the footsteps of indifferent husbands, Japanese wives are demanding lives of their own" (p. 2). It's true that the typical women who, in the past, gave up their own careers and relied on their husbands are disappearing. Women don't want to be in a rigid traditional marriage. They realize that they deserved to be happy by having and enjoying their lives beyond their marriage.

As a result of an improved economy in many Asian countries, women can become financially independent. This is the second reason why women's expectations of marriage are changing. For example, women in Japan now have more opportunities to get jobs and make money (Itoi, 1999). Having a job means not only making money, but also that women can establish independence. Nowadays, women in Asia have more experience earning, spending, and managing money. As a result, they have learned how to be self-reliant. This financial independence means that women can be more assertive. When they do not need to depend on a man for their financial security, they are able to express and expect that their own desires will be respected. Itoi (1999) writes that young women who were raised with financial security and have their own jobs now, understand that they have choices. They are learning that they are not required to end their arguments on someone else's terms to obtain what they need. They would like to express freely what they want to say and act how they want to act. Now that they have this leverage, they expect the husband to listen to them. So because the women have the ability to get more, they are accustomed to receiving more and have higher expectations of their husbands. Women want to look closely at their potential husband.

Asian women's ability to decide who will be their husband is the last reason for their high expectations of marriage. In the past, they couldn't select their husbands; it was out of their hands. Daswani (cited in Wark, 2003, p. 42) talks about arranged marriage, "[My parents] were brought together by their families, engaged within the day and married within a couple of weeks. That was 40 years ago and all is well." Like Daswani's mother, many women in Asia had to marry an unfamiliar man, picked by their parents or the man's parents. Like India, Korea has a long history of arranged marriage too. It was common that parents chose their daughter's husband or men decided who would be their wives. Women in Korea were required to wait for their husband patiently. However, increased financial independence for women has meant that choosing a partner to live with is becoming one of the important decisions a woman makes in her life. Single women who have a professional job tend to have high expectations of their future husband and their marriage. Robert Levine (1993), a professor of psychology at California State University in Fresno, writes in "Is Love a Luxury?" that marrying someone for love instead of for practical reasons such as financial security or family status is more common in wealthy countries that value individualism. Women are beginning to look for a husband who will respect their independence and share an emotional bond.

In conclusion, there are several reasons why women in Asia have these higher expectations of their marriage. They are transitioning from the traditional way of thinking about marriage (dependence on husband) to the western way of thinking (seeking their own career in addition to taking care of their family). Women are rethinking not only their own role in marriage, but also their husbands. They are looking for equality and hoping for a new way of living. ●

References

Itoi, K. (2000, July 19). I take thee, for weekends only. *Newsweek, 134,* 2.

Levine, R. (1993, February). Is love a luxury? *American Demographics, 15,* 27.

Wark, P. (2003, July 9). What does life tell us about love?. [electronic version]

    The Times, 8, 42.

Example Essay 3

Research Question: Why do people choose to be vegetarians?

Vegetarianism?

"Do you want to have this?" I offered the beef jerky to my friend. "No way! Don't you know it's from a dead animal?" I had this conversation when I was at a party in Japan with some foreign friends. Obviously, this person is a vegetarian. She does not eat any kind of animal flesh, does not drink milk or eat cheese, and does not wear leather fabrics. It was my first time to talk to a vegetarian. I was surprised and asked curiously. "Yeah, I know it is from a dead animal, but almost everyone eats it here. Why don't you?" She explained seriously that when she imagined it was from a dead animal, she felt very sick. She did not like depriving anything of its life.

It does not seem easy to become a vegetarian. You have to create ways to cook delicious food without the tastes from animals, like consommé, and bonito soup. Furthermore, you have to be careful of the menu when you order in a restaurant. For me, this activity seems like a pain. I love animals, but I also like eating some of them. So far, I have not felt like I should quit eating meat completely. However, as a result of my conversation with my friend, I began to wonder what makes some people become vegetarian. Improved health, ethical issues, and ecological concerns are three reasons why people become vegetarian.

First of all, many people try to be vegetarians to maintain good health. Vegetarianism can prevent people from getting certain diseases. Castleman (1995) mentions that many studies prove that meat, especially beef, pork and lamb, likely increase the percentages of heart disease and cancer. He states that the number of vegetarians who die from heart disease and cancer is definitely lower than the meat eaters. For example, from heart disease, 28 percent fewer vegetarians die than omnivorous do, and 39 percent fewer die from cancer. The National Cancer Research Institute has found that meat-eating women get breast cancer almost 4 times more than women who do not eat meat or eat little ("Why Be a Vegetarian?" 1999). Moreover, there are other diseases which meat eaters are more likely to get than vegetarians, such as hypertension, gallstones, constipation, and diabetes (Cerrato, 1991). Consequently, vegetarians may live longer than omnivores. Dworkin (1999) cites a Loma Linda University study that says vegetarians live an average of 7 years longer than those who eat meat. Another positive health point of vegetarianism that Dworkin gives is the fact that vegetarians tend to be slim and their bones can last longer. Recognizing these health benefits, many people are becoming vegetarians.

However, although people know these positive points of vegetarianism and want to be healthy, there are some opposing opinions concerning the health benefits of vegetarianism. Some people are concerned about the lack of nutrients in a diet without meat. As we know, protein is indispensable to live. Meat, eggs, and dairy products cannot be ignored in the diet, because they are the only source of vitamin B12 (Cerrato, 1991). The deficiency of vitamin B12 causes anemia and serious neurological damage. In addition, we also need to get essential amino acids, and nine of these can be absorbed from animal proteins. If we eat only vegetables, we have to carefully combine certain kinds of foods, such as red beans or lentils and rice, to get these nutrients. Meat can satisfy nutritional requirements easily, and people who don't like to spend time thinking about their meals prefer the easier way of eating meat.

In addition to health benefits, ethical beliefs lead some people to become vegetarian. Religious practice and animal rights are two ethical arguments commonly made. First, religious belief usually has a powerful influence in the believer's life. In an effort to persuade people to become vegetarian, the People for the Ethical Treatment of Animals (PETA) has argued that Catholic priests, Southern Baptists, and even poultry producers who call themselves devout Christians should be vegetarians because Jesus himself was a vegetarian ("Preaching Christian Vegetarianism," 1998). Another example of vegetarianism in Christianity is in Genesis. Adam named the animals, but he was able to eat only the "green plants" as food in Eden (Gen. 1:29). When these examples are used as arguments for vegetarianism, they imply that Christians have an obligation to follow the examples given in the bible if they want to consider themselves true followers of Christianity.

A second ethical argument that some people consider is animal rights. Imagine how chickens who are going to be slaughtered are crammed into cages. According to Moran (1989), these chickens have had their beaks cut with a hot knife. This painful process includes destroying sensitive tissue in the beaks. Poultry producers use this method to stop the chickens from committing cannibalism. However, farmers cause this cannibalistic behavior by forcing many into tiny cages. The chickens never fly or walk freely until they are killed. For pigs, it is also a nightmare to be born in factories. Today, many pigs bite their tails off (Why Be a Vegetarian?, 1999). They are bored and frustrated, and finally go insane. In cases where the farmer cannot solve the biting problem, the mauled pig might be attacked and killed by the other pigs in the small pen. This pig cannot be sold, and it becomes troublesome for the producer. As a result, pigs' tails are routinely cut off. They are also forced to stay in darkness until feeding time. I believe that nobody can say that this treatment is humane. People who support animal rights to advocate vegetarianism consider animals as living creatures that are the same as humans. They were not born to be killed or treated in inhumane ways.

On the other hand, in spite of knowing these unethical conditions, some people emphasize the supremacy of human rights which weakens the importance of vegetarianism. Christians who eat meat point out the contradiction of stories in the Bible. According to Witherell (1994), killing and eating animals is not only not forbidden in the Bible, but for some important occasions, it is advocated. For example, after the flood, God announced that there was a difference between humans and all the other creatures. The animals gave their flesh as food for Noah and his families (Gen. 9:3–4). This suggests humans' superiority over all others. In response to the argument that raising animals to kill them is unethical, Achor (1996) points out that some people justify eating meat by thinking this way, "at least the animals had happy lives before they were killed" (p. 68). Actually, we use this phrase when we argue owning pets, too. "They are fed and living safely. What's the matter?" For people who believe in humans' superiority, even religious and ethical reasons lose their strength.

There is one more practical reason to advocate vegetarianism. Meat eating seems ecologically quite wasteful. In research, it has been proved that raising animals to eat is surprisingly wasteful of land and food (Robinsong, 1995). Every minute, 20 acres of land are collapsed for our meat industry. Calculating the amount, it means that the destruction of the land is 28,000 acres per day. In other statistics, it is said that cattle require an incredible amount of water to mature (Castleman, 1995). Approximately 50 percent of the water consumed in the United States is used for domestic animals. In some areas, the rate is much higher. For example, 75 percent of the water from the Ogallala Aquifer, which is the main source for the High Plains, is for raising cattle. Thinking of water, we can compare it with meat. One pound of meat takes almost 2,500 gallons of water ("Why Be a Vegetarian?" 1999). One serving of chicken takes 408 gallons of water, and one pat of butter takes 100 gallons (Achor, 1996). Achor gives the astonishing result of a calculation of the cost for a pound of hamburger. She says that the real price is about 35 dollars. The cost includes, among other things, payment for water, which is required to produce enough greens to feed cattle.

However, somehow, people do not want to be vegetarians. Even though these statistics exist, most people do not want to know the truth or feel ambiguous when they learn what is involved in producing a piece of meat. When they buy a single pound of meat, they see just the "meat," but do not imagine the real cost of the meat.

After I finished this research, I felt that I was in a misty forest. What is important for me? What am I supposed to consider when I think of vegetarianism? Health and animal rights are convincing arguments. However, I still sometimes eat meat without hesitation. I dare to say that I do not even feel pity for the animals that are slaughtered to eat. How am I different from vegetarians? For them I might be a cruel murderer. Even though I do not commit the slaughtering directly, I do indirectly by increasing the demand for meat.

Likewise, if I become a vegetarian, I will indirectly improve life for others. For example, when people decide to become vegetarians in order to improve their health, it may also seem like they care about others. In fact, it is just fortunate that their lifestyle will not be harmful to other creatures. This is also true for people who become vegetarians for ecological reasons. They want to reduce wasteful activity, and it consequently helps animals' lives. Vegetarianism is a habit that allows us to reflect on our life. I cannot say that everyone has to be a vegetarian, but I am learning to respect vegetarians for their reliability as unselfish people. Vegetarianism could be one of the solutions that help this chaotic world become more humane. ●

References

Achor, A. B. (1996). *Animal rights.* Ohio: Yellow Springs.

Bloyd-Peshkin, S. (1991, June). In search of our basic diet: you may have heard that humans are naturally vegetarian. The evidence is convincing, but is it accurate? *Vegetarian Times,* 46–52.

Castleman, M. (1995, March–April). Flesh wounds. *Sierra,* 26–27.

Cerrato, P. L. (1991, March). Becoming a vegetarian: the risks and the benefits. *RN,* 73–77.

Dworkin, N. (1999, April). 22 reasons to go vegetarian right now. *Vegetarian Times,* 90.

Fossel, P. V. (1994, September–October). Letter from Plum Hill. *Country Journal* 8.

Ireland, C. (1992, February). Vegetarian timeline: a light and lively look at vegetarians through the ages. *Vegetarian Times,* 56–57.

Moran, V. (1989, January). Veganism: the ethics, the philosophy, the diet. *Vegetarian Times,* 50–53.

Preaching Christian vegetarianism. (1998, July 17). *National Catholic Reporter,* 8.

Robinsong, S. (1995, Spring–Summer). The butcher's secret. *Skipping Stones,* 29.

The vegetarian approach. (1991, September). *Current Health 2,* 19–21.

Why be a vegetarian? (1999, May 10). *Vegetarian Education Group of Northern Illinois University* [Online serial]. Available at: http://come.to/veg.

Witherell, T. D. (1994, April 23). Notes from the vegetarian underground. *America,* 16–17.